Diary
of a
Reluctant
Psychic

Ellie Duvall Thompson

Flying Horse Books

Published in 2014 by
Flying Horse Books
an imprint of
The Wessex Astrologer Ltd
4A Woodside Road
Bournemouth
BH5 2AZ
England

www.wessexastrologer.com

ISBN 9781902405964

A catalogue record of this book is available at The British Library

Cover design by Jonathan Taylor

I am neither a writer nor an author so please find it in your heart not to judge me for my grammar or style of writing. Judge me for not caring, judge me for not trying or judge me for giving up, but as I will always have hope and love in my heart, my epitaph will read:

"She Tried"

"The human way to evolve is not as a spirit but as a man, for the spirit of man does not need to evolve. Man in his many guises is still not perfect; he is still a being of malevolence, but he will soon learn that it is not by following others that he will attain purity and eternal life, but by seeing with his human eyes that all life is sacred, and all life is a gift."

The Keepers

Acknowledgements

I want to say a big 'Thank you' to some special people: to my mum and dad for always loving me; to my husband for marrying me – I will love you forever; to my daughters for choosing me as your mum, I am so proud of all three of you; to Michaela for the endless cups of tea and rather rude banter; and finally to Julie and Margaret – I couldn't have done it without either of you!

Prologue

November 1998

The glass doors of the hospital gleamed brightly in the morning sun. The over-flowing steel ashtrays on either side were like smelly, grotesque statues. As Dreanna got closer the doors opened automatically and she walked through them towards her mother's ward. Her head was flustered and confused and an uncomfortable feeling of fullness was trapped inside her mind. Death and dying was all around her; she could feel it, she could see it, and she could taste it. Black emotions entered her body, and a strong pain ate its way into her core. It wasn't the transition of death but the grief that it left behind that was using her body like a sponge, soaking up every piece of life she had left.

She stood still, closed her eyes and used her words as her weapons: sharp, angled spears that tried hard to defeat the emotions that whirled around in her head. Each word she spoke grew louder until in her own mind she inwardly screamed, 'Look straight in front of you. Don't look at the patients, don't look at the relatives. These people are not important to you, they don't care about you and you don't care about them. All they are is just more of your own species that are sick and dying. IGNORE THEM, IGNORE THEM!'

Her eyes were fixed on the door of the ward sister's office. She tapped on it gently.

"Come in," a woman's voice replied.

"Hi," Dreanna entered the room. "I'm here to see my mother, she was brought in yesterday – Iris…"

"Oh yes, please take a seat," the skinny but perfectly groomed woman answered. "Your mother is very sick you know. Her sores are badly infected and she has contracted septicaemia." She shuffled some paper. "Your father wants you to sign the 'do not resuscitate' forms. To be honest with you we were expecting you yesterday, but I suppose you were too busy?" Her tone was sarcastic and she frowned at Dreanna.

Dreanna looked at her and the energy she was generating in the room. Sarcastic, often thinks highly of herself, self-absorbed, controlling, hiding a secret that's kept her prisoner all her life, arse-kisser, likes being tied up in sexual games… hmm. Dreanna's thoughts made her smile. "I don't have to explain anything to you as to my whereabouts yesterday, and yes, we as a family do understand how sick our mother is, and excuse my candour but your nurses – or should I say the district nurses – have been coming in daily for the last couple of months, so in all honesty the fault lies with them as they should have known the severity of my mother's wounds and sores. So please pass me the forms so I can sign them." Dreanna returned the same sarcastic smile she received and signed the papers that were passed over the desk to her.

"Now may I please see my mother?" Dreanna's eyes never left the gaze of the Sister.

"Did your mother never tell you it's rude to stare?" the ward sister asked.

"Did yours never tell you to be careful about getting tied to the bed? One day you might lose the keys to your handcuffs – now that would be a reason to stare wouldn't it?" Dreanna pulled her gaze away and smiled as the Sister's cheeks began to glow a bright crimson. "Bay four isn't it?"

The Sister stuttered, "Yes, but how did you know? I haven't told you yet, and how...?"

"It's on the board behind you, derr!" Dreanna sucked in her lips in a bid to contain her smile. "Thank you so much for all your help. It's been such a pleasure meeting you, keep up the good work."

Iris lay alone in a four-bedded cubical, highly sedated. Her breathing was deep and shallow, her weightless, child-like body covered by a white sheet and a bright pink duvet. A drip had been inserted into one of the frail veins in her hand, and she had a vacuous expression on her face. Dreanna moved a plastic orange chair from the corner and placed it next to her mother's bed. She held her hand in hers and stroked each finger in turn, examining their deformity and the tautness of the thin pale skin that encased each bone. She could find no words to say to her. She had no words in her mind, even her thoughts had disappeared. The darkness in her mind moved around her body and before long all she could see was the obscurity of blackness. The whole ward and hospital had disappeared from her sight. Was she now in her mother's head?

Dreanna blinked and rubbed her eyes, but the dim shadows of obscurity didn't leave her. She was in nowhere-land; a state of total limbo where she could move neither forward nor backward. There was no fear, no happiness, no movement; everything was at a standstill, everything was stagnant and halted. Iris's mind was immobile like the pathetic vessel her body had become. She was paralyzed from the neck down, wearing nappies like a newborn baby, and now her body, her vessel, was fighting for life against a rampant infection eating its way through her like maggots feeding on necrotic tissue. How strong was her mother's body to keep fighting in this way? Dreanna knew she would have to be the stalwart figure here, she would have to be robust and resilient. Whatever was to come, whatever was to happen, there had to be a reason. There is always a reason, isn't there? She was brought back to earth by her mother shouting one solitary word.

"Glenda!" Iris was clearly incensed.

Dreanna gazed, astonished that her mother had actually said something, but why Glenda, her neighbour?

"She sees all that is going on Dreanna." A voice came from nowhere.

Dreanna repeated, "She sees all that is going on? So she really is split between the distance of time and the transition of death. She really is stuck in limbo, isn't she?"

"Yes my child she is."

Dreanna shook her head like a dog shaking water from its fur; reality had returned and so had the ward, the bed and her mother's unnatural state. She kissed Iris's hand and left the hospital, knowing wherever and whatever was going on in her life, her mother somehow observed it all from afar.

First Breath

December 6th 1967
Patrick picked up another nail and hammered it into the un-planed piece of wood. His mind was on other things that day; all he could think about was the imminent birth of his child. If he had his way he would have twenty children, but we don't always get what we want in life do we? The images of his own childhood filled his mind when the midwife, who had not long cycled in from the local cottage hospital, shouted from upstairs.

"Patrick, your baby is almost here, do you want to come and watch?"

Patrick shouted back nervously, "Not bloody likely! You stay upstairs and do your job. I'll stay down here and do mine."

Patrick and Iris had spent seven long years trying to conceive their fourth child and had just about given up hope of adding to their brood. Maybe it was fate, maybe it was just luck; either way all Patrick was thinking about at that precise moment was a jumble of memories from his past, the pain his wife was going through, and getting that blasted desk he had started building finished before his other kids returned home from school.

His hammer hit the nail for the sixth time, finally joining the old pieces of wood together to form the legs of the desk. It wasn't the best bit of carpentry in the world, but it would serve a purpose and at least stop his squabbling brood arguing about having nowhere to do their homework. Patrick put his hand into the rusty old biscuit tin that stored the different nails and screws and begun rummaging around for another four inch flat-headed metal spike, then heard the midwife's voice ricochet around the tiny box room upstairs. Patrick stopped his work, his heart missed a beat. What would the outcome be?

"Come on Iris, you know the routine. Chin on chest and push! Now pant, there's a good girl, and with the next contraction put all you've got into it. Come on Iris, push like you've never pushed before!"

With one final push Iris completed her task. Lying between her legs was her slightly bloody, slightly small, but alive and breathing newborn child, with ten fingers, ten toes, and eyes wide open ready to explore the new world. Iris's eyes filled with tears and her heart beat faster. She reached down between her legs for the new life that lay there. Finally, after so many years, she would feel another child nestle at her breast. How she longed for this moment – a desire and a need unlike any other she had ever felt. Iris knew that the length of time they had waited for this child, the constant vomiting for nine months and the pain of child-birth were all going to be distant memories in a matter of days. She now had the responsibility of nurturing four children. "A mother again," she sighed, and smiled an exhausted smile.

The midwife reached down to grab hold of the bloody bundle, wip-ing the body clean with a fresh piece of lint. Her voice echoed around the house, loud enough so Patrick could hear her. "It's a girl!"

With these words still ringing in Patrick's ears, his new baby daugh-ter filled her lungs and belted out a screechy cry.

"Not another one," he smirked. Patrick actually meant what he said; he knew that he would love her, but couldn't hide the fact he was hop-ing for another son. All his life he had been surrounded by women. With five sisters and now three daughters and only one brother and one son to continue the family name, he had hoped that luck would favour him with at least one more male. But unfortunately it was not meant to be.

He stared around his tiny kitchen; washing hung on an airer close to the open fire, the mangle resting against the back wall. He shook his head. God, how he hated doing the washing and now there would be the endless supply of nappies to wash too! Walking over to the sink, Patrick turned on the tap and splashed water over his face, then slicked back what was left of his balding hair with his wet hands. He looked at him-self in the mirror that hung on the wall. His hair was already white and the lines around his eyes seemed deeper than usual; stubble grew on his face with only a slight hint of his original colour left in it. "I may be get-ting old but there's still a bit of lead left in the old pencil," he grinned.

No matter how old he was looking, nothing was going to stop how he felt at that moment in time. He was proud, so very proud, and even though age seemed against him, time had at least given him another chance to be a father. He ventured up the staircase, his hand jingling the change in his pocket. As he headed to the little room where his newborn daughter lay he realised they may not be able to give her the best of everything, but one thing was for sure: this child would be given was so much love she was going to be suffocated with affection.

The bedroom smelt of disinfectant and human blood. Normally it would have made him retch but there were more important things to think about, like where was his new baby daughter? His eyes scanned the room. The midwife was busy stuffing all the bits of used cloth into paper bags ready to be burnt in the open fire down stairs. His eyes fell on the neatly wrapped bundle lying in his wife's arms. The baby was quiet now and Patrick finally met the gaze of his new daughter. A wisp of fair hair peeked out from under the blanket and her deep black eyes penetrated his soul; the love he felt was instant and any earlier thoughts of wishing his newborn child was a son seemed insignificant. His arms opened for this tiny bundle and with one swoop lifted her close to his chest.

The midwife couldn't help but stare at the joyous scene. It was these moments that made her rejoice in her chosen career; this was her destiny, this is what she was passionate about, and more importantly this was what life was all about. Holding back her own emotions and tears, the midwife teased, "Is that a tear in your eye, Patrick?"

Patrick didn't even bother to acknowledge her – he was too busy admiring what he and Iris had managed to produce. He looked back over his shoulder and winked at his wife. A single tear fell onto his cheek, and with the softest of voices he smiled and said, "Thank you".

The midwife laid Dreanna back down next to her mother. The events of the day had taken their toll and mother and daughter both drifted off into oblivion, their breathing synchronized, their hearts beating as one. Patrick smiled down at the two tired females. With tears in his eyes and a heart full of love he turned and walked away, pulling the bedroom door to behind him. Patrick made his way back down to the kitchen with the midwife following close behind. His tools were still strewn round the floor, the desk was only half made and in five minutes the rest of his family would be home from school wanting their tea.

"Come on Patrick, clean this mess up and put the kettle on." The midwife's voice was calmer now as she began to throw the soiled bedding and bits of used cloth onto the fire. She watched as the flames blazed higher and crackled in the roaring amber.

The wind was howling down the chimney and the flames of the fire seemed to breathe of their own accord with each gust, but the strange hypnotic pulse was soon broken by the loud crashing of three very wet, soggy children falling through the front door.

William was the eldest; ten years old and named after his grandfather. He had the same fair hair as his father had in his youth, but was taller, with a confident manner about him. Iris's only son. She could not help but to favour him and in her eyes he could do no wrong, even though he did, and actually quite often. Dawn came next, the only one of their family that shared her father's crystal blue eyes. Her hair was long and blonde and Iris loved her, but couldn't help feeling jealous of the bond that she shared with her father. When Dawn entered the room, Patrick's eyes seemed to light up and Iris would feel guilty of being so envious. She couldn't help herself as she loved Patrick greatly and was scared of losing his love, even if it was to one of their own children.

Patrice was their third-born child and her eyes and hair were dark. She resembled her mother but to some extent her appearance reminded Patrick of one of his sisters. Patrice never had the same interests as her sister Dawn, but preferred climbing trees, rolling about in the mud and being the tomboy of the family. And now they had a third daughter, another mouth to feed and body to clothe but more importantly another child to love.

Patrice broke the silence as their wet rain-soaked bodies hurtled into the kitchen. "Is it really a girl? Have we a sister? I wanted a brother, can we give her back and get a boy?" She didn't take a breath and her words flowed freely as the raindrops ran down her hair onto her pure white skin.

"Where is she? What does she look like? Can we see her?" Dawn's voice was full of curiosity and she was eager to see the new baby.

The three young siblings threw their coats into an untidy bundle on the dining room table and kicked off their wellington boots, each boot landing in an opposite direction to the other.

William was not interested in finding out more about his new baby sister, he wanted to know what the midwife was doing. "What's in the paper bag?"

The midwife tweaked his nose. "Nothing for you to worry about. Stop being so nosey."

William was soon followed by his sisters' prying and inquiring minds as to the secrets hidden inside the bags.

The midwife, Helen, hadn't been qualified for long and Iris's child was only the second she had delivered alone. She was young but her approach was old-fashioned and she believed that women should stop their whining and screaming and put all that energy into getting the baby out as quick as possible. Giving birth has been done for years so in her words you 'just get on with it!' It was an approach that not many midwives accepted but it seemed to work, even with the screaming banshees that saw childbirth as a time to be mollycoddled and wrapped in swaddling themselves. Helen had a compassionate side too and had cried many times as a student midwife. She had often been left to deal with the dead babies that had been carried for nine months but for whatever reason hadn't managed to survive, while the qualified midwives dealt with the formalities of such sad outcomes. These times were hard for her; she was always the first to offer love and support to the grieving mothers, and more importantly, opening her heart to them, feeling their pain.

With the eyes of the three young children upon her she thought a distraction would be the best way forward and decided to give each one their first lesson in origami with the help of the clean paper bags left over. All eyes were soon on her nimble fingers as she moulded the bags into various shapes and sizes. Laughter erupted from each child as they folded the paper, not quite getting to grips with the exact position of each crease and crinkle.

Distraction achieved, Helen was ready to move on. "Don't you want to see your new sister?"

Dawn threw down her wrinkled paper bag, a bubble of excitement in her stomach as she danced around the kitchen, arms waving in the air. "Me first, me first!"

Before anyone could blink she was waiting at the bottom of the stairs, her fingers twisting the edge of her cardigan, her feet unable to keep still. She hopped up onto the first step then jumped down again, then up again, then down again. She was like a child on Christmas Eve, filled with hope and expectancy as to what new gift lay hidden away in the valley of the staircase and beyond.

Patrice stood quite still by the open fire, her cheeks turning a deep crimson with the heat, her face screwed up and her nose twitching as she announced quite sternly, "NO! Didn't want a girl, it's not fair!"

Patrick swept the last bit of sawdust into the corner of the room, and looked at his son. "William, do you want to see your new sister?"

William screwed up his nose, his expression one of total boredom at the idea of seeing a new baby. "Spose, if I have to."

With his three eldest children lined up at the bottom of the stairs, Patrick looked intently at each of his off-spring. His soft voice made them hang on his every word. "You can all go together, but you must be very quiet. Your mum is really tired now and needs her rest."

All three stood quietly watching as their mother held Dreanna in her arms. Each child in turn observed their new sister, but it was only Dawn who stroked her arm, caressed her head, and asked to hold this new baby.

Patrice stood quietly against the back wall, picking off flaking bits of paint. William was also picking, but it was his nose that was given attention not the paint, and whatever was coming out of his nostrils was being carefully rolled into a soft ball between his fingers.

Patrice, with hair still damp and boredom in her eyes, asked in a jaded way, "Can we go now?" The monotony of the events didn't please her at all. She was cold and hungry and her legs were still stained with the mud splashed on them from the journey home from school. She smiled for the first time that day when their father gave the go-ahead to leave the room, and she and William made a hasty retreat. Only Dawn remained, still captivated by what she was holding in her arms.

"You'll make a good mother one day," Iris said.

"I hope so," Dawn smiled.

"But not for a few years yet, eh? Marriage first child, marriage first. Don't want any sluts in this family do we?"

Dawn stared, questioning what her mother had just said. Not understanding what a slut actually was and why she would talk about marriage when she was only eight years of age. With some reservation, Dawn answered her mother. "No Mum, we don't...I'll let you rest now."

"Good girl, go help your Dad with the tea."

Iris nodded her head and winked at her daughter, as once again she cradled her newborn baby in her arms, closed her eyes and drifted back to sleep.

October 1968
Time passed quickly as it generally does when there is a growing baby in the house, and before everyone knew it Dreanna was crawling around. The one thing that this petite package required was heaps of affection. She was not satisfied with the occasional cuddle – she needed constant love and would crawl onto anyone's lap if they sat still for long enough. The house was always busy and excessively noisy. Her siblings began their transition into early adolescence; Patrick worked as hard as he possibly could, leaving the house at the crack of dawn and not returning until darkness fell. He had no particular trade but could turn his hand

to anything that was asked of him. 'A handyman with many skills' is the way Iris described her husband. And as for Iris, her days were spent washing the family's clothes by hand, cleaning their home and aiding the development of her growing offspring. After giving birth to Dreanna she suffered chronic anaemia and bouts of severe lethargy, but with the help of her own mother, Matilda, she managed to continue to raise this hungry brood.

The family home was a typical council property on Stone Quarry Estate, with no heating except the coal fire in the kitchen. The wooden frames of the windows rattled in the wind and most of the furniture was either given to them or bought second-hand from flea-markets. The family survived on the bare necessities. Wallpaper peeled from the walls, the floorboards were bare and stained at the edges, there was a mottled-coloured rug in the centre of each room, and curtains that never quite fitted hung precariously on a thin wire fixed by rusty old nails. But it was clean, warm and with an air of homeliness about it. The front door was never locked and the small estate where they lived in East Grinstead had its own sense of a community. Everybody knew everyone else; they stopped to talk or gossip about other neighbours, children ran rampant in the street, and every corner you turned was filled with laughter, a barking dog, or the marital arguments that occurred daily. But this noisy and somewhat boisterous estate, with the occasional brassy and flamboyant resident, was home and it gave each resident a semblance of security, no matter how little they owned.

The estate was growing rapidly and now three shops greeted you at its entrance. The newsagents, where Dawn worked at weekends, was owned by a grumpy man who had no patience, was rude to his customers and would often try and brush up against the younger female members of his staff. He was not meaning to be rude but he was a letch and a pervert and spent a lot of the time ogling the breasts of any woman that came in. The grocery shop next door was owned by Dreanna's godparents. Iris and Patrick had known them for years and Iris told them they could be godparents if she ever did manage to get pregnant again. They accepted. The final shop sold fish and chips and it was was owned by a funny old couple, a husband and wife team both rather large and a little scruffy in their attire. The husband never said much and left most of the talking to his wife who always for some strange reason had a wad of tissue protruding from her nose. At some stage this rolled-up toilet paper must have fallen in the fryer. What a horrible thought!

Further up the street from the shops on the right hand side was St Lukes church, where many of the children from the estate were baptized. The whole point of being baptized was of course that the children could then attend Sunday School, which gave their hard-pressed parents a welcome break from their noisy antics. The hedges of this religious establishment were used by the youths for 'hedge jumping', one of their favourite pastimes. Another favourite was tormenting the kids who attended the Brownies and Guides Club that used to meet there. It's a wonder they weren't scarred for life by the verbal abuse they received. And on the left was the Guinea Pig Public house, a place that would supply plenty of ale and beer to those who wanted to partake in the pleasures of getting tanked up and paralytic after their wages were paid on a Friday night. The landlord and landlady were characters in their own right; he was tall and a little bit on the round side which isn't uncommon for a landlord, but he was a decent man and knew exactly what his punters wanted. His wife was occasionally a little harsh in her manner but her heart was in the right place, and the couple were well liked in this community.

There were many alleyways running through the estate where teenagers could grope each other without interference from adult or parent, as they explored the passions of a youthful mind and body; the nearby woods harboured the occasional flasher who would show any person, young or old, the shape, size and quality of his manhood. There was also a funny old rogue of a man that used to live in the woods, nicknamed Catweasel after the TV show. Not many had seen him but all were told he was there. Maybe it was just a tale to stop the kids getting up to mischief but everyone believed that he was real and stories about how he survived in the wildness were always being told. It was no more than just a typical estate of the late sixties – not polished, no finery, but fulfilling the needs of a growing town to provide the working classes with a home.

Dreanna had her very own cot that was positioned against the back wall of the front bedroom she shared with her sisters, but she very rarely slept there. She was at her happiest sleeping between the two people who gave her life. Their warm bodies and the reassurance of them being close by was all she needed to drift off into a deep trancelike sleep night after night. Her waking hours were no different; she was quiet and serene, and never demanded to be fed or cried inappropriately. She was contented knowing that whenever she felt the need for affection it would be given by a member of her family.

Patrick and Iris were very laid back in their approach to bringing up their children – there was never a set bedtime. Patrick hated the idea of making his children sleep if they weren't sleepy so they fell asleep wherever and whenever they wanted and were carried up to bed later. Dreanna had spent every night since the day of her birth sleeping in between her parents but Iris had decided it was now time for her to be transferred to her cot once she fell asleep. Iris kept to the same routine she had established for her youngest daughter: Dreanna was bathed in the kitchen sink with the open fire roaring and dressed in her nightdress that had been warming over a chair in front of the fire, but instead of being snuggled into her parents' bed once she fell asleep, her small body was placed gently in her cot. Dreanna woke up as she was laid down, and her eyes filled with tears. Iris's heart beat faster. She knew that leaving her daughter in the cot for the first time in her life was going to be as hard on her as it was on her baby and she couldn't help but feel she was in some way abandoning her own child. But she knew what she was doing was the right thing; doesn't this make a child stronger and more self disciplined? She tiptoed out of the bedroom.

Iris and Patrick lay motionless in their own bed, hoping that Dreanna's cries would awaken their other children and this could be the excuse they were looking for to carry her back to their bed. But there was no loud ear-splitting scream – the only noise they heard was the whimpering cries turning into laughter, a gurgling baby laughter that could light up the coldest of hearts.

Patrick pulled his body out of the warm bed into the coldness of their room. The chilly air outside the confines of his bed made him shiver. He never wore pajamas, and didn't even own a dressing gown or slippers, but the need to know what his fourth-born child was doing was too much for him to bear; the freezing house became totally irrelevant. "I have to see what's happening."

He peered into his daughter's room trying not to let his chattering teeth disturb her or wake her sisters. His youngest daughter was sitting upright in her cot smiling and playing what looked like 'pat-a-cake' with an invisible pair of hands. He watched for a moment, mesmerised by her tranquility and then smiled to himself as he returned to the warmth of his bed and his wife's body.

The Silence is Broken

March 1969

Night after night the giggles and chuckles came from Dreanna's cot. Iris and Patrick began to wonder if their nights would ever stop being disturbed, not by a screaming baby but by one whose spirits seemed to soar each time she was put down for the night. Neither pouring rain nor clap of thunder could frighten this child; she was happy just to be part of their lives and they were happy she was part of theirs.

"You know she's going to change, don't you Iris?" Matilda said in her broad London accent.

Iris slammed the last plate angrily down on the draining board. She loved her mother so much and always listened to what she had to say, but she didn't want to accept the fact that maybe one day this docile little child would change. She reached down and pulled the plug from the sink, her teeth chewing on the inside of her mouth as she watched the dirty dish water drain away. "I know you mean well Mum, but I can't see her changing. Look how happy she is – there aren't many kids that would sit on their own entertaining themselves the way she does."

Iris beamed down at her youngest. Dreanna sat on the rug at her feet, happily playing with a wooden spoon and an old saucepan, undecided as to whether it was better to bang the two pieces together or stick the spoon in her mouth. Either way the giggles were never too far away, which always made Iris smile and feel content.

Matilda's tone was blunt, her eyes squeezed tight at the corners. She dragged on her cigarette, and both women sat in silence watching this baby play, coo and chuckle into what seemed to be an empty space.

"Iris my love, look at her, really look at her. That child is not on her own. Look at the way she stares. Look at the way she seems to acknowledge something we can't see. I'd give my last tuppence if I'm wrong, but I really don't think that kid is on her own."

Matilda carried on staring at this tiny bundle of joy, trying in any way possible to see just what the baby was watching. She was watching and listening for anything that seemed a little out of the ordinary and hoping in her heart of hearts she was wrong.

Well, what can be said about Matilda? She was a well-loved member of the community and somebody that would defend her own to her last breath, but she held a secret that only a certain few people knew. She talked to the dead. In her younger years she would read tea leaves for anyone who asked her, or read their palms, and could tell you who was trustworthy, who was a complete liar, and who needed that little bit more help to carry on with life. No money would ever exchange hands. In her words, "It's my gift to give with love, for allowing me to have another shot at life".

Matilda grew up in the heart of London and all her children were born and lived there until the start of the Second World War, when her children were sent deep into the safety of the countryside. Only Matilda remained in London while her husband, a sergeant in the army, was fighting abroad and defending his British heritage. How she longed for her husband to be returned to her so her family could all be together. After the War was over Matilda and Burt decided to move to this tiny market town in East Grinstead, which meant they were reunited with their children and could at least try to give them the sort of security they just couldn't have in London.

Matilda was a strong woman with a big heart. But she had the worst cackling laugh that could ever be heard and when she laughed her eyes almost shut tight and it wouldn't be long before the tears ran down her face. She was a fun lady to be around and everybody loved her.

April 1971

Days, weeks, months and years passed. Dreanna had outgrown her cot two years previously and now shared a double bed with her oldest sister. Dawn didn't mind the endless cuddles that Dreanna gave her every night, she was all too happy to oblige. Maybe it was because of the coldness of the house, as all they had covering them each night was a sheet and two blankets. Or maybe it was because the affection her mother once gave her had finally stopped and this was Dawn's way of getting the attention she longed for. Either way the two sisters lay side by side, night after night, holding each other close for warmth, comfort and reassurance.

Dreanna was now ready to start her first day at nursery. She was still a ray of sunshine to her family, and not once had she lost her temper or cried in anger. She was a pleasure to have in any household, always smiling and showing affection, always being Dreanna, a child that wanted nothing or demanded nothing.

The playschool was situated on the estate in an old wooden hut and run by some of the mothers who had taken it upon themselves to have a place for all the young ones to go. It was inexpensive and freed up some time for the other mums to have a well-deserved rest from their growing children.

This was going to be the first time Dreanna mixed with lots of other children, some of whom she already knew, and these she usually played with hap-pily when their mothers shared a cuppa and a gossip. But most of the children that went to this playschool were from streets away, so she had never met, played with or touched them before.

She grabbed hold of her mother's hand as they had a leisurely stroll up the street. Her long fair hair was brushed and pulled into two separate bunches, held in place by elastic bands. Her dress was deep red and neatly ironed, and on her feet were the highly polished black shoes normally only worn for special occasions. Iris looked down on her child trying to jump the cracks in the pave-ment. "We might not have a lot kid, but you are going to look smart for your first day at nursery."

She stopped to rearrange Dreanna's dress, pull up her socks and wipe a bit of dirt off the tip of her shoes. As she bent down she cupped Dreanna's face in the palm of her hands and stared into the innocent eyes of her youngest child. "Now Dreanna, you won't be here for long and you are going to have such a wonderful time. Lots of children to play with and lots of toys. The only thing I ask of you is to say 'please' and 'thank you'. You must remember your manners young lady."

Dreanna lowered her head briefly before lifting it once more. "But why do I have to go Mummy? I want to stay with you and Nanny."

Iris thought for a moment as to why she really did have to go; it wasn't as if she was a handful at home and she needed a break from her. Iris really didn't know what to say, there was not going to be a good enough reason. She paused and stuttered her answer.

"B-b-because it's going to be fun and you will have such a good time." Part of Iris knew she was unsure of the words she had just said as she pushed open the door of the hut.

The hut was dark and musky inside; its high beams covered in woodworm were sure to be the building's demise one day, but it was holding its own and had been for many years. The floor was made from bare plywood, stained where many feet had trampled on it; the small windows had been painted to shield people's eyes inside from the daylight. Over time the paint had be-come scratched and glimmers of sunshine now peeked through. One single 100-watt bulb with no lamp shade dangled high above. The place was full of children screaming and fighting over toys, running around with not a care in the world.

Dreanna pleaded desperately with her mother, her heart beginning to beat faster and her eyes growing as big as saucers. "Mummy... I don't want to go in there; please don't make me go in there. I don't like it, it's scary and horrible. Mummy please take me home, please Mummy I don't like it!"

"Enough Dreanna! You will enjoy it I promise you."

The sternness in Iris's voice made Dreanna stop in an instant. She wasn't used to anyone talking to her in such a sharp way, and this alone shocked her into not asking again.

A well-built woman grabbed Dreanna by the hand and heaved her into the centre of the room. The grasp she had on her tiny hands made Dreanna's puny fingers tingle. Her apron smelt of old socks and was tied tightly around her waist making her stomach fat protrude over the top of it. Dreanna was confused at the tone of her voice; she said the nicest words but her voice had no feeling, no affection and no love.

"Come on precious, you are going to have such a good time. Look at all the amazing toys we have."

Dreanna's eyes locked into this woman's gaze; the woman's eyes were dark and wrinkled. Her face? Where was her face? All she saw was those deep dark cold eyes. She blinked and rubbed her own eyes – all they could see was a distorted, expressionless void of physical nothingness. The woman's voice seemed to change from offering words of support to anger, so much anger. Her words weren't kind and considerate anymore, but were words of hatred and rage, the words that Dreanna was told never to say. Dreanna's ears could only hear this woman's anger.

"Fucking hell, you're useless! Lazy bastard piece of shit! That's what you are!"

Dreanna shook her head hoping the words would stop, hoping the face of nothingness would disappear from her vision. She stared around searching for her mother, hoping to find her amongst the noisy children, but she had gone. She turned to face the playful children, her mind filling with their shouting and noise and words that she couldn't understand or interpret. She put her hands over her ears. Everybody was talking at once. The sound was deafening. Her small body started trembling and shaking, the tears fell down her face, and all she wanted was to get away. Her voice was wavering, her arms lashing out at any person who tried to give her comfort. "I want my Mummy, I want to go home. Please let me go home!"

The faceless woman tried to grab her but Dreanna sidestepped out of her path and began to turn in circles looking for some way to escape the feelings and noise she was experiencing. The faceless woman tried again; again Dreanna moved her arms waving frantically. The woman held out her hand to this sorrowful mess. "This child is crazy. Someone go collect her mum quickly before she has some sort of seizure. Come on now love, you have to stop crying, nobody's going to hurt you, come on now."

The woman's hands drew nearer and nearer to Dreanna's tear-soaked face and before she could react, Dreanna bit her hard, bit and held on, her milk teeth sinking further into the woman's fat fleshy hand as if she was some sort of animal feasting on its daily kill.

"Why you little bitch!" The woman pulled at Dreanna's hair until she let go of her hand, her arm raised high into the air as if her next strike would be to slap her hard across the cheeks."You need to be taught some manners you little bitch. Spoilt, that's what you are, you are nothing but a spoilt little brat. Your poor mother, I feel sorry for her, you…"

Before she could finish her sentence Dreanna heaved herself free and ran. She escaped to a corner of the room, her head buried in her knees, her hands placed tightly over her ears. The tears that had flowed now stopped as total shock took over. Her eyes did not blink as she looked for some sort of solitude, some way to escape from the prison without bars.

Iris had just arrived home and was pouring herself a cup of tea, when her silence was interrupted.

"Iris? Iris where are you?"

She recognised the voice of Margaret, the neighbour who occasionally helped out at the playschool. "In here love, do you fancy a cuppa?" Iris shouted as she reached for the tap to fill the kettle.

"Not a good idea. I think you better get yourself up the road – your daughter has just bit Sue. I think she's gone a little crazy. Well actually that's an understatement, she's gone fucking barking mad!"

Puzzled and bemused, Iris turned off the tap and put the kettle back on the worktop. "What, my Dreanna bite someone? Never!"

Margaret leant in the doorway between the kitchen and hall, lifted her right arm and blew her nose into a small pristine white hankie with an initial 'M' embroidered into one of the corners.

"Well you better believe it. She was screaming like a banshee and then just seemed to lose it. I've never seen a child behave in that way, it was a little freaky. Bloody crazy Iris, bloody crazy!"

Iris rushed past Margaret and shot out the front door. Even for a twenty-a-day smoker she managed to arrive at the hut in record time. Tears filled her own eyes when she saw her child, her head hidden from the prying gazes around her.

Sue, the obese woman with no face, grabbed Iris by the arm. "Your kid needs a good hiding. You should have warned us how aggressive she was. She's only been here half an hour and disrupted every kid in the place. A right royal smack on the arse is what she needs. Please Iris, just take her home and never, ever bring her back!"

Iris grimaced as she bent down and grabbed Dreanna's arm. "Come on poppet, let's get you home." She glared at the women looking on, knowing that her daughter's antics would be the talk of the estate for many days to come. But Iris held her head high. "Just for the record Sue, Dreanna never has behaved like this before. Maybe you should check your own skills in looking after kids, or maybe she just didn't like what she saw in you as a person." She added under her breath, "Stupid fat bitch!"

The walk home was quiet. Dreanna wasn't her normal happy-go-lucky self, and something in her personality seemed to have changed. Matilda was sitting at the dining room table when they got in, a cigarette hanging from her creased mouth. "Told you didn't I girl? I warned you it would soon change. I didn't expect it to happen quite like this, but I knew sooner or later she would become a handful." Matilda inhaled her cigarette deeply.

Iris looked at her child for a long time. She felt angry and let down. She wanted to shake her daughter, scream at her and demand from her the reason behind her behaviour, but all she could see was this perfect child; a perfect child who for whatever reason was now sad. For the first time in her short life Dreanna was expressionless.

"Mum, what should I do? What's happened to her? Why did she bite Sue? She's never bitten anyone, she's never cried like that before. What's the matter with her?"

"Listen to me Iris," Matilda said. "I'm thinking that there's a great possibility that this is going to get a lot worse, so prepare yourself and get ready for a bumpy ride ahead. Are you going to Elsie's on Sunday? See what she has to say about all this. You never know – she may be able to see her future – 'cos in all honesty my girl, I don't have a bloody clue as to what to say to you."

Iris looked at her mother with desperation and apprehension; as much as she loved Elsie that woman put the fear of God into her. She always felt a little uncomfortable around her, as if she was on trial for something when left alone with her too long.

Elsie was Patrick's mum. Her dark Roman gypsy hair was always pulled back off her face, which was slightly chubby, as was her body; it was her penetrating dark eyes that held her beauty. In her hey-day she had been one of the town's lay people who delivered many of the local babies, but Elsie was known by many more as the town's oracle. She held a gift similar to Matilda's but with a crucial difference: Matilda would never tell anybody their future, while Elsie occasionally relished the fact that someone she disliked "would get what was coming to them". Elsie's words were few, and if she liked you, you would class yourself as lucky, but if she didn't you made sure you stepped out of her path. It was whispered that many a curse was fashioned in her parlour, and bottles and jars of unknown ingredients were mixed to either give life or take it away.

Sunday came around quickly enough; the day was warm and sunny, a typical spring day. Buds were beginning to appear on the trees and the primroses and bluebells had just started to flower – their scent filled the air as the family began their two-mile trek to Elsie's house.

Dreanna was as usual being carried on her brother's shoulders; Dawn and Patrice idly walked behind their parents. Patrice had picked up a large stick and was poking the back of Dawn's legs with it.

"Stop it Patrice, that hurts."

Patrice smirked and continued thrusting the stick into Dawn's shins.

"Mum, Patrice is hitting me," Dawn's voice was squeaky and persistent.

Iris tutted and gave her two daughters the glare that only mothers can give. "Now girls, enough is enough. Patrice put that bloody stick down! What is Elsie going to say if you turn up covered in mud and looking grubby? She'd think I can't look after my own kids." Deep down she knew Elsie would never judge her if her kids looked untidy, as Elsie always said, "A clean kid is an unhappy kid, but a dirty one knows just how to have fun." Iris grinned as she remembered these words, but all the same she didn't want them turning up at their nan's house looking like latch-key children.

They arrived just after one o'clock. Elsie's home was always full of children; some were her own grandchildren who used to live with her, others were the neighbours' kids. Her door was always open and if anyone had a problem Elsie's was the first place they would go.

Dreanna's Auntie Bet handed her a plateful of food with a warm smile. A homemade sausage roll, a slice of cake and a lovely big chunk of freshly baked bread smothered in Marmite. "Come on Dreanna eat up. Your mum said you love Marmite, so come on, down the hatch."

Dreanna stared at the piece of bread covered in black spread. Just the colour of it turned her stomach. Dreanna whispered in her father's ear, her hand cupped so no one else could hear. "Daddy, I do like Marmite, but it's too strong. I don't think I can eat it, it's all yucky."

Patrick gave his daughter a wink and shoved another of his mother's homemade pickled onions into his mouth. Out of the corner of his mouth he whispered, "Don't worry Bubs, Bet won't force you to eat it."

Iris's eagle eyes caught her daughter and husband and wondered what they were whispering about. The one thing she hated was secrets. "Don't you eat too many of them damn pickled onions Pat, you know what they do to your insides!" she laughed.

"I think you're just a little too late with your advice Iris, clear the decks, I'm coming through!" Patrick made a hasty retreat, and shot upstairs to the bathroom, not even bothering about the cup of tea he'd knocked over in the process.

The bathroom had just been moved from outside to inside. This was one of the first houses the council had decided to renovate. An indoor bathroom made a nice change from the toilet in the garden and the old tin bath that was used by all the members of the family on a Sunday evening.

The older children went straight outside after tea and played in the yard. Dreanna sat next to her dad, her head resting on his lap as he rubbed his bloated stomach. "You've really done my guts this time," Patrick looked straight at his mum. "You bloody old witch!"

The room shook with laughter.

Elsie sipped her tea and with a proud mischievous grin announced quite matter of factly, "Never a truer word my son, never a truer word."

Once the amusement had passed Patrick turned to his mother and looked straight into her eyes. His expression was now one of concern, burden and unease. "Mum, I need to ask you something about Dreanna."

Elsie's eyes were as dark as coal. Nobody ever questioned her. She always had the last word and even her own grandchildren were petrified of this powerful figure. Dreanna lifted her head and met Elsie's gaze and the two females stared at each other for a long time. It was Dreanna who looked away first, but Elsie continued to search for a clue as to what was going on inside this young girl's head. "An inquisitive child if ever I'd seen one. Not really sure about this one Patrick, she certainly has something and there are all sorts of energies around her, but I'll be honest son, I just don't know. She's going to be a handful, and mark my words, you'll end up pulling your hair out!" Elsie hated the fact that she couldn't see beyond this particular day and that this child's future was going to be written one day at a time. "What did your Ma say, Iris?"

Iris stared at her husband, her eyes locked on his. He could tell how desperate she was and how badly she needed to know what the hell was happening to her youngest child.

"She hasn't said a lot really, she just keeps telling me how much she's going to change. The other day when we took her to nursery she bit one of the ladies' hands. To say we were shocked was an understatement. When we got her home Dreanna was unusually quiet and solemn, but after a couple of hours, well it was like that morning never happened."

Elsie's glare moved away from her granddaughter as she reached for her son's cigarette packet. She broke the tip off a cigarette and threw it upwards into her open mouth. "Bloody nurseries. What's the world coming to? A child should be with their mother. Just another way for a parent to get rid of their kids for a couple of hours, that's all them places are. Bloody new fangled bollocks, prisons for kids, bloody prisons! But as for Dreanna, time will show us Iris, time will show us."

October 1971

Six months later Elsie passed away sitting in her chair in the family home. It came as a big shock to the family as she hadn't even been ill. Obviously she had creaking bones and found walking a little hard, but at her age that was to be expected. She just went to sleep in the chair in the parlour and never woke up again; she always said she would never die in a hospital bed, so her wish was granted. She died in the home that had seen the births of her seven children, the beginning and end of the Second World War, and the return of her husband, complete with a medal of honor after fighting for king and country.

The day of her funeral saw the whole street lined up, patiently waiting to give their last respects to this pillar of the community. Some, it has to be said, were there just to make sure the 'old witch' had finally perished; they would have had her burned at the stake if it was still legal, and had her travelling family put in prison just for dirtying the streets with their presence.

White roses spelling out her name were lying on the top of her coffin. Every single person was dressed in their Sunday best, with neatly pressed shirts and collars, polished shoes and hair brushed, set and Brylcreemed. As the hearse stopped outside the family home, Dreanna grabbed her father's hand, her eyes already moist with the tears that others wanted to shed but couldn't, as each one remembered the words that Elsie said: "Laugh at a funeral as they will now be at peace, cry at a wedding as the silly sods don't know what troubles lay ahead."

A booming voice sounded behind father and daughter, and broke the deafening silence that filled the air. "A saint your mum was, a true saint."

"Thanks Fred." Patrick turned to shake his hand then let his eyes fall back to the gaps in the pavement.

Dreanna began pulling at the rim of Patrick's jacket. "Daddy...who is that man over there, dressed in uniform?" Dreanna's voice was but a whisper.

"W-w-what?" Patrick stuttered.

"The man, he's waving to you. He's standing by the car with Nanny's flowers in. He looks like you, Daddy." Dreanna smiled up at her father and squeezed his hand tighter than before.

Fred looked down on this curious child, as he began rolling a cigarette between his fingers. "Is your daughter seeing things that we can't Pat? Looks like she's got your mother's talent." His voice broke off into a short burst of laughter and before long Patrick joined him. Soon their quiet chortles turned into loud, almost oppressive guffaws.

The funeral was over soon enough and the doors of the family home were left wide open; anybody who wanted a slice of cake, a pint of stout, or just somewhere to go to pass the time of day was welcome. It was almost as if Elsie was still there welcoming all and sundry into her home for one last time.

The Doorway Opens

August 1972

The hot summer sun shone down on Dreanna as she happily played in the garden, dancing in and out of the vegetables that Patrick had planted earlier in the year. With nimble fingers she carefully pulled off the slugs and snails eating their way through the green leaves, and then she walked slowly to the bottom of the garden and threw them over the fence into the bracken below. As disgusting at it may sound she kissed each one before launching them to their fate.

Iris was doing the washing at the kitchen sink, her soapy hands scrubbing a pair of Patrick's work trousers with an old brush; the pile of wet clothes ready to be put through the mangle was growing higher and higher at her feet. There was a knock at the door. It was Dreanna's friend.

"Dreanna, Dreanna!" yelled Iris, "Cathy's at the door. Are you going out to play?"

Dreanna appeared at the kitchen door. In the palm of her hand sat a juicy fat slug that had spent the morning nibbling Patrick's lettuce. "Yep, hold on, I just have to say goodbye to the slugs and snails. Now you be good, Mr. Slug, and don't eat too much of Daddy's lettuce, or he will put salt on you." She gently placed the slug back onto a fresh leaf and headed up the garden path towards her waiting friend.

The parents had no concern in allowing their offspring to wander outside; there was hardly ever any traffic apart from the occasional ice cream van, and there were always enough prying eyes around to check that no mischief was going on. Dreanna and Cathy skipped hand in hand up the road and played for the next two hours at the edge of the woods. They collected yet more snails and put them into groups; each snail was given a name and a job to do. The girls' hands were getting covered in the sticky oozy mess, and their once-clean clothes were covered in mud and grime; the remnants of what they'd wiped off their hands was now down the front of their jeans. Their once-white cheeks had taken on a summer glow, and their hair stuck to the backs of their necks where the summer heat had made them sweat.

Iris leaned over the same fence where just a few hours ago Dreanna had thrown the slugs and snails. "Dreanna, Dreanna! Time to come in now."

Dreanna sighed. She was so enjoying her time under the summer sun with all her new slime-making friends. "I have to go now Cathy. Daddy will be home soon and my belly is making growling sounds which means it must be dinner time."

The two sweaty children sped up the road, saying their goodbyes as they reached Dreanna's home. She nudged open the front door with her backside and ran into the kitchen. Iris was upstairs getting ready for her evening at work and Matilda was busily putting the rest of the clothes through the mangle. Dreanna watched as the water was squeezed out of the garments and she tried catching the droplets that fell in her hand. Her hands began to change colour as the dirt she'd collected mixed with the fresh clean liquid.

"DON'T touch the clothes Dreanna, you're filthy. C'mon let's get you cleaned up before you ruin all the hard work your mother's done." Matilda lifted her granddaughter up onto the workspace by the sink. Dreanna waved her dirty hands close to Matilda's face almost touching her and sharing the grime with her.

"Oo you are a bugger," Matilda chuckled.

Dreanna giggled. Matilda reached for the dish-cloth and began wiping the day's dirt from her granddaughter's hands and face. Matilda stared right into Dreanna's eyes and Dreanna began reading her nana's thoughts. She crawled and probed every corner of this woman's mind, scrutinising every word and every image she saw there. "Nanny…why do you want to die?" Dreanna asked, perched on the side of the work surface, her feet dangling into a sink full of warm water.

Matilda was taken aback at the matter-of-fact way her granddaughter spoke to her and shocked that she would even ask such a personal intrusive question. "What a silly thing to ask child, I don't want to die."

"Yes you do. You're sad, Nana. Why are you so sad?"

Matilda didn't quite know how to respond. Should she lie? But there was something in this child's eyes that told her even if she did she wouldn't believe her. "I just miss your granddad that's all. He was such a special man." Matilda's eyes began to fill, but the last thing she wanted was to let this child see her cry. She swallowed her pain and with it the memories of the only man she had ever loved. "Come now, let's finish getting you cleaned up. Your dad will be home soon."

The evening passed much the same as any other. Patrick arrived home and shared a pot of tea with his wife as they talked about their day's events. Iris then left for work at the local hospital, which was at the far end of the estate. A pioneering young doctor in World War 2 had made an astonishing break-through in plastic surgery and the hospital specialised in burns victims. It also had a Casualty department that was always full of bloodied, broken and injured bodies, an old people's ward where most of its occupants spent their final days, two general surgery wards for mundane tonsillectomies, appendix-removals and in-growing toenails, a children's ward and an eye ward. It was the eye ward that Dreanna hated. It had very dim lighting and all the patients walked around wearing glasses or eye patches. How she hated not seeing their eyes.

Iris arrived back home at around 9 o'clock, where a fresh cup of tea awaited her as she walked through the door. The older children were still playing outside, but Dreanna was already dressed for bed. She was sitting in her favourite place between her father's legs, her head gently resting on his chest, brushing her fingers through his white nicotine-stained beard. The rest of that evening was spent watching the fourteen-inch black-and-white television that sat in the far corner of the living room. Dreanna as usual fell asleep downstairs and was put to bed at the same time that her parents decided to retire. Her siblings were fast asleep when Patrick softly lay her down next to Dawn in the large double bed they shared. Patrice slept in a single bed at the far corner of the room; she had never wanted to share a bed with anyone, including this child who would wrap herself around her each time they got close.

Dreanna's breathing was slow and steady, her eyes tightly closed and Dawn's arm moved to drape across her chest as if trying, even in her unconscious state, to protect her in some way.

A strange sensation shot through Dreanna's sleeping body; a feeling of lightness, a floating awareness from the tips of her feet to the top of her head. She felt warm and calm, composed and peaceful. She became aware of being lifted upwards, higher and higher. Her eyes opened and she looked around her bedroom. Instead of lying down she found herself standing upright on top of the blankets that covered her bed. She looked behind her and saw her sister with her eyes tightly closed and her arm still across her physical body.

"Well it's about time." The voice came from another child that stood on the floor beneath her.

"Eh? I don't understand. Who are you? What... what's happened?" Dreanna's inquisitive tone begged for an answer. She wiped her eyes and examined her fingers. "I'm all sort of see-through and glowy," she giggled.

The mysterious girl winked as she responded, her face suffused with light as if lit by a hundred light bulbs. There was an urgency in her voice. "You'll soon get used to that. Come on and don't worry, I'll have you back by morning. Hurry up – we have lots to do! Don't be frightened, I'll take care of you, I promise."

Dreanna reached out her arm and held this newcomer's hand tightly, still unsure what was happening to her.

An aura of the purest light appeared, right in front of the chest of drawers. The light seemed to fill the whole room and its glow held compassion and empathy. Even though it was so bright it didn't make Dreanna's eyes squint; it didn't hurt them in any way. The two girls walked slowly into this all-embracing luminosity. The light saturated their bodies, and they became the light that surrounded them. It didn't take long for the lustrous glow to disappear and Dreanna stared down at her hands; her body again resembled something solid yet she felt strangely different and somewhat peculiar: warm, contented, blissful and heavenly. She opened her eyes wide, taking in the new sights that became clearer and clearer. Long flowing grass, flowers so colourful, so bright, a sky of deepest blue, everything so clean so fresh so pure. Wherever she was, Dreanna didn't have a care in the world; she was peaceful and the place was peaceful. It felt like home – it felt like she belonged.

"Where do you want to go?" asked the stranger.

Dreanna stared into open space, not quite knowing what to do or say next.

"You look a little shocked," the girl laughed. "You see that tree over there? Let's go there." She pointed to a giant oak, its branches spread across the whole meadow, its leaves gently rustling in a warm breeze. "I think it's going to be a nice place for you." The girl stopped talking abruptly as the figure of a woman appeared by their sides.

"Hello my darling. How are you my sweet child?"

Dreanna turned her head; she knew that voice, there was no mistaking it. It had to be, it was! "Nanny?" she screamed. Dreanna rubbed her eyes, not understanding why she could see and hear Elsie. After all, everyone said she would never see her again. She was, as they say, dead. Dreanna saw them put the coffin into the fire with her body inside it. This couldn't be Nana Elsie, could it? Was this a dream? But it felt so real, it felt so natural. It felt wonderful.

Elsie laughed mischievously. "Didn't expect to see me again so soon, did ya? I haven't got long, but make sure you give Patrick and Iris a big kiss from me. Come here child, and give your old Nan a big squeeze." Dream or not, Dreanna didn't care and walked closer to her grandmother, and before she knew it was engulfed in Elsie's plump arms. Elsie had never once hugged her before, unlike Matilda who constantly showed affection to her grandchildren.

Elsie's hands held Dreanna's cheeks. "Now be good. It may be hard, but promise to be good." And within the blink of an eye Elsie was gone.

Dreanna turned to her new friend. "Where did she go?" Dreanna paused, confused by everything. So many questions raced around her young mind and she looked around again at her surroundings. Everything seemed so real. Nana Elsie had seemed so real, but how could she be? She was dead and people can't vanish that quickly, can they? Her head began to ache. She opened her mouth again and asked, "Where am I?"

The young girl stood head and shoulders above Dreanna. Her hair was long and her eyes were black, as black as the coal that Patrick placed in the hearth each morning. She was very pretty with a kind face. Not once did Dreanna feel frightened, she only felt free.

"You are wherever you want to be. Imagine whatever you want and it will be here, but I think that's enough for tonight. Things are better done in small doses. Come take my hand."

They stepped back into the space where the lights had been and were once again standing in the bedroom with Dawn snoring and the family dog curled up at the bottom of Patrice's bed.

Dreanna stared down at her sleeping body. "What do I do now?"

The girl led Dreanna to the edge of her lifeless form."Just touch your body – any part of you – it doesn't really matter, and I will see you really soon. I will be back before you know it, I promise."

Dreanna reached down to touch her own cheek and as her fingers pressed against the soft skin, she felt an enormous pull downwards. Her breath was taken away sharply, and as she inhaled her eyes opened wide.

She lay motionless in her bed and all she could hear was her sister's breathing. Dreanna turned to look at the place where the light had appeared. All that was left was a twinkling of stars and in a couple of seconds even they were gone. Her body felt heavy and deeply tired, and as much as she tried to keep her eyes open, she lost the battle and a deep slumber took hold.

Watching her father make an early morning pot of tea, she wondered if she should tell him the events of the night before. Dreanna stared straight at the back of her dad's head. "Daddy, Nanny said to give you her love, 'cos I, erm, saw her last night in a field and there was a really big tree and a little girl who had long hair and black eyes and she said that I can see her again soon and I was in bed and ..."

Patrick hunched his shoulders, concentrating on pouring the tea. "Dreanna, take a breath. You're the only kid I know that can talk for England. You suffer from verbal diarrhoea, you do!" He picked up a spoon and stirred the tea-flavoured water. "So you saw my mum did you? That was nice. We'll have to talk later, I have to get to work kid. Your mum's upstairs. Give your dad a kiss."

Patrick bent forward and kissed the top of Dreanna's head and handed her the fresh cup of tea he'd just made. She watched as he pulled his bag onto his back and headed out the front door. She hated this time of day, as everybody seemed to leave so quickly. It made her feel so very sad and lonely.

Dawn was the next to appear in the kitchen. Dreanna, like most kids her age, got distracted easily and the thoughts of Nana Elsie were soon gone from her mind and all she could think of was what her father just said. "Dawny, Daddy said I have verbal diarrhoea. Does that mean I have to see a doctor?"

Dawn's tone was more impatient. Usually she would listen to her youngest sister, but this morning she seemed irritable and tired. Dawn didn't even look at Dreanna but carried on staring into the mirror while her fingers gently squeezed a large spot on her chin. "God, Dreanna you are so stupid. Dad means you talk too much, you're not ill. So shut up. I can't be bothered to listen to you this morning; you kept me awake last night, you were freezing. Plus just look at the size of this zit! How can I go out of the house with this thing on my face? Jesus! It looks awful!"

Dreanna sat on the dining room floor oblivious to Dawn's moans and carried on sipping her tea, thinking just how yucky it would be having diarrhoea coming out of your mouth. She cringed at the thought.

All three siblings left the house at much the same time. It was nearly the end of the summer holidays and the three oldest children where off to the nearby outdoor swimming pool. The French exchange students were over in England for a few weeks giving the local female teenagers a good excuse to bare their skin and flaunt their young bodies at any French boy they could.

William was now fifteen and often used to fight with other boys. Nearly every day he would come home with a bloodied nose or someone else's blood down his shirt. Dawn was turning twelve in September and Patrice would be eleven in the same month. Dreanna was due to start infant school as soon as the summer had finished. Iris had never bothered to send her back to nursery, not that she would have been allowed back anyway, and she put her freaky behaviour down to her daughter simply having a bad day. But in the back of her mind she didn't believe she had seen the last of it.

September 1972

The end of the summer holidays saw the worst thunderstorm of the season, and Dreanna's first walk to her new school was an adventure of its own. Iris held her daughter's hand tightly as they stepped in and out of the puddles. Their walk to school took them through a small wooded area, and the dry mud was soon turning into a watery bath of russet-coloured slop. They reached their destination in record time, fifteen minutes from start to finish. The school gates were wooden and kept in place by two iron catches that held them safely out the way of the hoards of children and parents that poured through them. Dreanna's grip on her mother's hand tightened as she entered the playground. The older, more boisterous children were running round, coats held high above their heads, never minding the rain soaking their clothes; their parents shouted at them to put their coats back on, but their comments fell on deaf ears.

A tall thin lady walked out from one of the entrances, a floral headscarf tied tightly around her head. She held a large brass handbell which she yanked up and down. The noise stopped all the children in their tracks and silence fell on the playground. Even the mothers stopped their chatter and looked over at her. The older children made orderly lines and filed through the same door that this woman had appeared from; the younger ones stood still, not knowing quite what to do next.

Another lady appeared. Her frame was small and her skin dark. "Follow me children. Let go of your mummy's hands, come now quickly, quickly."

The rain was still pouring down and you could see how much this woman hated being outside. Iris bent down and straightened the collar of Dreanna's coat, then kissed her tenderly on the cheek. "Now Dreanna, you are going to love school. It's not like that nasty nursery. The teachers are really nice here, and Mrs. Martin teaches in the school next door. You remember Mrs. Martin, don't you? Daddy did some work for her and she gave you chocolate cake. You remember her, don't you?"

Dreanna nodded. She was so unsure of how she was feeling. The size of the building scared her; all the other children filled her with terror, and the memories of that stupid fat lady at nursery made her stomach churn. "I have to go, don't I Mummy? Will you pick me up later? Promise to pick me up later Mummy, promise?"

Iris stroked her daughter's head and with a reassuring smile replied, "At 3.15. I will be here and Nanny will be here as well, I promise. Now run along and mind your manners, 'please' and 'thank-yous' at all times remember?"

Iris watched as Dreanna made her way into school. Part of her was happy that all her children were finally out of the house during the day as this was her opportunity to work at the hospital full-time to earn some much-needed extra cash, but part of her was frightened for her youngest daughter. She was half the size of the other kids and Iris was scared that school would indeed change this mild-mannered child. She quickly turned and left the playground trying not to think of the concerned look on her daughter's face when they parted.

The day went exceedingly well. Dreanna came out of school holding a creased piece of paper that she had painted, her face beaming as she searched around for her mother.

Matilda was the first to see her grand-daughter. "Dreanna, Dreanna, we are over here!"

Dreanna ran as fast as her little legs could carry her into the open arms of her mother. Verbal diarrhoea took hold. "Mummy look what I done, I drew this picture for you, and I played in the playground and I ate all my lunch and I saw Cathy, and Janet, and Rose and I saw Mrs. Martin and we played in the water and in the sand and…"

Iris couldn't help but laugh. The fears that she had at leaving her daughter seemed foundless. "Dreanna, slow down! So you had a nice day then?"

Dreanna's excitement didn't stop all evening. Every person in the house got told the day's events over and over again. Until everybody shouted together,

"WILL YOU SHUT UP!"

Dreanna was exhausted and she edged her tiny form closer to Dawn's as they lay in bed that evening. It wasn't long before the ghostly figure of the unknown girl was again standing by her side and Dreanna was staring back down at her physical shape in the bed.

"What's your name?"

"Susan. My name is Susan."

"Where are we going tonight Susan? Can we go to the field again?"

"No, we are going to your own special room, and you can play there all night." *Susan's face beamed with a knowing smile.*

As the girls approached the end of the long fluorescent tunnel, Dreanna found herself in a large room bigger than her own bedroom and filled with so many toys. A doll's house as tall as her sat in the centre of the room, and a grey rocking horse stood proudly at the far corner.

"WOW" Dreanna gasped as she scanned the contents. "Let's play!"

Susan and Dreanna played all through the night; it was as if they had known each other for years. Dreanna was never a child to hold back her thoughts and spoke freely. Some would say she was nosey, but her family liked to think she was just inquisitive.

"Where's your mummy?" she asked.

Susan's eyes were fixed on the rocking horse, her nimble fingers twisting and turning the hair of its mane into a tight plait. "I don't have a mummy or a daddy. I don't need anyone. Everybody here takes care of everybody else."

Dreanna didn't quite understand what Susan meant, and to be honest she really didn't care – her only interest lay in playing, and then playing some more. The night finished all too soon for her, and before she knew it she was back again in her solid physical form. But at least she had the next night, and the next and the next and the next…

Goodbye for Now

The school days passed quickly and before anyone knew it the half-term break was upon them. Iris was relieved that her fear and worry over Dreanna starting school was unfounded; she had settled in so well.

When the new half term began Dreanna was allowed to make her journey to school with Cathy, Janet and Rose. She hung up her coat in the changing rooms outside her classroom and changed her wellies into the black plimsoles they had to wear then took her seat inside with the other children. Some of the boys were busy picking their noses and wiping what they found onto the nearest back that came into range. Mrs. Duke, the school's head mistress, strolled into the class, her glasses fixed firmly on the bridge of her nose, her grey hair nicely set. Everybody liked her and she had taught each one of Dreanna's siblings in turn. Her voice was gentle but firm and she had the respect of pupils and staff. "Now settle down class. Unfortunately, Mrs. Jones is poorly and won't be able to teach you this term, so we have a new teacher for you. This is Miss Beachly. Now you all behave and I will see you in assembly."

Mrs. Duke left and Miss Beachly sat at her desk in front of the class. She was short and stout, her hair scraped back into a tight bun. Her shoes were highly polished and her clothes nicely pressed. Dreanna could not tear her gaze away from her new teacher's shoes – they must have taken a lot of polish to look that shiny. Her eyes began to travel upwards and she glimpsed at Miss Beachly's silver speckled glasses and then their eyes connected. Dreanna's head began to ache and her stomach started to do somersaults. She felt dizzy and began to sweat, as if she had spent too long on the roundabout in the park.

"I don't think Dreanna feels very well," said Rose, her hand raised straight in the air.

Miss Beachly looked concerned. Dreanna was silent, her eyes filled with tears that soon streamed down her face.

"Don't you feel very well little one? Little one, are you okay?" The teacher's hand was now touching Dreanna's forehead.

Dreanna glared deep into her eyes. "I want to go home. I need to go home," she shouted. "Please, I need my Mummy." Dreanna jumped out of her chair and ran to the door.

Miss Beachly reached out her hand, waiting for Dreanna to grasp hold of it, but Dreanna pushed her hand away fiercely.

"Okay, okay my dear, let's take you to reception. What's the matter?"

Dreanna's breathing was hurried and rapid. "Leave me alone," she shouted. She moved her body further and further away from the substitute teacher; Miss Beachly could do no more than usher her to the reception area of the school. Dreanna sat down outside the main office while her new teacher tried to explain to the secretary just what had happened.

"Don't worry," the receptionist said, "leave her to me, we'll soon have her sorted."

As Miss Beachly left, the secretary came and crouched down beside the tearful child. "Now Dreanna you must tell me what's wrong. Are you feeling sick? Shall I get you a bucket?"

Dreanna's voice was weak, as if she had been ill for days not minutes. "Yes... My head hurts and my tummy and I want my Mummy." The tears that had stopped now flowed freely again.

The kind receptionist patted Dreanna on the back and smiled comfortingly. "Sit here for a moment and if you feel better later you can go back to class, okay?"

Dreanna's head bowed and nodded in approval. The secretary left and returned with the ominous red bucket. Dreanna wondered how many times children had thrown up into it. She lay down on the put-you-up camp bed that was used when children felt unwell, closed her eyes and immediately fell into a deep sleep. She was interrupted by the sound of the bell ringing for morning break, and as she opened her eyes she saw the smiling face of the school secretary.

"Feeling better honey?"

Dreanna shook her head. "No, my head still hurts."

The receptionist placed the back of her hand onto Dreanna's forehead. "Well there doesn't appear to be a temperature but let's call your mum anyway to come and collect you, shall we?"

Dreanna was back at home before she knew it, and was soon curled up on the settee, a blanket thrown over her. The sound of the familiar lunch-time radio show was playing in the kitchen.

"She's been asleep for at least two hours," Iris said, drawing on her cigarette.

The second voice was Matilda's. Dreanna was always reassured when she heard her nan's voice. "Well that's a sure sign she is ill Iris...you know flu is going around, don't ya? Best get some of them antibiotics just in case."

"Think you're right Mum. Can you keep an eye on her while I nip to the phone box?"

In an instant Iris was out of the door, but returned just as quickly. "The doctor's popping in later when he's doing his rounds. Hope he bloody gets here before work tonight."

Dreanna snuggled beneath the warmth of the blanket; it had the familiar smell of Lux flakes and it smelt like home and she felt secure. As she stared blankly out of the front room window, she saw the familiar figure of the doctor walking down the garden path. After a brief examination and the dreaded wooden stick being shoved into her mouth to observe the back of her throat, he explained that it was most probably just some sort of virus, and left a prescription for antibiotics to be given if she became worse.

Dreanna couldn't wait for night to fall and bedtime to arrive, as she knew that once she could escape from her physical body she would feel so much better. Instead of falling asleep curled up on the settee, for the first time in her life she took herself to bed early. As usual it wasn't long before she was playing happily in her own private little nursery, with her new companion by her side.

"Dreanna," Susan paused. "Promise me you won't be sad, but I have to go away for a while. It doesn't mean you can't still come here, but I just have to go. You need to be a little girl."

Dreanna screwed up her face. "Susan you are so silly, I am a little girl but when I'm ten I will be a big girl."

"No, you don't understand. I can't come and play with you anymore."

"What? Why? Have I been naughty? Don't you like me anymore? I will try harder I promise, you are the bestest ever friend and I like playing with you and..."

Susan's face was solemn, her body held stiff. "No, stop! You haven't done anything wrong, and you're my best friend too, but I have to go away. I'm so sorry... but you can still come here whenever you want to, you know what to do. I need to take you back now." Susan grabbed Dreanna's hand and led her down the all too familiar path. Dreanna was still bemused and unsure of what her friend had just said – she didn't understand why Susan couldn't come and play with her again. As the girls reached the end of the bed, Susan leaned forward and kissed Dreanna on the forehead. "I love you my friend, and I will miss you. Please try and be good and remember you can go wherever your heart desires, but you must leave yourself plenty of time to get back."

Dreanna looked intently into Susan's eyes and watched as they took on a shimmering glaze as if they were about to cry. Susan's tears looked like the first flakes of winter snow; they were so beautiful, and each drop shone and glistened like a tiny crystal, each one so perfectly formed. Dreanna raised her hand and with her fingers gently wiped away each crystallized snow flake that she could. "Please don't cry Susan, you make me feel sad."

With one final touch of Susan's hand the two good friends separated. Dreanna was back in her own body, and Susan was gone.

It Hurts

December 1972

After a few days recovering at home, Dreanna was back to her old, inquiring self. She returned to school feeling relieved that everything seemed absolutely fine, the traumatic experience that she had days before seemed just a distant memory.

Her fifth birthday soon arrived and like most kids at that age she couldn't control her excitement. She woke earlier than usual and ran to open her presents – a Winnie the Pooh sketch book, crayons and pencils, a new jumper lovingly knitted by her mother and some soap-on-a-rope from her siblings. Her face beamed as she immediately began drawing in her new book. She was looking forward to going to school that day to tell her friends what she had received. In morning assembly the school tradition was to sing Happy Birthday to the recipient who then blew out the candles that were fixed inside a hollowed-out log. Today was Dreanna's special day. Her name was called and she jumped up off the cold wooden floor and headed towards the stage. Her audience began singing as she stood smiling and watching the naked flames of the candles rise higher and higher.

"Happy Birthday to you, Happy Birthday to you, Happy Birthday dear..."

As the birthday rhyme finished, Dreanna's gaze met that of a young boy sitting in the front row. At first he looked happy and then his face seemed to change and he started to cry. She looked deeper into his eyes; he wasn't in the school hall any more but running up some stairs. The carpet on the stairs was green with brown swirls running through it – then she heard the voice of a woman shout, "Get back here! Jesus fucking Christ, you are gonna get it this time, you wait till I get my hands on you!"

Dreanna blinked, then blinked again.

"Dreanna my darling, you have to blow your candles out. Can you hear me? Everyone is waiting – blow your candles out honey."

Dreanna turned her head in the direction of the voice and almost immediately she started to cry.

"Oh, have you got a little stage fright my dear?" Mrs Duke was smiling down at this bewildered child.

Dreanna closed her eyes and pouted her lips ready to blow out the candles. THUD. She felt as if she had just been hit hard around the back of her head. THUD. The forceful pain seemed to strike the side of her face. She opened her eyes and couldn't see the rest of her class or the teachers, all she could see was this one boy in the front row, crouching, crying, hurting… She blinked her eyes over and over again, for what seemed like minutes but in reality was only seconds – the hall was once again full of gawking eyes waiting patiently for her to blow out the five candles.

"Shall I give you a hand? Come now let's do it together, after three, one, two, three!" With one big puff from Mrs Duke all five candles had been quickly extinguished.

Dreanna still stood quite still, tears now falling faster down her cheeks. She slipped her hand into the strong grip of her head teacher. "Mrs Duke, I don't feel well."

Mrs Duke's voice was calming and reassuring, her hands were soft and she smelt of lavender and marigolds all mixed into one. "Oh, don't you my darling? Then you can come and sit with me in my office for a while. I think I would feel a little poorly if I had to blow out my candles in front of the whole school, and at my age my dear that would be an awful lot of candles!" Mrs Duke laughed quite openly, as if she had just amused herself.

Dreanna sat in the big comfy chair, her head resting on the padded arm. The feelings she had a few days ago had returned and she began shivering and clutching her stomach tightly as if to try and comfort herself in some way.

"Are you feeling better, little one? I must say you are very pale. Shall we call your mum?"

Dreanna could do no more than nod her head, she felt so very tired; sleep was all she really wanted. Dreanna's poor mother yet again made the walk to school in the freezing cold and biting wind to collect her child. The first of the winter frosts was still hard on the ground and the wind ate through their clothes on the journey home. The dead wood of the trees filled every space around them, and the air was pure; the smell of winter had finally arrived.

"Well it looks like we're going to have to get that prescription after all. You'll be up and about before you know it," Iris smiled down at her pasty-faced daughter.

Once back at home it was the usual routine of the favourite blanket, a hot water bottle and a glass of orange squash – and Dreanna wrapped up like a turkey on Christmas day, nestled on the sofa. She tried to force her eyes to stay open but of their own accord they shut tight together.

She managed to escape her listless body and was soon standing on the arm of the sofa staring down at herself. The normal light that beckoned her into its presence was nowhere to be seen, she was just standing in the recognisable surroundings of her front room. Try as hard as she could to move, her feet were fixed firmly to the velvet arm of the settee. Her impatient little body bent and twirled until she managed to break free. She made her way into the adjoining room. Iris and Matilda were busy peeling potatoes for the family's evening meal. A pot with its bubbling contents of neck of lamb, vegetables and dumplings, was simmering on the stove.

"I bloody hope this illness goes soon. I start full time work next week and just don't know what I'm gonna do if I have to keep going to get Dree from school. I hope the others don't catch it, I'll be screwed if they do. I'll get some Jeyes Fluid when I go up the town and disinfect the whole house, that'll soon kill off those germs." Iris scraped the skin off another dirty potato.

Matilda nodded firmly. "Good thinking Iris, it's better to be safe than sorry. Kill them little buggers before they kill you, that's what I always say."

The two women looked at each other, not knowing that they had an audience of one listening to their every word.

There was a strange pull dragging the translucent child backwards, hauling her further and further back to her sleeping form. She was too tired to fight it, too tired to try, and so allowed the wrenching sensation to grab hold. As soon as she was close her body became a magnet and the parts were finally together again as one.

Dreanna appeared to recover in record time and was soon busily drawing in her new book.

Iris was dressing in her winter clothes as Patrick was taking off his rather clumsy steel-toe-capped boots. "We might as well keep her off the whole week Patrick, there's no point going back for one more day," Iris said as she pulled her mittens on.

"I agree, see you later, and don't work too hard." Patrick pulled off his socks and loosened his belt buckle.

Sunday arrived and Dreanna was back to normal, rushing about the house and talking that endless waffle that her family had now become accustomed to. "Daddy," she shouted, as she pushed each foot into a wellington boot, "I'm going out to play down the woods with Janet and Cathy, is that okay?"

"It looks like the weather is changing. Are you sure you wanna go down the woods? You could stay in and help your dad cook the dinner?"

"Erm, no, Daddy, I have to go down the woods as we found a dead frog yesterday and have to go and chop it up, 'cos Janet wants to see what's inside his tummy, and then we have to go to the streams and..."

"I get the picture Dreanna," Patrick laughed. "Off you go and make sure you stay warm, don't want you catching another little lurgy do we?"

Dreanna made her way to the opening of the woods with Janet, Cathy and some older children from her street, each child chattering away like they hadn't seen each other for weeks. The fallen leaves crunched under their feet and the wind blew through the branches of the trees. The gaggle of children made their way to a pile of rotten wood where they had hidden the decomposing amphibian; they pushed the shards of wood aside but the frog had disappeared.

"Oh no! The frog's gone," cried Janet. "What are we going to do now?"

"Let's make a camp, a really big camp under the ground, and we can cover it with sticks and then nobody will know it's there," suggested John, one of the older kids.

Before long all the children were on their knees, mud clinging to their faces, hands and finger nails, as they dug deeper and deeper into the sod.

Dreanna lifted her head. "Cathy I think we should go home."
Cathy's dirty face questioned hers, "Why? I don't want to."

"Because there is a thunderstorm coming and you are scared of thunder, and we are going to be squashed by a tree."

Cathy's tone was abrupt. "Dreanna you're so stupid! You don't know that. If you want to go home then go, but I'm staying here – we're not going to be squashed. You're being silly!"

"I'm not allowed to go anywhere on my own, you know that! So, so I suppose I'd better stay, but you will be scared and we ARE going to be squashed." Dreanna took a deep sigh and returned to scraping the mud towards her.

An hour passed and the children's hole was deep enough for them to climb into. Dreanna staggered out, mud filling every one of her orifices, including the corners of her mouth. The air filled with rain and an enormous rumble of thunder echoed through the trees. The rain drops grew larger and flashes of lightning shone through the gaps in the foliage.

"Quick everybody, run!" one of the older children screeched.

"Cathy can't get out of the hole, she keeps slipping," Janet answered as she looked back and saw her friend sobbing as she tried to scramble out.

Cathy's feet were slipping more with each movement. She was somewhat bigger than the other youngsters, and her own fear made the situation far more terrifying for her. Another clap of thunder made Cathy scream at the top of her voice, the rain now pounding down around them.

"You get her out, we're outta here!" John shouted, his shoulder length hair soaked with the driving rain.

Janet and Dreanna lay flat on the mudded ground, their clothes now saturated and filthy; they pulled and tugged at Cathy's jacket until they finally managed to free her from her sludgy prison. Cathy, still crying, began running with her friends towards the top corn field. From there it would only be a few minutes until they were out in the open and nearly home. One more ominous roar of thunder sent Cathy into a hysterical frenzy and the fear became too much for her. The contents of her bladder began trickling down her leg.

"Cathy you must keep running, don't stop!" Dreanna sounded almost desperate.

"I can't. I'm scared."

"Well you gotta." Dreanna pulled at Cathy's coat urgently. "Do you understand me? You gotta run!"

The three girls reached the opening to the top field as the sound of the crackling electricity filled their ears. The lightning had struck a tree to their left that was beginning to sway frantically and it began to fall in their direction.

"RUN!" Janet screeched.

Just as the girls reached the outer perimeter of the woods the tree fell, crashing fiercely to the ground. Their bedraggled bodies were finally free from the darkness of the trees and Dreanna turned to her friends. "I told you, didn't I! Next time you must listen." She tried her hardest to square up to her friends who were all so much bigger than her in height and size.

Janet grabbed hold of Cathy's hand and held on to it tightly until they reached the concrete pathway that led them back home. "How did you know 'bout the tree Dreanna?"

"Dunno, just knew." Dreanna sighed and ran the short distance home still questioning herself. In her mind the tree had fallen moments before it actually happened. Her confusion was leading to frustration, and her frustration was leading to a fear she couldn't escape from.

Monday arrived just a little too soon. Dreanna awoke already anxious about going to school that morning. She sat in front of the coal fire that had been burning since 5 o'clock, and watched as her mother made her lunch for school. "Mummy, do I have to go to school today? It's scary."

"Dreanna, don't be stupid, you know you do. It's the law and it's not scary."

Iris seemed a little out of sorts that morning and the last thing she needed was a whiney five-year-old.

"Mummy school is horrible. It hurts me."

"Don't be so bloody ridiculous child; school doesn't hurt you. Come on quickly, go get your wellie boots. That rain has made the woods all muddy and your friends will be here soon."

"But it does hurt, it makes me feel horrible."

"I'm not going to tell you again. Get your boots, stop being a baby and go to school."

"But Mummyyyyy!"

"Enough now, you're going to school!" Iris screamed at her child.

With a tut Dreanna made her way to the front door, and instead of the normal "Goodbye Mummy, see you later," Dreanna looked at her mother and said, "School does hurt, it does!"

July 1975

Time seems to pass so slowly when you are a kid, but the last three years had gone all too quickly for Patrick and Iris, and most of their young family were now in their teenage years. William was now eighteen and not a day went by when the police didn't knock on the front door because he had been in some kind of trouble. Normally it was just fighting with another group of young lads, but when Patrick was called to the local police station this particular time to collect his son, William was given one final ultimatum.

"Either go inside boy or join the army," the custody sergeant told him.

It really wasn't a hard decision to make and in a few months their oldest child was off for military training.

Dawn was nearly sixteen and her main interest was the Osmonds and of course, boys. Patrice still acted like one of the lads and spent the majority of her youth hanging around with the other young boys on the estate. The estate by now had changed considerably – new houses had been built and new faces were all around. Dreanna was eight years old and was still the smallest in her class. Her long fair hair had been cut short and her eyes were still the deepest brown. Facially you could see which family she belonged to but her other siblings were so much taller than her at that age. Dawn constantly used to tease her, saying that she was the runt of the litter and if their mum had been a pig she would have eaten her quite happily.

Each night Dreanna would still make the separation from her physical form and either go to her special room, her field or simply move from room to room watching as her family slept soundly in their beds. Not once did she allow herself to venture away from the boundaries of her home. Something inside told her not to go too far, so she always stopped at the front room window to peer outside, and watch the darkness and the occasional fox rummage through the dustbins. On the nights that she chose to stay inside her body, the dreams began. Not dreams of play or even monsters under her bed, but dreams of children begging for water, men and women being disfigured; dreams so full of hate and pain it's no wonder that every night she choose to escape her body. It gave her freedom from the trauma she saw each night in her dreams, but it also gave her the freedom she needed from reality.

Susan was by now a distant memory – she had never returned even just for a quick visit – and in her waking life, school was something Dreanna just had to deal with. Every now and then she had the same experience as at nursery and in the first two terms at infant school, but they were becoming more and more sporadic. It was now the dreams that affected her more and the pain she felt whenever she woke from them affected her during the day. She couldn't stand seeing pain inflicted, even on small creatures. On this particular day the

family were going on their annual holiday and were busy loading the minibus. Dreanna shouted as her sister walked up the garden path carrying her
small green suitcase that had seen better days. The brief summer shower had
filled the garden path with snails galore, and Dreanna was getting crosser and
crosser as each person came bounding up and down the garden carrying their
luggage and boxes of food, not caring whether or not their feet crunched on an
unexpected snail. "Don't tread on the snails!" Dreanna shouted at each of them
in turn.

"Dreanna SHUT UP! It's a bloody snail!" Patrice bawled.

Dreanna stuck her tongue out at her older sister and continued picking up
each snail and placing it carefully back in the undergrowth.

The family were going on their yearly holiday with their uncle and aunt,
their two sons, and another of their cousins who tagged along. Dreanna never
minded this jaunt away; Matilda was coming with them this year and Robin
her cousin would be there. How she adored him. He never made her feel insignificant or annoying; he made her laugh and would often just hold her in his
arms. This was the one thing she loved more than anything else.

The minibus was packed, the families boarded and empty chatter filled the
vehicle until they reached Pontins Holiday Village at Camber Sands. Someone
would shout out, "Look I can see the sea! Can you smell that air? Taste that
air!"

She never quite understood how you could taste the air and would often
open her mouth wide, gulping in mouthfuls to see if the air actually did have a
taste. It never did.

The first night in the caravan was the same as it had always been. Dressed
in their finest clothes, they made the short walk through the holiday park to the
entertainment hall. The men drank their usual 'holiday stout', the women their
'snowballs' – a funny drink made up of advocaat and lime – and the kids some
cheap fizzy pop that more often than not was not fizzy and contained more
than enough sugar to rot their teeth. Then after a lovely evening at the club-
house they called in for fish and chips at the shop before returning to the caravan where there was no room to sit, let alone sleep. On this holiday Dreanna
was to sleep side by side with Matilda in one of the make-shift beds that by day
was a sofa. The caravan had only one room with a proper double bed and that
was shared by Dawn and Patrice. William was sleeping on what during the day
was the dining room table which folded flat, and Patrick and Iris pulled their
bed down from a cupboard.

Dreanna held onto her grandmother's hand, as she slowly drifted off to
sleep.

"*Hey you,*" came a voice in the dark.

"Er what? What...? Who...?" Dreanna asked.

The silhouette of a tall young man dressed in uniform stood before her. "*Yeah you, come with me. I know you can so don't pretend you can't.*"

"Oh, I don't think I should. I'm not allowed to go anywhere with strangers," Dreanna answered.

"*But I have something to show you.*"

Curiosity got the better of her and a few moments later Dreanna was staring back at her body. She searched the darkness for the figure she had briefly seen moments before.

"*I'm here.*"

"*Well I can't come with you if you're gonna hide over there, can I, you plum! But I don't really, really know if I wanna come with you, you look sort of ...scary.*"

"*You have no choice ..! This way,*" *he ordered, as he reached for her tiny hand.*

Before she could stop herself she was moving closer to him. The dark surroundings vanished and she was standing on a concrete parade ground. Buildings of two storeys stood in front of her made of red bricks. She couldn't move, she felt vulnerable and scared.

"*Just watch, learn and remember,*" *the man said. Then he was gone and Dreanna was left alone, unable to break free of the sights and sounds before her.*

The soldiers were standing in orderly lines, their shoes polished, their uniforms pressed, rifles hung over their shoulders. The young men in uniform marched towards the open metal gate. The second to last soldier was one she knew, it was her own brother. It was William. His feet followed the same rhythmic march as all the other soldiers, she tried to call his name but no sound could escape, she watched, not being able to move as the young men left the confines of the barracks. Then the image changed and she was standing at the corner of a terrace of houses. Children were shouting and screaming at the soldiers who stood nearby. Their rifles were now poised in front of them, the soldiers' eyes were concentrating hard, watching every movement, watching every person that came into their vision. Her brother was standing chatting quite openly to a mother pushing a young child in a pushchair. William's eyes looked up staring straight at his sister, she tried again to call his name but he looked straight past her, she was invisible to him. Something caught William's eye, he pushed the women he was talking to, to the ground, and began to run. "*Noooooo!*" *he screamed.*

Dreanna turned to see what and who he was shouting at; a young child no older than she was handing a box with a huge bow on it to one of the other soldiers.

"*It's a present from my mum to you, it's just biscuits, she made them special.*"

The soldier took the box and ripped the bow free from its contents.

William was still screaming and running faster and faster, shouting with every step, "*DROP THE BOX! Drop the box! Don't open it, fuck, don't open it! Don't fucking open that box, put it down!!*" *William was just feet from the soldier.*

"Hi Wills, do ya fancy a biscuit? That cute kid over there just gave them to me." The soldier was still ripping at the inner layer, his fingertips tugging at the lid.

"Don't open the fucking box," William screamed. *"Put it on the ground. Put the fucking box on the ground!"* His words fell on deaf ears as the young squaddie lifted the lid off the box.

There was a deafening explosion. The soldier's body was blown high into the air; his arm was on fire and as he hit the ground, his mangled shredded body trickled blood. His burning arm seemed to extinguish itself as it ran out of flesh to burn. The other soldiers began running towards the casualty and Dreanna looked around frantically for her brother but she couldn't find him – he wasn't there. She tried to scream his name, but no sound came out of her mouth. As tears poured down her face, the pain in her heart burned; her innocent eyes had just seen the pain of death and the fear in others, but her own fear felt so much worse. She wanted her brother back, she wanted to find him, she needed to find him.

"Will you wake up?" Matilda shook her grand-daughter. "Come now sweet-ie, open your eyes. You're having a bad dream."

Dreanna's eyes were wide open, the tears cascading down her face. "Nanny, I couldn't find William. I couldn't find him, a man was on fire – there was so much blood Nanny – where's William? Where's William?"

Matilda held her close, rocking her slowly and stroking her hair. "It's okay precious. William's asleep and it was just a dream, a nasty dream." Matilda kissed Dreanna's forehead. "Rest now my little one, rest now. Nana will take care of you."

A while later Dreanna was still lying under the blanket that was gripped tightly in her hands; the events of last night were still vivid in her bewildered and jumbled mind. She searched the small van from her safe haven, looking for her brother. 'Kiss me quick' hats that belonged to her siblings were lined up on the window sill. Her huge brown eyes still searched for William – she knew she wouldn't believe it was only a dream until she saw him with her own eyes. Then there he was, opening the caravan door that squeaked on its hinges; he had already been to the shower block and was washed and dressed ready for a day at the beach. The relief surged through her body; she spent the night think-ing he was lost, but now he was safe, she had found him.

Seven days passed and the holiday came to an end. The rain was lashing down. Bloody British weather! They busily packed up the minibus for the jour-ney home. Suitcases were piled high on the roof, secured by two lengths of thick rope. The normal arguments were already breaking out as the cousins began the big fight for who would sit in the front seat. Dreanna as usual sat by her father further back in the bus, sharing his affections with the family dog.

It wasn't until they had returned home that Dreanna found the courage to tell her mother about her dream. They were standing in the queue in the newsagent's when she started recounting the vivid dream and its events. Iris handed her daughter the Curly Wurly she'd just bought and Dreanna ripped it open and started to devour the contents. With her mouth full of chocolate she concluded her story.

"It was so scary Mum, I couldn't find William anywhere."

"Don't speak with your mouth full," her mother said.

Dreanna swallowed sharply. "Sorry, Mum, but did you hear what I just said? I couldn't find William anywhere!"

"It was only a dream Bubs, just a nightmare; it was just your imagination, that's all. Just your imagination."

"But Mum it wasn't my imagination, it was real. You don't understand. I go to – erm – somewhere when I'm asleep, I don't know where but I know they are real. Mum are you listening to me?" She knew that she shouldn't speak to her mother like that, but she wasn't paying attention to her, she just wasn't taking her seriously.

"Whatever Dreanna, now stop talking and eat your chocolate and hurry up, I've got to get dinner on before work tonight."

Iris wasn't listening.

October 1975

William had one final day at home before leaving to join the army. His bag was packed and he stood leaning against the back door, a cigarette between his fingers. Dreanna sat on the step beneath her brother, pulling and tugging at the weeds that were sticking up out of the concrete ground.

"Bubs, I've got a present for you, but promise me you will only use it if you have to. The estate's changing and you will need to protect yourself."

Dreanna continued prodding at the weeds, taking her aggression out on each one and ripping it to shreds. "What you talking about? You are so silly, I don't need protecting. You're just leaving me, I hate you!"

"Don't be angry with me Sis, I'll be back soon." William reached into his back pocket and handed his sister a silver knife. "This is for you. If you need to, use it. I won't be able to look after you for a while, so you have to take care of yourself. You understand, don't you?"

William's words meant nothing to her. All she knew was he was leaving her and she didn't want him to go. "William," Dreanna paused and inhaled, "You will come home won't you? You won't get blown up, or something... please say you're coming home."

William bent down and cradled her in his arms. "I'll be back kid. We're not at war you know."

The two siblings sat holding each other until Patrick told them it was time for William to leave. Dreanna moved the folded blade between her fingers, flicking it open and closing it back down over and over again. She had always been just that little bit closer to William than her sisters and now he was leaving her. The only one that didn't see her as invisible or just annoying was now going and again she felt deserted and alone just like when Susan said her final goodbyes. She watched as William walked up the road to the bus stop. Her heart was breaking as he turned the corner.

August 1976

Dreanna returned home from playing out with her friends to the usual sound of her mother and Dawn arguing. They had been arguing a lot of late, it was becoming a normal occurrence. If they weren't arguing then both were moaning about what the other had said or done. This time though the voices of the two women were loud, so very loud. Hatred, aggression, revulsion and disgust filled the house.

"What do you think you were playing at? So you had to turn into the town bike, did you? You just couldn't keep your legs crossed – you're nothing but a common whore. What are the neighbours going to say?" Iris screamed, her voice turning more croaky with each word.

"But Mum, I, I, I..." Dawn tried her hardest to explain but her mother didn't want to know. All that concerned her was the family's reputation and her eldest daughter's pregnancy.

"I told you not to be a slut, but no, don't listen to me, will you? I'm just your mother, you common little whore! You strut around here, with your high-heeled shoes and make up all over your face like some cheap prostitute, I s'pose I should really understand why some bloke shoved his cock inside you. You make me want to vomit! You dirty bloody tart!"

"Stop it, stop it, stop it!" Dreanna yelled, "you're hurting me!" Her head had the all too familiar feeling of being stabbed, her stomach was churning and she felt giddy and woozy. But the two rivals paid no attention as they continued to bicker amongst themselves. Dreanna fled the house, running as fast as she could. The throbbing ache in her head slowly left her as she reached the opening to the woods. She sat down on an old oil drum and wrapped her arms tightly around herself. This was the only way she felt safe.

Patrick did not share his wife's concerns about one of his children being in the family way; it was the word abortion that made him want to vomit. This caused many a heated debate between them. "A child has been conceived and has a right to life, and no one has the right to take this away. And anyway, if a woman doesn't want to get pregnant then she should keep her bloody legs crossed or the man should take the necessary precautions, end of. This baby is being born, Iris, whether you like it or not, so you better bloody get used to it!"

April 1977

Patrick and Iris didn't have a phone, so Patrick rushed over to one of their neighbours when he heard Iris was calling from the hospital. "It's a boy, a happy bouncing baby boy, 7lb 3oz, a mop of dark hair and he is bloody gorgeous. They will be in hospital for a week b..." The pips went before she had time to answer any more questions.

A week later the neighbour's car pulled up outside their home and Dawn handed the baby to Patrick who was waiting patiently.

Dreanna's face grimaced as she looked down at her first nephew. "He looks like a rat!" She paused staring at this baby wrapped in a blanket with only his head poking out. "Well he does!" Her eyebrows rose, "Can I hold him pleeeease."

Patrick handed his new grandson to his youngest daughter. "Make sure you support his head, and give him back to me if he becomes too heavy."

Dreanna's eyes locked onto those of her nephew, her arms holding tight to its precious cargo. "I'm not alone any more. You're going to be my best friend forever and ever." Her lips gently kissed her nephew's head, "I love you already."

Everything had changed so much; William leaving, Dawn having a baby and Dreanna's dreams becoming more painful than life, but right at that moment in time all she could think about was this new friend and this precious new life she held.

It was a moment in time when the outside world all but disappeared. The love she had inside her for this new baby made her senses lighten; it was a love she had never felt before and it made her cherish life that little bit more. Even through all the dirty nappies, sleepless nights and the alterations the family had to make to their routines to accommodate him, this baby was going to be the one thing that kept Dreanna going even at such a young age. He was her respite. He gave her hope.

Distance of time

January 1978

Dreanna kicked off her shoes and threw her school bag down in the corner of the hallway. But hers wasn't the only bag on the floor. William's khaki-green army duffle bag was leaning against the wall. She didn't understand why he was home – he wasn't due for any leave yet, so why was he here? She ran up the narrow hallway screaming her brother's name and exploded into the kitchen. Her dad was sitting on his chair close to the cooker, and other members of her family were around the table. Andrew was crawling on the tatty carpet, his fingers holding a teething ring which he forced into his mouth.

"William! What you doing home? You weren't supposed to be home for another week!" She threw herself at him and they clung tightly to each other.

"Hello Sis," his grip on her tightened. His head turned to his father. William was begging his father for help. "D-d-dad I can't. I don't know how... "

Dreanna looked at each member of her family in turn and tried to pull away from her brother's grasp. "What's going on? Why is everyone at home? What's happened?"

"Bubs, it's your Nan," Patrick's voice broke into a whisper. "She died this morning."

"Don't be silly, Nanny isn't dead," Dreanna gave a nervous grin. "She's just poorly that's all. You said that the doctors were gonna make her better, you promised!" Dreanna tried to free herself again, but her brother held her tighter than before.

"Dreanna, stop being so fucking stupid, Dad wouldn't lie. Nan's dead, okay? She's dead." Patrice screamed as she wept.

Dreanna escaped William's grasp and sank to the floor, staring around the kitchen. "Nana can't be dead, she just can't. I need her."

The family sat in silence for the next two hours; Andrew's gurgles and baby chatter were the only things to break the stillness that surrounded them. Dreanna's body felt numb. At ten years old she didn't understand the full circumstances about why her nana had died.

The funeral took place a week later. Dreanna so desperately longed for Matilda to come and see her, but nothing happened; there was no sign of her anywhere. She just didn't understand, she loved her so much, so why didn't she come to see her?

Night time fell and Dreanna had already decided to go to her green field with the old oak tree that stood so proud. As soon as she could she took herself off to bed, wishing that Matilda would grace her with her presence, but again nothing. She had spent night after night in the vast expanse of her field just sitting, waiting and longing for a glimpse of her nan. But there was zero, zilch, not a sausage, no reassuring voices, no translucent image, nothing. The loneliness and isolation returned; Dreanna's days were spent yearning for her nan's special touch, her nights hoping and searching for her.

Matilda's death tore Iris apart and her health began to falter – something inside her had changed and Dreanna started to think that if all her kids vanished Iris wouldn't even notice they were gone. Something inside Iris had died also.

There were many times that Dreanna would find her mum sitting, rocking and crying, holding a picture of Matilda close to her chest. She often joined her, hugging her mum tightly. No words were needed, just the reassurance that there was someone there. But Iris's sorrow lasted for many more years, and her physical health continued to weaken. She found the strength from somewhere to continue working full time, looking after her family, and would chat and smile to the neighbours, but behind closed doors her tears flowed without hesitation. Her zest for life was gone.

March 1978

Dreanna held the sides of the bowl tighter as her stomach wretched for the third time; stomach acid was all that was left to bring up. Her mother held her hair back with one hand and was gently patting her daughter's back with the other. "It's okay Bubs, the doctor's on his way."

Dreanna tried to look up at her mother before the cramps in her stomach hit again and she vomited more and more. Her eyes were red and swollen, her face pale and white, her listless body exhausted.

Iris handed her a clean tissue. "Have you finished sweetheart?"

Dreanna wiped her nose and slumped backwards, too exhausted to speak. She had now been vomiting every day for almost two weeks and she was losing weight at an alarming rate. A week ago the doctor had said she was suffering from stomach flu and would be up and about in no time. But another week had passed and the continuous vomiting didn't stop. Everything was tiring, and she couldn't even venture to the toilet unaided in case she collapsed. The doctor explained that he would only give Dreanna one more day, and then she would have to be hospitalised.

"I can't go into hospital Mum, I just can't. Please make me better. Please... ?" Dreanna's voice was a whimper as she begged and pleaded with her mother.

"Don't be silly child, they will make you better and you'll be back at home in no time... I'm going down stairs to do the tea, just shout if you need me, okay?"

Dreanna nodded.

If only Dreanna had been brave enough to give the real reason she didn't want to go, maybe her mother would have understood a little more. But she wasn't brave and her fear of others' emotions had grown until it was almost overpowering. She could smell the family meal cooking downstairs and her stomach heaved. 'Please not again,' she told herself.

"Now precious, I'm with you. Let's get you sorted out, shall we?"

Dreanna lifted her head from the bowl and turned to where the voice came from. "Nanny is it you? Where have you been? I've been so worried about you, why didn't you visit me before?" Dreanna swallowed deeply pushing the bile from her stomach back down to where it belonged.

Matilda's face looked so fresh, the normal lines and wrinkles had all but disappeared. Her skin looked so soft, so young. Matilda spoke in her usual comforting and soothing way. "Calm down, I'm here now. Let's just see what's going on, shall we?"

Matilda placed her ghostly hand on Dreanna's head, and the other on her stomach. "This is what I want you to do. Each time you think you are going to be sick, you must think of a place that makes you happy. See yourself there smiling and content, breathe deeply, but remember to smile, do you understand, you must smile. Concentrate hard on your favourite place, don't let any other emotions stand in your way. Use your imagination my precious, use it, it's yours, you own it!"

Dreanna nodded, her favorite place was easy; it was in the security of her grandmother's arms.

"I must go now precious, please keep an eye on your mum for me, and best not tell her just yet that I came to see you. Remember this is not goodbye, just see you later. I love you."

Matilda's words were few but they meant so much. Dreanna did exactly as instructed and before the end of that evening she had stopped vomiting and managed to keep down a whole glass of water with glucose. She was finally on the mend. Her recovery was slow and after another week she was back on solid food, but the awful concoction of raw eggs and milk her mother made her swallow was enough to make her vomit again, especially if it hadn't been blended together that well. Dreanna's normal inquisitive self soon returned. Her nan's visit had given her so much more than she realised, as it proved there are never really goodbyes, just a distance of time that splits the two dimensions.

You're Scum

April 1978

"Have a great Easter everyone!" Dreanna's teacher bellowed above the din. No one was really listening. The children headed for the door full of excitement. With no school for two weeks their heads were full of all the antics they had planned over the coming days. The walk home with her friends was no different than any other day, but Dreanna felt edgy, slightly fearful and apprehensive about going home. She suddenly became hesitant about going back to the only place that really made her secure.

Janet noticed her silence. "You okay Dreanna?"

"Yep, I'm fine," forcing a smile. But these words seemed to stick in her throat. She had become accustomed to saying "I'm fine" when she knew she wasn't or when something unexplained was about to happen. But it kept everyone off her back, and stopped them from asking probing questions.

The children reached Dreanna's garden gate and finished their conversation before saying goodbye. Her mother was working full time at the hospital now, and as the school finished early for the Easter break, Dreanna had been allowed to have a key so she could go inside instead of waiting on the doorstep.

But Dreanna wasn't on her own. Paul was there. Paul worked for the local council authority and was one of a team modernising houses in the area, fitting new windows and doors, central heating and modern bathrooms.

The only person who didn't want the changes was Patrick. "Central bloody heating!" he had moaned. "You watch, we'll all get ill now. False heat that's all it is. Bloody false heat, not natural, not bloody natural!"

Nevertheless the changes were being made, and Paul was one of the men fitting the new copper pipes around the house for the shiny new white radiators. "Hey child," he said, as she was taking off her coat.

Dreanna nearly jumped out of her skin. "Oh! You made me jump. Why are you under the stairs?"

He manoeuvred his body from a crouching position and turned his head in her direction. "Gotta attach this pipe here, see?"

"Oh right." Dreanna's usually inquisitive nature was for once not interested in the bright orange copper tube.

Paul waved the pipe high in the air. "Hey, why don't you give me a hand?"

Dreanna's stomach churned. "Erm no, it's okay, I've got to go and see one of my friends in a minute."

"I insist, young one, come closer to me and hold this spanner."

Dreanna didn't move.

"No? Shy are you? You know me, I've been here for two weeks now. Don't be scared – c'mon, come help me for a bit." His eyes never left her young body.

He walked towards her. "Okay, if you won't come to me then I'll have to come to you!" His voice was colder now. "Aren't you a pretty little thing? Look at your big brown eyes, and your skin is so smooth, so soft, so young." His hand began stroking her cheek. The stale smell of nicotine on his fingers filled her nose, his breath smelt like stale beer.

Dreanna inwardly retched. "What are you doing? Please don't stand so close to me, your breath smells and I don't like you touching my face!"

Paul leaned into her, pinning her against the wall. He stroked her hair and grabbed a handful, smelling it deeply. "Mmm lovely."

"Please let go of me, you're squashing me and I can't move."

Paul tittered. "I will let go of you when I'm good and ready young lady, not a moment before." His hands began stroking her face again. He looked deep into her eyes, his fingers toying with her lips, the lingering expression of pure lust moving down his body. His hand slid down to her neck, then his fingers reached inside her jumper and began massaging her juvenile breasts while his other arm still held her tight against the wall. He let his hand slide slowly off her breasts and grasping Dreanna's hand in his, placed it on his penis. "Can you feel this, my sweet little girl? Can you feel how much I want you? Can you feel my desire? Stroke it child, stroke it!" his hot breath whispered into her ear.

"NO!" Dreanna shouted, her fingers pressed into a tight ball.

He chortled. As his hand released hers, she began to squirm and wriggle but he held her tight to the wall. "Not yet sweet girl, you're not going anywhere yet." He lifted her skirt and began stroking the inside of her thigh. He searched for the top of her knickers then his fingers entered her body, invading every inch of her virginal flesh.

Dreanna screamed.

"Enough now child, enough now. Stay still and it will soon finish." His breathing became faster, she could feel his fingers stroking, rubbing, fingering her insides. She stood still. He sighed, a huge relieving sigh as his body, sweaty and smelly, contracted onto her eleven-year-old frame. "There now, all done." Paul smiled. "But I think I may have made a bit of a mess in my trousers." He grinned as he withdrew his fingers and released his grasp of her innocent body.

Dreanna started to cry, her tears sliding down her face.

"Now child, don't cry. You haven't done anything wrong. It's all what is supposed to happen – men touch women, women are for men's pleasure. You will learn in time, you will learn in time," he smirked.

Dreanna's feet were rooted to the spot, she unable to move. She felt dark inside, scared and hopeless. "But I'm not a woman!" she screamed, her face contorted.

"You will be soon, I can feel it, I can smell it." He lifted his finger to his nose and sniffed, he laughed. "Now sweet one, you mustn't tell anyone, 'cos if you do I will do it again, do you get me?"

A cough. Dreanna heard a cough. "That's Mummy home from work." Dreanna looked pleadingly into his eyes.

"Well then, looks like I'm done here for the day doesn't it?"

The key turned in the lock and her mother's face appeared. Dreanna, still crying, flew into her arms. "Mummy don't ever not be here for me, please Mummy!"

"Oi oi oi! What's all this then?" Iris asked.

"Think she was scared that you weren't home," Paul said gruffly.

"Yeah, first time home without one of us, that's what it is," Iris said, holding her youngest daughter close to her. Dreanna pulled away as her mother gently released her, heading for the kitchen. The door closed behind her.

Dreanna stood her ground and looked at her assailant. She watched as he gathered his tools and made his retreat. Dreanna's eyes were filled with hatred. She had stopped shaking and an angry sensation now engulfed her. Her body was rigid, her mind was dark. She took herself off to bed early that night and lay there thinking of what Paul had done. She wept silently in the darkness.

"*Dreanna.*"

There was a pause.

"*Dreanna my precious one, listen to me. You haven't done anything wrong. This is not your fault, please don't blame yourself.*" The voice was calm, serene, a woman's, but one she did not recognise.

"Why did you let him do that to me? Why did he touch me, why did he have to hurt me?" Dreanna asked openly, not caring if anyone in her house could hear.

"*We cannot control what people do. I'm sorry child, however hard this is for you, know that one day you will understand why.*" The voice repeated, "*One day you will understand. Now sleep my darling, dry your tears. I love you.*"

The voice disappeared and Dreanna was left alone in silence, alone with her pain. Finally she slept.

A Close Shave

April 1978

The following morning Dreanna awoke feeling very sore with a dull pain in her pelvis. She dragged herself out of bed, cleaned her teeth and went downstairs for breakfast.

Before too long Cathy was banging on her front door. "You coming out?" she asked Dreanna, hopping up and down off the front step as she spoke.

Dreanna thought for a moment before she answered; her mind was still confused from the previous day's events. "Erm, 'spose.Where we going?"

"Dunno, thought we could go knock for Janet and go down the woods, or stream jumping?"

Dreanna's response was short. "M'k ... Don't really know if I want to go stream jumping, I've got a bit of a tummy ache."

Cathy nodded as Dreanna put on her trainers. The two of them walked a short distance to Janet's house, but according to her brother, Janet was still in bed.

"Can you tell her we'll wait at the green?" Cathy asked.

"If I remember," he answered, puffing on an Embassy stolen from his mother's packet.

The green was just an area of grass that separated a few houses from the road, but most of the street's kids would gather there at some stage. The girls sat down on the dewy carpet, and it wasn't long before Dreanna was feeling like a normal eleven-year-old again. "Did you see the gymnastics the other night?" she asked Janet. "I wish I could do what they do." Dreanna stood up, arms in the air, and began prancing around, contorting her body, cartwheeling the entire length of the grass.

Janet giggled. "You look really stupid," She held her stomach as she fell sideways, her body now lying on the sward of grass. "Bet you can't do cartwheels on the wall," she shouted at Dreanna.

"My name is not Dreanna, I am Olga Korbut, Olympic gymnast extraordinaire."

"You're also mental," Janet said, now hysterical with laughter.

Still laughing, both girls jumped on the three-foot-high wall that bordered the houses from the green, running the entire length doing star jumps.

"Go on, do a cartwheel, Olga," Janet shouted.

Dreanna lifted her arms high in the air and proceeded to cartwheel herself along the wall. Her head felt dizzier with each turn, but she carried on, laughing louder and louder each time.

"STOP!" Janet screeched.

Dreanna didn't hear. The end of the wall was closer than she thought. As her foot touched the tip of it, she fell, her crutch landing right on the corner. An intense pain filled her pelvis and blood trickled down her leg. Crying, she turned to Janet, her hands full of blood.

Janet stared at her, her own eyes now full of tears. "Quick, let's take you home." Her voice was shaking with fear.

Dreanna was no stranger to the Accident and Emergency department. In the last year she had broken four toes, dislocated her thumb, broken her wrist and her elbow, had ten stitches in her head after playing piggy-back fights with her friends, smashing against the same wall she had just fallen off, had six stitches in her leg after a neighbour's dog bit her, had her eye scraped after a piece of tissue paper she was tearing up stuck itself to her eyeball – oh, and she had also trapped her finger in a neighbour's car door.

"Your daughter's very accident prone," the staff nurse commented to Iris, as once again Dreanna sat on the pristine sheets of a hospital bed.

Iris glared at her daughter, giving one of her disapproving mother looks. "Think we're gonna have to wrap you in cotton wool," she said.

Dreanna pointed to her womb. "Mummy it hurts, down there," then whispered, "in my private bits."

"Don't worry Bubs, the Doctor's gonna want to have a look at you. You'll soon be sorted."

The doctor was a tall man who smelt of coffee and soap. He gently moved Dreanna's legs apart, and for a few seconds just looked, not touching her. "Right young lady, I'm just going to insert a finger to feel if anything is wrong."

Dreanna's eyes opened wide, and the word inside her head was NO, but yet again she was powerless to stop a man touching her intimately.

"Okay." The doctor turned to Iris, "She's very bruised and very swollen, and to be honest," he raised his eyebrows, "I'm a little confused as to why an accident like this should have caused so much swelling. But the human body can sometimes be a mystery."

Dreanna knew exactly why, but couldn't find the strength to tell the truth. Could all of this really be because of a stupid fall or was it down to the molestation by the perverted builder?

The doctor concluded his diagnosis. "If the bleeding continues for more than a few days, please bring her back. I have to say this might affect her having children, but right now it's too soon to tell." He rubbed Dreanna's arm. "Stay in bed for a few days, okay?"

Iris nodded. Dreanna just looked to the ceiling and wondered, 'Why me?'

July 1978

Her home was buzzing with excitement; William was due home on leave and Dreanna's stomach was filled with butterflies as her brother, still dressed in uniform, walked down the garden path. She hurled herself at him as he walked through the door.

William hauled his little sister up into his arms, spinning her round and round. "D'ya miss me much then?" he asked, grinning.

"Nah, not much." Her smile filled her whole face.

"Think this is an excuse to have a party, don't you?" William winked.

Dreanna's face dropped. "Yeah." All the excitement drained out of her voice. She had always hated the family gatherings that occurred all too frequently in a family of her size. They made her feel so ill. Even her own family's emotions affected her. She tried so hard to ignore these feelings but they overshadowed every enjoyable aspect of a family getting together. However, a party there was going to be, and in no time at all the hall was booked, and the invitations sent out.

Like most old halls it had a certain stench about it. The off-putting welcome for a visitor was the smell of stale cigarettes and the sight of rotten floorboards and the musty curtains that hung at the windows. A couple of broken windows were amateurishly boarded up, and the ladies' and gents' toilets were only separated by a sheet of plywood, held up by rusty nails. At least there was toilet paper, even if it did crunch as you pulled each sheet free and the smell of cheap pine disinfectant suggested the toilets were at least cleaned from time to time. The older women would descend on the toilets to reapply their lipstick before taking their places at their chosen table in the main hall. A small glass of Guinness, stout or a snowball was cupped in their hands and their cigarettes and Swan Vestas were never too far away. Their eyes constantly searched the room keeping a look out for the youngest of their brood. The occasional bitchy comment was heard and gossip was rife, but the time spent together gave them all a chance to be reunited as one big happy – if happy is the right word – family.

As the guests started to arrive Dreanna knew she had to try and control her sense of foreboding. In some way all the emotions that were about to fill this place had to be suppressed. She stared round the room at the tables laden with food; the corner of the hall had been turned into a bar, with kegs, barrels, tins and bottles of all shapes and sizes. The decanter, filled with a concoction of all the spirits that Patrick could lay his hands on, was positioned at the front of the bar. It could easily have knocked a horse off his feet; this brew was for the bravest of men and they each had to take their chance when they drank it. Only the most courageous would sample this homemade brew but everyone knew that before long there would be one of the family who, instead of taking a sip, would drink a pint glass full and either vomit over the first available lap or turn into some form of Neanderthal man, abusing his spouse or picking a fight and end up throwing punches into thin air. This particular evening would be no doubt classed as a good family party; one that would go down in history and be remembered for years.

William had been at home a couple of days before the party and had brought another squaddie home with him. Both young men had just finished a stint in Germany and were on two weeks leave before their next posting. Iris and Patrick were not enthusiastic about their son's next relocation, a six-month stretch in Northern Ireland right in the centre of the IRA trouble spots. He would be one of the young men in uniform they saw on the news every night, guarding and roaming the troubled streets. They were so proud of him but terrified they could lose him at any time. Both had lived through the Second World War but when someone you nurtured and watched grow is put into a place where death happens quicker than life... Iris didn't even want to think about what was coming up, her only interest that night was for everyone to have a good time.

Patrice and Dawn were dressed in flared jeans and platform shoes, Andrew wore a sailor suit with blue buttons down the front and Patrick was in his one and only pair of good trousers, nicely pressed, with his shirt slightly open to reveal the familiar string vest underneath. Iris had had her hair done the day before and it sat nicely in a tidy French pleat. Dreanna was in her favourite party frock, which in all honesty was now getting too small for her growing frame and William was dressed in jeans, a tee-shirt and a pair of Dr Martins. It was William, with his head shaved so close his scalp could be seen, who greeted their guests on arrival.

The hall was bustling with people, their voices raised over the music that bellowed throughout the enclosed space. Children were running and skidding across the polished floor, knocking the older generation off their feet, some of them cheering when one of the cousins drank a half pint of Patrick's infamous brew and then legged it to the nearest toilet (where they stayed hugging the porcelain bowl for the rest of the evening). Dreanna did what she had always done; she played with her cousins skidding across the floor, her party frock covered in dust and grime, and smiled in the necessary places when a drunken uncle told a joke. But inside her body it was beginning to hurt, her head was full of distorted words and her heart was beginning to ache.

The alcohol flowed freely and emotions began to rise. She knew it wouldn't be long before the headache started to cause her distress. The noise of their fears would begin seeping into her mind and the trauma they had experienced at some stage in their lives would soon become hers. She was learning to live with this, but she was teaching herself to read the signs and knew instinctively when she couldn't handle any more. She knew she had to leave before her body sucked up all the emotion out of that hall and swamped her mind with fear and aggression. Her deep brown eyes locked onto that of Patrick's, her face told the story of her pain.

"Okay kid, you've had enough." Patrick always knew that his youngest daughter was a little different from his other children and his intuition spoke to him at exactly the right moment. "Come on then let's get you home, go say your goodbyes."

His patience was unlike any other person. He never raised his voice or his hand to his children no matter what they did; he spoke to them as an equal and was always there for each and every one of them.

"I'm sorry Pops, did you want to stay?"

"Don't be a daft bugger. Snooker's on the tele – it's Ray Reardon tonight, or Dracula, as you like to call him!"

Both of them giggled, knowing full well that if it wasn't for the commentator telling them which colour ball had just been potted they would struggle to follow the game on their black and white television.

"A nice cup of tea is what we both need now; I'll leave the young ones to drink that decanter. Rather them than me!" His reassuring voice calmed down her mind and body.

The party was over for Dreanna.

William's leave went all too quickly for Dreanna. She enjoyed having her big brother back at home; their jaunts through the woods where he would carry her on his back when the nettles became too high, were fun, but more importantly the smile had returned to her mother's face. Since Matilda died her mother's expression always seemed so sad but her son's return had lifted her spirits and made her come alive. William knew that this time round his goodbye was going to be the hardest, but he smiled even though deep inside his stomach was churning with fear.

"Now you stay safe, boy." Patrick glared at his son.

"No probs Dad, I'll do my best."

Iris enveloped her son in a hug, but the anxiety and fear filling her heart made her voice tremble. "Right, we need you to come back to us in one piece. Make sure you write at least once a week, and, and..."

"It's okay Mum, I will come home and with nothing missing."

William wrapped his arms tightly around his mother. Dreanna stood waiting at the top of the garden path, staring out at a neighbour's house; the twitch-

ing of their curtains and the occasional glimpse of their faces were such a giveaway as to what they were doing.

"This will be all around the estate by tomorrow, bloody curtain twitchers!"
Patrick said, as he placed a reassuring hand on Dreanna's shoulders.

"Some people are never happy unless they know your business," she muttered, eyes still fixed on the house across the road. "This estate should be known
as 'Gossip Heaven'!"

Patrick flicked his fag butt into the road and joined Dreanna in watching the
curtain twitchers watch them. "Well at least if they're talking about us they're
leaving some other poor sod alone." He turned to watch his son walk up the
garden path.

William's arms were outstretched to his kid sister. "Come give us a hug
then!"

The memory of Dreanna's dream from when the family were on holiday
was playing out in her head over and over again. She told herself it wasn't
real, it was only a dream, it meant nothing. Her brother was going to be safe
and he was coming home. She flung her arms around his waist. "Please don't
go. Please tell them you have a cold or a headache and you're too poorly to go.
Please stay here." Dreanna's tears flowed again of their own accord.

"I have to Sis, I'm sorry but I have to." William prised her arms from around
his waist. "Look after Mum, and I'll be home before you know it."

And he was gone. Dreanna stood motionless, wishing, hoping and praying
that her brother would indeed be home soon and that her dream was no more
than a horrible nightmare. She looked to the skies. "I hate you all. Everyone I
love you take away from me. Why do you have to make people go to fight each
other? It's not fair and it's not nice." She raised her tone, "I will change this
world, somehow, someway. I will change this horrible world."

October 1978

William's letters became more graphic. Patrick was clever at reading out the
letters to his wife, leaving out the bits he knew would scare her and make her
worry for her son's safety. William had spent the last two months patrolling the
grounds of Maze prison, but soon he was to go on patrol outside the confines
of the prison. The danger that involved was watched by every household in
Britain; it was covered in every news programme that came on. The fear was
felt by every parent of a serving soldier. Bomb blasts were headlining the news,
not just when they happened in Ireland, but also the streets of the UK. All the
family sat watching the news in horror, the fear for their son, their brother,
never far from their thoughts.

A loud knock on the front door made Dreanna jump. She was sitting on the floor with her nephew, by her dad's feet listening to him reading aloud another new poem he had written.

"Patrick! Patrick, you in?" The familiar voice of one of their neighbours was shouting through the letterbox.

"Yep I'm in!" The three generations of the family made their way to the front door, Dreanna almost dragging Andrew behind her.

"It's William – he's on the phone, he sounds a little upset."

Jean was one of the neighbours that the whole family liked; she rarely gossiped and was a good friend to Iris. She was also one of the only people in their street who had a telephone.

"Oh right. Bubs you stay here with Andrew, I'll be back in a minute," Patrick left his notepad on the table on the way out.

Dreanna took Andrew into the front garden, sat him down on the damp grass and began telling him the stories of her nightly travels. The good thing about having such a young nephew was that he never judged her but listened contentedly. To him it was just another story, another book without cover. "Is everything okay Dad?" she asked as Patrick returned.

"Let's get inside, shall we?" His voice deep and mournful.

"Dad, what's happened? William is okay, isn't he?"

"There's been a bit of an accident, but your brother is fine, just a little shaken up. There was a bomb blast and a couple of his friends died, but William is okay kid, he's okay. They're giving him a bit of extra leave so he will be home in a couple of days."

Dreanna's heart sank; she had seen this before it actually happened. She didn't understand why. Why did her dreams, her nightmares, become reality? But at the same time she was massively relieved.

Patrick picked up his fags and placed one in his mouth, his hand a little unsteady. "He's had a close shave Bubs, a very close shave."

The Turning Point

July 1980

Dreanna was now in secondary school, and it was only another few weeks until school would break up for the summer. When autumn came she would go up into her third year. Her brother had now left the army and was enjoying his new-found freedom. Andrew was three years old and the apple of everyone's eye. Dawn and Patrice were both settled into regular work, and Iris had started to find life a little more enjoyable again. Every Tuesday, without fail, she would buy a bunch of flowers in town and bring them home to place with much care and love by her mother's photograph. And as for Patrick, well he was just Patrick. He worked, wrote his poetry and relaxed by listening to his favourite music. He took life on the chin and got pleasure from just watching his family grow. Or did he? His poetry had begun to change. He wrote constantly about when he was going to die and of seeing his mother and father again. The jovial words that once flowed from his pen had changed in style and mood.

Dreanna was coping, although she battled continually with the noise and the hustle and bustle of school life; she tried hard to keep up with her class-mates, with the teenage world, and with the useless pieces of information the teachers shoved down her throat. Her secret world and life was hidden at all times. To everyone else she was just that child from Stone Quarry who meant nothing to anyone except the family she loved.

Dreanna's current teacher was different from the others; she had Down's syndrome and had spent much of her adult life fighting the system and trying to prove that despite her disabilities she still had the knowledge and ability to teach others. Miss Hartley was five foot nothing and had the typical appearance of a Down's person, but her heart was so kind and she was warm and friendly in spite of the jibes from her students that hurt her to the core. She knew she was different but she carried on trying. Maybe that's why Dreanna liked her so much, because with all the hate that was thrown at her she still continued to fight. Miss Hartley, the warrior with a heart.

"Class, I would like to introduce you all to Louise," she announced one day.

Louise stood at the front of the classroom, her head bowed, her embarrass-ment all too clear. She was a pretty blonde girl, her hair in a tidy bob, her finger nails nicely filed and polished. She looked like she was used to the best in life, unlike Dreanna, who was still wearing the same school jumper she'd had for two years. The repairs her mother had made to the seams and elbows were a complete giveaway. You could always tell the newbies, Dreanna thought to herself. Their uniform still had that air of crispness. Everyone else's by this time in the term had started to fade and their jumpers had thumb holes in the sleeves where they'd been pulled over their hands too often. The boys' trousers had frayed at the bottom, their shirts hung over top of their trousers instead of being tucked in, and their ties over the last few weeks had magically became shorter and shorter. The girls' skirts seemed to have got shorter too, where they had become a little braver and rolled them up at the waist – until they saw a teacher who demanded they roll them down again. The developing bodies of both genders had begun to take on a new shape, particularly the girls which seemed to amuse the boys considerably, especially when they noticed that one of the girls around them had started to wear a bra.

"Take a seat over there, Louise, they may all look like a wild bunch, but they are quite nice when you get to know them." Miss Hartley pointed to a spare chair.

It didn't take long for one of the testosterone-driven teenagers to make their thoughts known to the class, as Louise took her seat."Cor, she's a bit of all right. Nice tits!"

The class roared with laughter and you could feel the heat radiating from Louise's cheeks.

"Jason, that's enough!" Miss Hartley really couldn't shout loud enough but she tried, and with this class her throat must have been raw by the end of the day. Louise's blushes were saved as the bell rang, but the young men still gave her the third degree as they left the form room. Every teenage eye was on Louise's arse and the tightness of her skirt made it easy for the rampant young men to let their imaginations run wild.

The end of the day came soon enough, and Dreanna walked home with Janet, Rose and Cathy.

"What do you think of that Louise then?" Rose asked.

Dreanna's thoughts were elsewhere. She had been suffering from a headache all day and was struggling to work out if it was one of 'those' headaches or just a normal run of the mill one. "She seems okay. I didn't get to speak to her much, but she is very pretty."

After the initial question the girls' conversation seemed to cease abruptly. They were now more distant with each other; their journey to and from school was really the only time they spent together, and their relationship was more one of convenience than anything else. They were all growing up but were also growing further apart.

Dreanna's daily regime of getting in from school and lying on the sofa to sleep before dinner was beginning to worry her mother. Dreanna would come home, sleep, eat her dinner, sleep and then go to bed.

"You surely can't be that tired, Bubs?" was the regular question from Iris.

"I am Mum, school's tiring you know."

"It's just not normal; you sleep at least thirteen hours a day during the week, but weekends you're up at the crack of dawn and as right as nine-pence. I just don't get it, I really don't."

"Whatever, Mum," Dreanna responded as her eyes drew tightly closed.

The school term had finished and the summer holidays had finally arrived. The new girl, Louise, had made loads of friends and seemed to be everyone's favourite person. Dreanna saw her a few times when she was shopping with her sister, and the two girls always said hello, but that was that. They were now just ships that passed each other in a harbour full of daydreams.

That summer was one of the loneliest ever for Dreanna. Her three close friends on the estate were hanging around with other girls from their school and Dreanna felt deserted and isolated from nearly everyone. Even her own sisters seemed to get annoyed with her and her brother was only interested in his new girlfriend. Much of her time was spent at home looking after Andrew and they were becoming very close. During that summer Dreanna's headaches and stomach pains disappeared and her tiredness had gone, but she had a strange feeling that she couldn't put into words. She felt less connected to people, and at the same time incomplete. She had slowly got used to the horrific scenes she saw in her dreams, and she found the chattering of hundreds of voices could now be drowned out by listening to music. But her freedom still only came when she left her sleeping form.

She had begun to travel further afield in this way and would roam the estate night after night, often giggling as she saw the older teenagers doing things that they really shouldn't be doing. She tried to stay clear of the sheltered bus stop; it was a regular haunt for young unbridled and lustful bodies to begin their sexual adventures, but she was too scared who and what she might see there after she caught her sister's friend in a very peculiar position with an older, and it has to be said, married man.

Money was still in short supply but Iris decided that her daughter was in need of a new uniform and raided their savings to buy the necessary clothing before the new school term started. Dreanna's body had indeed outgrown the uniform she'd worn for the past two years – her body was changing and so was she.

September 1980

For the first time since starting secondary school Dreanna felt quite smart on her first day back. At least she wouldn't have to face the sarcastic jibes from the other pupils who constantly teased her about her clothes being tatty. She had learned the hard way to stick up for herself and defend herself when it was needed, but she would never resort to violence. She hated the way that anger made her feel, and hated the emotional black spot it caused that blocked her mind.

As always on the first day of a new term she was reminded of her very first day in this school when two older girls had hung her upon a clothes peg in the P.E. changing rooms, her tiny frame left to dangle like a pig hanging in a butcher's shop window. The caretaker had been her saviour – her other friends had run off, too scared to face the bullies. Her family had told her to stick up for herself, but she was frightened as these girls had a bad reputation and nobody messed with them.

Their teasing continued until the day Dreanna stood there and released the weeks of torment she had suffered in one massive punch, straight into the ring-leader's face. The girl's lip was cut and she started to cry. The shock on the other girl's face as she looked at her friend's bleeding mouth was enough to give Dreanna the courage to stand up to anyone who wanted to pick on her, but she vowed that day that she would never retaliate in such a manner again. The emotional anguish had made her suffer more than the recipient of her punch. It left her feeling sick to the pit of her stomach.

Morning registration was louder than usual, as everyone was talking about what they had got up to that summer, and it wasn't long before Dreanna felt the dull ache inside her head. She tried her hardest to ignore it and join in the conversations. The girls were discussing their new hairstyles, showing off their new shoes and doing their best not to let the other girls see what they really thought of them. Dreanna couldn't help but chuckle as one of the girls stared at her, eyeing her up and down as if she had just grown an extra head, when in reality all she had was a new uniform.

"You look smart for a change."

Dreanna just looked at her, showing no emotion. "Thanks."

The class mate still stared.

"Anything else?" Dreanna asked, her gaze not moving from the girl.

"Er, nope. Don't get defensive, I only said you looked smart. Not used to you wearing a jumper that your mum hadn't knitted," the girl laughed and poked her friend in the stomach with her finger.

"Hmm," Dreanna said, now looking out of the prefab's window. "And you're actually a bit of a slut who will get forced into having anal sex before this year is out."

The two classmates' faces dropped. Dreanna smirked.

Dreanna and Louise had their first proper conversation in a boring French lesson. Dreanna was surprised at how easy Louise was to talk to and how well they actually got on. Even though they were worlds apart, they were able to chat like they had known each other for years, and over the next few weeks they spent more and more time together. Their friendship blossomed and soon the two young teenagers were inseparable. It was hard for Dreanna when she overheard other kids saying, "Well you always get one pretty one and one ugly one together", but she enjoyed having Louise as a friend, even if Dreanna was seen as the ugly duckling of the duo.

The last lesson of the day was religious education which all the students agreed was the most boring subject of all, and the whole hour was normally spent ridiculing the teacher, passing notes under the desks, or pretending to make an obscure noise that sounded like a fart. The teacher was totally oblivious to what went on when his back was turned, and his dreary voice and the story he was telling drove them all to despair and utter boredom. If you were lucky enough to sit at the back of the room then sleep was the best option, but for the rest of the class their antics made sitting in his lesson worthwhile. A large white clock hung over the classroom door which Dreanna watched almost hypnotised as the hands moved from minute to minute. "Only another twenty minutes left," she thought.

Her mind counted down each second, tick, tick, tick, tick... Another minute went by, tick, tick, tick... Her eyes were fixated on the hands of the clock, her ears heard the ticking getting louder and louder, and then – nothing. Total silence. Not one sound did she hear, not the clock, not her class mates, not even the humdrum sound of her teacher's voice. She was surrounded by silence. Her eyes struggled to keep focus as the classroom had all but disappeared and she was sitting in nothing but light. There was nothing in front of her, nothing to her side and nothing behind; she was an insignificant child sitting in an insignificant place. The only thing that made her feel she was still alive was the pounding pain in her head.

"Dre...Dree...Dreanna are you listening?" the teacher shouted directly at her.

The sights and sounds of her classroom began to reappear, but with one main difference, the noise had increased as if each child was talking all at the same time.

Dreanna put her hands over her ears. "Stop shouting at me!" she begged.

"How dare you talk to me like that?" the teacher snarled.

All she could do was to shake her head, cup her hands even tighter over her ears and pray that the school bell would hurry up and ring. It did. And she ran the two miles home in record time, almost collapsing on the hall floor as she entered the family home.

"Are you alright Sis?" Dawn was worried.

"I don't feel too good Dawn, I'm going to bed."

The next thing she knew Iris was gently shaking her. "You coming down for some dinner, Bubs?" Her mother's face was so close to hers she felt her breath gently flowing across her cheeks.

"Yeah, in a minute Mum, just need to wake up a bit first." Dreanna's head was still throbbing but her stomach was growling so she forced herself to go downstairs. She hadn't eaten anything since lunchtime and maybe some solid food would make her feel better. She looked down at the sausage, mash and peas that filled her plate and knew she had to try and eat at least some of it. But the uncomfortable throbbing in her head made even eating an insufferable experience. She felt physically exhausted and just wanted to go back to bed.

Patrick shoved the last forkful of his dinner in his mouth. "Still feeling crappy?"

Dreanna pushed the food around her plate, her face sad and subdued. "Yes, Pops, think I'll try and go back to sleep."

Even though her body felt worn out her eyes would not stay closed, the afternoon's events were still spinning around inside her mind. She so desperately wanted sleep to grab hold of her and keep her in its grasp until morning, but every attempt she made to drift off was halted by the busyness of her thoughts.

The evening was soon over and she heard Patrick making the usual nine o'clock pot of tea for everyone. She climbed down off the top bunk but as soon as her feet hit the floor she began to feel woozy and giddy. She made her way carefully down the stairs to the kitchen, and the pot of steaming tea.

"You okay kid?" Patrick looked at his daughter as he stirred the pot one last time.

"Not sure really Dad, my head still aches and I'm feeling a little dizzy."

"Most probably because you haven't eaten enough. Do you want a cuppa?"

Dreanna nodded, leaning carefully against the worktop. After drinking her tea she went back up to bed but as hard as she tried she still couldn't get to sleep, She tried everything from counting sheep, singing to herself, even tickling the inside of her arm at the joint of the elbow, but sleep was not on the agenda for tonight. Dreanna lay there staring up at the ceiling, with the cracks and peeling paint; the sound of her sister snoring – which seemed louder than usual – and even the family dog licking himself began to annoy her. 'God, why can't I sleep?' she wondered, as she turned her head towards the landing light. She made her parents leave it on at night as she was scared of the dark. A spider dangled above her head and she became mesmerised at just how clever such a tiny creature could be, and wondered what it would be like to travel from place to place with nothing more than a thread attached to you, its duty to keep you safe and out of the way of other predators. She came to the conclusion that she was no different from that spider as each night she floated freely, away from prying eyes. And if need be, somehow a gravitational pull would throw her back into her sleeping body. Just like that spider using her thread to travel back to the safety of the web.

She must have dozed off, but was awoken abruptly by the sound of Patrick's alarm clock. Her eyes felt heavy, her body was worn out, and she hoped that sleep would take hold again, but her mind was too busy.

Patrick was making the first pot of tea of the morning when she wandered into the kitchen. "What the bloody hell you doing up? It's only five o'clock! Have you shit the bed or something?"

"I couldn't sleep Dad, haven't been able to all night." Dreanna yawned. "Shit the bed Dad? Really, that's disgusting! I'm not two anymore, thank you!"

"Well have a cuppa and then go back to bed. You can have the day off and try and catch up on some sleep. You may not be two anymore but you're still my baby girl." Patrick leaned down and kissed her head.

She was too tired to say any more and took her weary body back off upstairs and flopped down on her bed. The house was in total silence when she awoke. Her head felt more normal, but her stomach was demanding food. The autumnal wind howling through the ill-fitting windows was a giveaway that the seasons were changing. The sky outside had a dark grey tinge to it, but according to the weather forecast it was going to be a warm day even for that time of year. Dreanna was freezing, from the top of her head to the tips of her toes, and her body felt like she had just stepped out of a freezer. She made her way down to the kitchen and put two slices of bread under the grill and boiled the kettle, hoping that some food and drink would soon warm her up. Tea and toast carefully in hand, she went into the front room and sat on the floor with the family dog. If she sat close enough to him his body warmth would soon make her own temperature rise. The tea and toast stopped her stomach from growling but she felt colder than ever. She shivered as the coldness penetrated deeper and deeper inside her.

"*Dreanna, my sweet.*" There was a voice but no body. "*Dreanna, now listen to me, don't panic, you're going to be fine. It's all change from here on, try and just accept it, don't fight it. We are always by your side. No one will hurt you, you must be brave.*"

"What? Who? I'm going crazy aren't I? I'm just like the man over the road that went loopy. I'm scared. Who are you?" Dreanna's voice trembled and shook. The idea that she had lost the plot and would be sent away like her neighbour filled her with terror. But there was no response. No one answered her questions or spoke another word.

The journey to school the following day started with lots of idle chit-chat, which as usual turned into silence as the three girls ran out of things to say to each other. It was a great relief when they entered the school grounds and they could all part company and speak to their new friends.

Dreanna felt fine, no painful head, no stomach cramps, no woozy sensations; she felt totally normal. She placed her bag on the floor and took her seat next to Louise. The boy behind them kept interrupting their conversation, eager to show them the mark that 'ring worm' had left on his hand.

"You're disgusting. We don't want to see that!" Louise said, her face screwed up like she had just sucked the juice out of a lemon.

"Yeah but don't you think it looks cool? I think it's brill. Dree what do you think? You think it's cool, don't you? Dree. Dree?" Roy raised his voice, but Dreanna wasn't responding. Her face was pale, her body cold and her head spinning as the usual pain returned and ripped through her body.

"Louise, I don't feel good, I need to get outta here."

The teacher still hadn't arrived so Louise took her hand and led her outside. "What's up? You still feeling shit?"

Dreanna sat on the top step of the prefab's stairs, her head bent and her eyes closed trying her hardest to make it all go away. "I wasn't Lou, but I am now. I think I need to go home."

Louise joined her and draped an arm over her shoulder. Her heavily rouged cheek pressed against Dreanna's. "It's okay, I'll take you to the nurse." Louise stood up and rearranged her skirt, brushing off the dust from the skanky old step. "What's up then?"

Dreanna took a deep breath, stood up, and with sad eyes and a heavy heart walked down the remaining three steps. "I don't really know, but I know I have to get out of here, before it gets out of control."

"Huh?"

Dreanna met her gaze. "Doesn't matter, ignore me."

After plenty of pleading from Dreanna the school nurse finally allowed her to go home after stuffing two large paracetamol tablets down her throat. But the school would not allow Dreanna to leave the premises without a responsible adult, so Iris had to leave work and get a taxi to fetch her daughter. Once back at home Iris went upstairs, pulled out 'the blanket', laid it on the sofa and headed into the kitchen. A sad faced Dreanna sat at the dining room table, her body already calming down and feeling more like her normal self.

Iris poured Dreanna a glass of squash. "I've got to go back to work, are you gonna be okay?"

"Yeah, think so Mum. I'll be okay tomorrow."

All Dreanna could do was curl up under that blanket and sleep, praying in her heart that tomorrow would never come. But of course it did.

Another day had come! Dreanna walked through the school gates relieved that she once again felt okay, she felt normal, she felt ...

"Hi Dree, you okay today?" A girl's voice took her by surprise and she turned to face her.

"Yeah, I'm feeling a lot better." Dreanna paused as she made eye contact with Tricia, a typical teenager with a few spots and long dark hair. Most of the time she was happy, but today something was different about her.

"Are you sure you're okay?" Tricia asked.

Dreanna couldn't hear her, she couldn't see her, and the world around her faded. Then the image of Tricia filled her mind. She wasn't dressed in school uniform, but jeans and a tee-shirt. A woman's voice was bellowing at her.

"You are such a lazy fucking bitch, I asked you to do one thing and you couldn't even do that could you? God, what have I done to deserve such an ugly lazy child. I'm sure they swapped you in the hospital, because you can't be mine." The woman's hand swung and landed on the side of Tricia's face.

"Dreanna come back to us. Is there anyone there?" Tricia giggled as she waved her hand in front of Dreanna's face.

"Sorry, I was miles away." Her mouth opened again before she could think of what she was saying, "Why do you let her hit you like that? She was drunk. You could get away from her, she wouldn't be able to keep up with you – you could run."

Tricia stared angrily. "I don't know what you're talking about. Are you some sort of freak? Yeah you are, aren't you? You're just a weirdo, freaky girl, so shut up weirdo."

Dreanna so wished she had kept her mouth shut. Now everyone was going to think she was some sort of psychological reject. "I'm sorry, I'm not weird, I don't know..." Dreanna kept her head bent as she went into her English lesson as she knew Tricia was going to be sitting close to the classroom door. As she pulled her chair out the ominous words of 'freak' and 'weirdo' came from Tricia's direction. Dreanna swallowed back her tears; the last thing she wanted was to be known as a cry baby as well as a weirdo. The whole lesson was a total blur. Dreanna couldn't concentrate as she felt Tricia's eyes boring into her body.

She walked home alone that afternoon, stopping at the local park, trying to work out why she said what she had. Why hadn't she just kept her big fucking gob shut? The tears she had held back that day flowed without restraint.

"My child, don't upset yourself. She won't tell anyone, she's too afraid — go home now child it will be dark soon." The reassuring voice came again.

The Autumn term continued and the time spent at school was becoming more and more unbearable for her. Everyday was the same: she would see and hear the other children's pain and problems, she could pin-point who had just had an argument with their parents, who felt unwell and who was being abused either mentally or physically. Her mind was full of pictures, her body full of pain, and Dreanna was drained and exhausted.

"Mum I'm feeling sick, can I stay at home?" Dreanna begged her mother.

"What again? You know this really must stop kid, you've had so much time off school. But if you're really feeling bad, I suppose one more day won't harm anyone." Iris couldn't be bothered to argue, and chose to believe her youngest. But that one day off turned into days, then weeks. Dreanna was too scared to tell anyone the real truth behind why she didn't want to go to school; she thought no one would believe her. Or they would say she was crazy like her neighbour's son over the road, and send her to some mental hospital far away, so for now she just kept telling the same story.

Enough is Enough!

February 1981

Dreanna sat in the hospital cubicle, her body covered by a gown – meanwhile her mother was checking the room for dust.

"Mum! What are you doing? Mum!"

Iris's fingers were wiping the top of the window sill. She had spent sixteen years working, cleaning and scrubbing at the hospital near their home and was proud of the standards it had. "We wouldn't've been allowed to leave this room in this condition, it's a disgrace. Cor, you wouldn't have to be sick when you came in here, but when you left you soon bloody would be!"

"Shhh! Someone will hear you!" Dreanna felt the heat of embarrassment sweep across her face, as the doctor entered the room. He was a well spoken man, with glasses and receding hair. His name tag was crooked on his jacket and Dreanna was tempted to straighten it up for him. He spoke in a deep voice that reminded her of an advert on the television, but she couldn't place which one. His crisp cotton coat was creased and far too small for his frame. You could see it stretch at the seams as he went to shake her mother's hand.

Dreanna lay on the bed, her dignity just about covered by the floral backless gown. The doctor approached her slowly, his hands covered by a pair of latex gloves. Dreanna breathed in deeply, wondering how many more times her genitals would be touched without her permission. Her legs were wide apart and they began to wobble as he pushed his gloved fingers inside her. His other hand was pushing on her stomach. Dreanna tried hard to swallow back her tears – she felt dirty and used as she relived the painful memories of what Paul had done. She was trapped in her mind, her memories haunting her every second. But the doctor did what he was supposed to do – he did no more than what was asked of him. He examined her thoroughly, both externally and internally and chacked her blood pressure as well as her urine, faeces and blood. After the examination both mother and daughter sat in his office waiting patiently for the results.

"Well – we have some good news and some bad news. The good news is that you daughter is not suffering from any serious disorder; the bad news is we are still unsure of what she actually is suffering from. She's showing some form of discomfort in her pelvic region but this is only to be expected with someone of her age and all the hormonal changes her body would be going through right now. The only thing I can think of is that she's suffering from some form of migraine – these are common in adolescent girls. She is, like I said, very hormonal and could well be having some anxiety or panic disorder too. So I'm going to give you some anti-spasmodic medicine for her which needs to be taken three times a day. I'll also give you are prescription for a sedative but she must only take it when these episodes of panic are severe." He rose from his seat and opened the door. Iris shook his hand and they left.

The bus journey home was awful; the skies had opened and the bus was packed with soaking wet people who just wanted shelter from the rain.

Once home Iris turned to her daughter. "Right kid – now all you have to do is take this medicine. You can't have any more days off school – the school authority have already been in touch and they said that if you don't go they'll take you away, and you don't want that do you?"

"No Mum but..." Dreanna sighed. "It doesn't matter... yeah, I'll take the medicine, I promise."

It was Friday, only one more day to go before freedom, Dreanna thought as she brushed her teeth, then no more school for two whole days. She sorted her bag out and placed it by the new telephone that had just been installed.

Dawn and Andrew were sitting in the front room and Iris was washing up in the kitchen. As Dreanna walked towards her mother something inside her head snapped, like the twang of an elastic band. The agonising ache filled her head and she squeezed it tightly between her hands. 'No more,' she begged. 'Please, no more!' She rubbed her temples and her heart pounded in her throat. 'I just can't do it,' she told herself. 'I just can't go to school today. Oh my God, why can't I? Why am I feeling like this?' "Mum," she stared longingly into her mother's eyes "I'm not too good, my head is hurting. Please... help me."

Iris reached for the drugs on the table and took a teaspoon out of the drawer next to the sink. "Well take this medicine then, but you are bloody well going to school, do you hear me? You are bloody well going to school." Iris's hand was shaking as she forced the bitter medicine into her daughter's mouth.

Dawn began shouting at her sister as she walked into the kitchen. "Is she complaining again? Come on you little bitch, Mum doesn't need this. Get your coat and go."

There was a knock at the door.

"Mum please, I can't go, please don't make me, Mum. Mum!"

"For fuck's sake, you are such a selfish little bitch. If my Andrew turns out like you and doesn't go to school, I'm gonna blame you – you know it will all be your fault." Dawn grabbed the back of her sister's collar, and thrust her out of the door.

Her friends didn't bother to ask what the matter was anymore, to them this was just a daily occurrence and they were used to it, but to Dreanna this was turning into one of the biggest battles of her life. She could cope with so much but carrying everyone else's emotions was making her ill, an emotional wreck, and she was so alone, so isolated and so scared.

The weekend came and went and Dreanna had spent nearly all of it sleeping. The two days' respite helped her to gather strength and by the end of it she almost felt normal again. But Monday arrived all too soon, and even before anyone had the chance to tell her to take this so-called marvellous tonic, she had already poured it onto a spoon. She had got used to its acrid taste, but it didn't work, it never bloody worked! The next school day came around so fast it might as well have had fire and brimstone surrounding it, because this is how she saw it; a hell on Earth, a secret hell on Earth. Her friends knocked as usual, but this time Dreanna hadn't brushed her teeth, combed her hair or even dressed in her school uniform. She sat, refusing to move from the settee.

"God, not again," Dawn shouted. "I've had enough of this bollocks. Tell her friends just to go Mum, I'll sort her out." Dawn threw her sister to the floor and waved her finger frantically in Dreanna's face. "Enough is enough, you are going to school whether you like it or not. Mum, call a taxi." Dawn stood over Dreanna's motionless body.

"You don't understand, I can't go. I just can't...Please Dawn, don't do this to me, please don't make me go."

"Well you're fucking going. Get up. Look at the state of you. Don't you know how ashamed of you we all are? Don't you know what this is doing to Mum? You are pathetic. You're a pathetic selfish little bitch!"

The taxi had arrived and hooted his horn; Iris went to the window, her arm raised to acknowledge him.

"Come on, get up," Dawn screeched. "For fuck's sake, get up."

Dreanna looked up at her sister with bloodshot eyes and tear-stained cheeks. "But I'm still in my nightie."

No amount of pleading was going to work – Dawn was too angry. "I don't give a fuck. You're going and you're going right now, dressed or not!"

Dawn pulled on the sleeve of Dreanna's nightdress to get her to move, but there was a loud ripping noise and the sleeve now hung down over her arm. Dreanna tried to sit still on the floor, determined not to cry again, but Dawn hauled her into the hallway by her arms. Iris opened the front door, her eyes not once meeting those of her dishevelled daughter.

"You've brought this on yourself, Dreanna," Dawn snarled, as she forced her outside in the winter rain and icy wind. Dawn saw the neighbour watching as she threw her sister inside the waiting taxi. "Get in the car. Get in the fucking car! And what are you looking at, you nosey old goat?"

The taxi driver stared at his messy shambolic cargo. "I'm not taking her anywhere. Look at her – she's still in her pajamas, and she doesn't have a coat – she's really upset."

"Good, she deserves to be upset. You don't know what she's done to this family; she's pulled it apart and she is an evil little bitch, so take her and dump her somewhere, we really don't care, just get her out of my sight!"

The driver muttered something under his breath as he pulled away from the kerb. Dreanna didn't even look up. She didn't know where he was taking her and she didn't care. All she knew was that her family had had enough of her. She was a horrible child who didn't know how to explain to her family why she was the way she was; she was once again alone and ashamed of who she was.

"You're Patrick's daughter, aren't you?" he asked as he pulled out of the estate.

"Yes." Dreanna's head hung low and she looked straight at the dashboard.

"I used to work with your dad at the builder's merchants. Good bloke, your dad." He paused. "My name's Glenn by the way. Look I don't know what all this is about but there's no way I'm taking you to school looking like this. In fact I actually don't know what to do with you right now, but I need to fill up with petrol and then we'll see if we can sort this mess out, okay?"

Glenn reached behind and grabbed something off the back seat. "Here put this on. It's going to swamp you, but you must be freezing." He handed her a navy blue sweatshirt, which did indeed engulf her, but she was glad she had something to cover up her shoulders. She had tried to cover her teenage breasts but the ripped nightdress didn't have enough material left to cover her bare skin. "I'm just going into the garage to pay, you promise to stay in the car?"

Dreanna nodded, her head still bent towards the floor.

Glenn returned with a packet of salt and vinegar crisps and a can of Fanta. "Here – take this. I assume you haven't eaten or drunk anything yet. Do you fancy a drive around before I take you home?"

"Please don't take me home, they hate me. Please... don't take me back there, they don't want me anymore." As Dreanna stared out of the window the ghostly figure of a man stood in the doorway to the entrance of the garage. His piercing eyes gazed back in her direction.

"I'm sure that's not true," said Glenn. "What have you done anyway, murdered someone?"

"No, I didn't want to go to school." Dreanna's voice was soft and embarrassed, but her eyes were still focused on those of the deceased male.

Glenn laughed, knowing full well he didn't have the complete story from this disorganised mess of a girl. "Jesus! Is that all? By the way your sister was going on at you I thought you must have committed a crime! Look, I need a break anyway so let me radio control and tell them I'm taking it now, and then we can try and sort this out. Smile kid, you've gone all pale. You're not gonna puke in my car are you? What's up? You look like you've seen a ghost!"

Dreanna made eye contact with her driver. "How can I tell you I have?" she said. "And even if I did, you wouldn't believe me."

Glenn looked puzzled and could do no more than nod his head. He drove to the local reservoir and parked the car. Both of them stared out of the front windscreen at the stillness of the water. The only noise came from the wind and the squawking birds bobbing in and out of the cold water.

"Lovely here isn't it?" he asked as he looked down on his cargo. "I always come here when things aren't going so well and I need to get away. It's a good calming place – somewhere to hide away and let things just float on by."

"Thank you."

Glenn smiled back at her.

The rain had started to fall again and Dreanna was becoming mesmerised by the windscreen wipers moving from side to side. Their hypnotic movement made her eyes close and soon she was peacefully sleeping. Her mind made no effort to dream, her body made no effort to move. For now at least she had some peace.

Glenn's warm tones disturbed her precious moments of recovery. "Hey kid, time to wake up."

They were back at her house. The neighbour across the road stopped washing the inside of her windows and peeked over the edge of her glasses in their direction. Dreanna knew it wouldn't be long before her family, and especially her, were the talk of the estate once again. This was becoming a habit. This woman spent every waking hour gossiping about others, their problems and their hardships, and was so busy looking into the lives of others that she was often blind to the imperfection and dysfunction that went on behind her own closed door.

"I'm sorry," Glenn said "I just couldn't take her to school."

Iris ushered her daughter in. "It's alright. Things have calmed down a bit now. How much do we owe you?"

"Nothing, it doesn't matter. I needed a break anyway and she was a good excuse. See you later, young one." He was gone. Dreanna's knight in shining armour for the morning had ridden away on his four-wheeled steed.

"I'm sorry Mum, I just don't know what to do. I'm so sorry." Dreanna reached out for her mother.

"So am I." Iris looked coldly in her daughter's direction, not paying any attention to Dreanna's yearning to be cradled in her arms. "I've been in touch with Mrs Hatter – she'll be around this afternoon. You're going to have to go away. We just can't take this anymore."

"No – Mum – please, NO!!! I'll try harder I promise, please don't send me away."

"Sorry Dreanna, it's too late. We have to pack you a bag. You're going today."

"B...b...but Mum, the reason is because, because I, I..." but try as hard as she might she still couldn't tell her why she behaved the way she did.

At two-thirty on the dot Mrs Hatter arrived, a short rather chubby lady, whose lipstick was smeared across her front teeth. She smelt of some sickly cheap perfume that women of a certain age wore. Her crimplene skirt hung just above her knee, her flabby stomach dropping over the top like a cupcake that had gone horribly wrong. The rotund face wrinkled and twitched as she fumbled with her oversized bag. The handbag suited her; it was as large and ugly as she was. Dreanna took an automatic dislike to her.

"So you're the one that's causing all the trouble are you?" Her voice was stern and arrogant. "Well a few weeks spent with us will soon knock you back into shape; we will soon mould you back into the perfect child."

"Who are you, Hitler?" The disgust and disapproval Dreanna had in her voice showed on her face at the same time.

"Dreanna, manners!" Iris screamed.

"Well who does she think she is? She doesn't know me, she said she's gonna mould me. How can she mould a person! She looks like she's eating all the moulds as well as all the kids." Dreanna's words were bitter. She felt let down not only by her mother but by all the dead and deceased who had been with her since the day she was born.

"I'm so sorry, she is never normally this rude." Iris glanced down at her daughter, a frown now appearing on her face.

Outside the house, Iris climbed into the front seat of Mrs Hatter's car and an unwilling Dreanna climbed into the back. Their journey took about two hours. It actually would have been a nice car ride, as the scenery was pretty and Dreanna enjoyed going out in a car as the family had never owned one. But this journey was ruined by the overweight dictator sitting in the driving seat; it was also ruined by Dreanna feeling her world had finally been destroyed. She didn't understand how, why or what she had done to be so abandoned by the people both living and dead that she loved the most.

"Come on child, out you get. That's right – one foot in front of another."

"I do know how to walk you know, I've been doing it a long time." The bitterness was still in Dreanna's voice but something about this woman made her stomach churn. "Probably all the kids she's eaten," Dreanna chuckled in a low voice so no-one else could hear.

Dr Cuttels was the first to introduce himself. "Hello Dreanna, glad you could join us. First things first – say goodbye to your mum."

Iris tried to grab hold of her daughter, but Dreanna moved away. She felt her heart was tearing in two. She loved her mother so much but how could she dispose of her like that? How could she discard her like an old newspaper?

"We'll see you soon – come on, give us a kiss," Iris begged.

But Dreanna showed no response. She stood firmly on the same spot and for one brief moment she hated her mother with revulsion and disgust. She hated the rest of her family and she even hated Andrew for being the perfect little boy that her parents adored. She hated him for taking her place sitting in between her father's legs at night whilst watching the television. She hated the world, she hated everything.

Dr Cuttels showed Dreanna around her new home, finally ending up at the small two-bedded room where she would sleep. "This is your room. You will not be allowed to watch television, you will be up at six o'clock and in bed by eight, you will shower with the other girls only when supervised. You will not be allowed to listen to music and you must speak only when spoken to. Do you understand?" The previously nice tone in the doctor's voice had become aggressive and controlling. "Answer me girl, do you understand?"

"Yes, yes, I understand." The doctor left.

Dreanna lay on her bed. The blankets were smooth but smelt stale and musty. The room was dark and dreary apart from one single photograph positioned on the bedside cabinet by the other bed. It was the picture of a child of about four years, smiling, with the happy faces of a man and a woman crouching down by her on either side. Whoever it belonged to, this picture showed a happier time, back when life hadn't grabbed hold and sunk its fangs into the young flesh of that smiling child. Her roommate entered the room.

"Hi, my name's Corinne. Why you here? I'm getting off the drugs, been on them since I was eleven. It's shit here, so many rules, but at least you get fed. I can get you some ganja if you want, do you want?"

"No, No! Go away. Leave me alone." Dreanna didn't want to talk. She didn't want to see or feel why Corrine had gone from being a contented child into one of society's dope addicts.

"Chill, will ya? I only fucking asked."

A bell rang loudly in the hallway outside, and there was a bustle of rushing feet. Dreanna got up from her musty bed and made her way into the hall.

"New girl, grub's up," a boy so much taller than Dreanna shouted as he passed her.

She followed the hoards of teenagers down the corridor to a large open dining room. Two white tables were laid with a jug of water placed in the centre of each one. A large clock hung on the grey-painted walls.

"Out of the way, bitch." Corrine stood behind her. "Come on move your arse. If you don't want the food, get out of the way, 'cos I'm starving."

Dreanna edged sideways to let Corrine pass and lifted a tray. She really wasn't hungry and the food looked so unappetizing. The chicken was anaemic, the vegetables were stuck to the sides of the silver bowls and mushy, and the gravy was thick and lumpy, but she filled her plastic white plate and moved to the end of one of the tables and sat down. All the other kids were chatting between mouthfuls. Dreanna just pushed the rancid-looking food around her plate, the bewilderment rising in her chest as she stared around the room. Her mind began to feel dizzy, the usual pounding inside her skull sent electrical currents through her body and the mixed-up jumbled words of each child in the room got louder and louder. Visions of needles, bottles of beer, clothes being ripped from innocent bodies, blood, shouting, screaming and begging surged around her. She felt like her whole aura was being suffocated.

"I need to get out of here." She didn't realise just how loud she had spoken as she run back to the sanctuary of her room. The other children watched as Dreanna bounded out through the dining room doors to the safety of her claustrophobic room.

"Are you okay?" The boy who had told her about dinner was standing in the doorway.

"Yes… yes I'm fine thank you."

"You ran outta there like your arse was on fire. I know the food is shit but never seen anyone run as fast as you did… My name's Joel."

"Dreanna." Her hand reached out to shake his.

"Someone's got some manners," he joked. "So why you here then? Most of us are in here 'cos we have a problem with the booze or drugs, and the rest of us are here 'cos our parents can't control us."

"That explains a lot," Dreanna said. She paused, "I wouldn't go to school."

"What the fuck? What do you mean? You're in this shit hole 'cos you wouldn't go to school? Well that sucks. Think someone's taking the piss personally. This place is for fruit loops – you know – kids that have problems, the nutters. I'd get out as soon as you can if I was you – before you turn into one of us!"

"Don't worry, I intend to. Is there a phone somewhere I can use? I really need to phone my dad… but… but I don't have any money."

Joel fidgeted his feet, his hands stuffed firmly in the pockets of his tracksuit trousers. "That's not a problem, come with me. Everyone will be in the main hall, including the carers stuffing their faces…We can go to the office, but will have to be quick." Joel took Dreanna to the front office and led her to a desk with a phone. "Hurry up. If we get caught, they'll take away my privileges and yours, so please speak real quick!"

Dreanna took hold of the receiver, placed her finger into the first digit, praying no one would interrupt the pleading conversation she was about to have.

"Dad, DAD! It's me, Dreanna. Please come and get me, please take me home. I promise I will go to school, Dad. It's scary here, Dad... Dad...?"

"Calm down kid, I'm not leaving you there, I just need to sort out how I'm going to get there and pick you up. NO bugger is taking my kids away from, me no-one!"

"Ask Glenn, he will do it. Tell Mum I'm sorry. I'm so sorry for hurting her, I promise I'll stay out of everybody's way, you won't know I'm even there. I love you Dad."

"Don't worry kid, somehow, someway I'll get you home, don't worry about anything, just stay strong. You understand me? Stay strong."

Footsteps rapidly approached the office and Joel grabbed hold of the phone in the middle of Patrick's sentence and slammed it back onto its base. "C'mon, get your arse back to your room." He shoved Dreanna out through the door.

It took two whole days and nights before Patrick could get his daughter home, and those two nights for Dreanna were the most frightening experience she had ever had. The pain, trauma and fear she felt in that prison made her realise what it was like to be a child that had nothing and was nothing; what it was like to be condemned by a society that, instead of helping, found it easier to throw these kids into a place where they were the ones in the wrong. They were seen as an embarrassment, a waste of time and effort, and a waste of fucking space.

The house was silent as Patrick pushed the front door open. Only the family dog greeted his master as he strolled into the kitchen. Dreanna walked slowly behind him.

"Tea and then chat, okay Dreanna?"

She nodded, but all she really wanted was for her dad to cradle her in his arms and make the last few days vanish.

"Right," Patrick said. "This is what the plan is going to be. I was speaking to Glenn, the taxi driver, and he said that maybe hypnosis could help you. I don't really understand it, but I've found a man that does it. Rose's mum is going to take us there tonight, but don't let anyone know that it's costing all my wages for this week. That will have to stay our secret."

"Does Mum know I'm home?"

"Yes, Bubs, but Mum's a little delicate right now. She's struggling, don't know why, but she is – you've really taken a lot out of her and she just doesn't know what to do with you. We will sort this, I promise."

The hypnotist sat opposite Dreanna, his legs crossed. He held a fancy pen in his hand and a A4 notebook rested on his lap. His room was full of books and pictures of Victorian men and women. It smelt of wax polish like Iris used on the stained floorboards at home. It was a soothing room, one to tranquilise your feelings and calm your mind.

"Now Dreanna, tell me what's been going on – but I need to know everything."

"You have shining eyes, kind eyes, eyes that can tell a story," Dreanna replied.

"Erm, thank you," he fidgeted in his seat. "Now can you tell me what's happening? What's been going on?" He looked into Dreanna's big brown eyes and she looked straight into his.

For the first time in months Dreanna felt calm and relaxed. She felt this stranger would listen to her. She trusted him and for the first time in her life she told another person absolutely everything without feeling silly or stupid or mentally deranged. She didn't feel alone anymore.

"Do you feel better now you've got everything off your chest?"

Dreanna smiled. She did. "Yes." The corners of her mouth actually turned upwards. "Yes," she said again, "I feel empty and free."

The man with the shining eyes smiled with her and took a deep breath. "Firstly I don't think you have, nor do I believe you have ever had, an anxiety attack. You may very well be hormonal, after all you are a teenager, but I need you to listen closely and pay attention to what I'm going to say. You have to remember some things in this life cannot be explained; some things happen for no rhyme or reason, and some people are born with abilities that are, how can I say this, erm, different to others. One day you'll know why, one day you will understand, but for now I will teach you to control it, okay?"

Dreanna nodded.

"So, I want you to take a deep breath, and hold it... now release it... Close your eyes and see yourself in your field. Over by the oak tree is a red balloon with a long string attached to it. Walk over to it and grab hold. Are you holding it?"

"Yes."

"Each time you start having these feelings and sensing pain, close your eyes and picture your field. Take hold of the balloon and allow it to lift you gently up in the air through the tops of the trees. Each time you get higher you become calmer and calmer. This place you are in is yours and no one or nothing can hurt you. Understand?"

"Yes."

"Good. Now walk back to the sound of my voice. Are you with me?"

"Yes."

"Open your eyes. How do you feel?"

"Strange. A little tired, but I feel good."

"My last piece of advice for you is this. Others around you, even those you love, will assume they know better than you. They'll try and make you believe that they know what's best, and they will at times be unbearable. You'll feel confused and angry with them, but one day you'll know what to do and what to say. You will make enemies, so watch out for them, but be patient. One day it will all make sense."

Dreanna never saw this man again, but his words would stay with her always. She knew that somewhere inside him he had shared her experiences, and she was so grateful to him for allowing her to be just who she was, even if only for an hour. He was her hero with shining eyes.

For the first time in ages she was back at school and was finally being what she should be: an inquisitive teenager. The dreams didn't stop, and she still picked up the emotions of nearly everyone she met, but for now at least she could cope – and she was finally able to relax and experience the thrills of being a teenager.

The Kiss

October 1982

By the time she hit fifteen, Dreanna's friendship with Louise had ended. They were in different classes at school now which meant that Louise had met new people to hang around with. Dreanna felt lonely again, and missed her so much. She loved her like a sister and Dreanna's family adored her too. She would be eternally grateful to Louise for giving her a chance to feel what a juvenile friendship can give a person and so held a special place in her heart as a thank you for being her friend.

She still had a few friends but most of these were merely acquaintances that she hung around with so she wasn't constantly on her own. However, there was one girl in particular whose company she adored, although she was no replacement for Louise. This girl made her laugh and they sat together in their English lessons never really getting any work done, because they were constantly talking and mucking around. Dreanna trusted her and treasured their friendship, but the rest of the time she spent alone or with her sisters. Since the trials and tribulations of the last year their bond had grown stronger and they were not only sisters but best friends. Dreanna had even forgiven Dawn for her actions and spiteful words. She was her sister after all and loved her with the whole of her heart. She was only fifteen but her weekends were normally spent with her siblings at the local pub. They even took her to her first male strip show. Dreanna didn't know where to look when the male exotic dancer removed his undergarments and began gyrating in her face. It was surely a sight that any fifteen-year-old girl would never forget! She had never felt more normal in the whole of her life, and she loved it.

School was just school, a place she had to go to. Her only real problem was trying to conform, and once or twice her non-conformity had got her into trouble – with one of the teachers especially.

She was changing back into her uniform after a PE lesson, chatting to her class mates when one of the PE teachers grabbed hold of her arm and tried to pull her outside. The teacher was shouting about the state of her uniform and how the blouse she was wearing was not the right attire. Dreanna stood there, staring at her and listening to her sarcastic jibes. Over and over again the teacher repeated herself, then she began flicking Dreanna's ear lobes, telling her that having four pierced holes in one ear was not school policy. Dreanna just stood there. The teacher grabbed Dreanna again by the collar, her voice getting louder and louder, until silence fell in the shabby changing rooms. Dreanna looked up into her eyes, smiled and said, "You're a very angry lady aren't you? And me, well I may not be what you want or expect a student from this school to be, but when I'm older I will make a difference and you…let's just say you're going to turn into an angry lesbian and the only pussy you'll get to stroke will be your black and white cat."

Needless to say she was suspended for a week, for in the words of the head-master, "She should not have talked so abruptly and uncouthly."

Dreanna handed her suspension letter to Patrick when she got home that day. He did what he always did – he laughed, shook his head and made a pot of tea.

December 1982

The local disco was holding its annual Christmas party and the room was packed. Hormones were flying free and the more adventurous teenagers downed bottles of cider outside, hiding the evidence under a bush if one of the adults were about. Dreanna never drank alcohol, unlike many of her friends, and had only had one sexual experience with a boy and didn't enjoy that much either. Very clumsy and not quite what she was expecting. The Earth didn't move.

The girls she had arrived with were all trying to outdo the other on the dance floor, shaking their backsides and waving their arms in the air to attract the attention of some horny boy. Dreanna sat perched on the edge of a shaky table that had seen better days, wondering why she was there. She couldn't dance, didn't drink, and didn't even enjoy it that much. She began playing with a thread hanging loose on her jacket.

"Look up Dreanna, look up."

"What?" She knew she had spoken aloud and tried to pretend she was sing-ing along to Frankie Goes To Hollywood's *Relax*, but was desperately hoping no one noticed that her lips didn't move in sync to the music. As she looked up and scanned the room her eyes stared straight into a pair of green gemstones – and he was looking right back at her. They both seemed absorbed in each other, and then he was gone. "Pleasant!" she laughed.

"Hello."

"Er, hello," she answered. The eyes she had stared into were now by her side. Boy and girl stood still looking intently at each other and then, before she knew it, they were kissing, a long lingering kiss; the kind of kiss that she'd only ever dreamed of having.

"What's your name?" her snogging partner enquired.

"Dreanna. What's yours?"

"Callum."

Their lips touched continually throughout the rest of the evening, not talking, not acknowledging any other person in the room. They were totally absorbed with each other; it was as if nobody else mattered. Just the two of them and the gentle touch of their mouths caressing each other.

Early afternoon the following Sunday the phone rang.

"Hi, can I speak to Dreanna please?" a young man's voice asked.

"Speaking. Who's this?"

"Er, it's Callum. Hope you don't mind but I got your number off one of your friends. Are you busy? Can we meet?"

Dreanna punched the air. She never in her wildest dreams thought he would want to see her again. "Yep I s'pose I can. Where do you wanna meet?" She tried so hard not to allow the excitement be heard in her voice.

"How about the park near the police station?"

"Okay, I'll be there in 'bout ten minutes."

Dreanna couldn't help herself, she punched the air AGAIN. "Yes!" she screamed.

Callum was already sitting on one of the swings when Dreanna arrived. Her heart began to pound as she edged closer to him. He held out his hand and Dreanna placed hers in it. He pulled her closer and kissed her tenderly, their bodies pulled tight into each other. Dreanna had never felt these strange sensations seeping through her body before. Her groin began to ache as shivers ran down her spine. She felt heat rising through her as each kiss took more of her breath away. Callum's hands moved unsteadily down her back and under her coat. He reached for her firm breast; she knew she should stop it, but couldn't, she wanted him to hold her, and she wanted him to satisfy this fire that was building inside her loins. He stroked her skin and began unbuttoning her jeans. His hand slid into place. Dreanna sighed a deep sigh, his lips kissing her neck. She was a teenager experiencing her first full throes of lust and passion.

"Stop, please you must stop...I, I shouldn't be doing this," she said, her breath shallow.

"I'm sorry, I'm so sorry." Callum's reaction was full of embarrassment as he withdrew his touch.

Both had to control the urges that had been growing inside them. They composed themselves and sat side by side on the swings.

Dreanna lifted her gaze from the ground and stared at him, a warm sense filling her whole body. "Whoops!" she said. Both of them began to laugh. She was the ugly duckling that may still not turn into that beautiful swan, but he made her feel like she didn't have a care in the world. She was happy.

January 1983

Dreanna's friends often told her, "He'll only use you; you know he's only interested in one thing, you'll get hurt!" But Dreanna couldn't see what they saw, something inside just made her yearn for his touch. Before long she was head over heels in love with him; he made her feel special, he made her feel free and he made her feel excited. Callum's friends didn't make it easy for her in the way they looked at her or the way they dressed; their middle-class upbringing was worlds apart from hers and they made sure she knew it. She often heard bitchy comments about her when Callum left the room. The main difference was that Dreanna knew exactly how and what they were thinking, but for the first time in her life she didn't give a damn. She lay in her bed smiling to herself.

"*Dreanna,*" the voice asked, "*are you happy?*"

"Yes," she answered.

"*Good, he will be yours for many years to come. Isn't he what you asked for?*"

"I don't understand, what do you mean what I asked for?"

"*Cast your mind back – did you not ask for a boy, green eyes, muscular build, kind, accepting?*"

"Yes." They really had been in her head! All those nights of wishing for her green-eyed hunk, and here he was!

"*Well here he is. Admittedly he doesn't have all the traits you desired, but he is very similar isn't he?*"

"Yes… But I don't understand. Are you saying because I asked for him he came to me? I'm confused, please explain."

"*In time, my precious one, in time.*"

Then the voice was gone.

November 1985

Dreanna found herself perched on the edge of her bed, watching, staring and hoping that the little window would not produce a solid blue line. The last thing she wanted was to be pregnant at seventeen.

"Nan, if you're there, I wish you… you could help me a little here!"

"*It's the way it should be,*" the voice said.

Dreanna screamed as the ominous line appeared in the window. "Fuck!" She was definitely pregnant. "Fuck," she said again as Patrice entered her bedroom, staring at the test in her hand.

"Shit," said Patrice, pulling her face into a grimace. "Don't wanna be in your shoes when Mum finds out! You know she won't be happy don't you?"

Dreanna could not take her eyes of that bloody blue line, willing it to disappear, but of course it didn't. "I know Pat. Oh fuck, fuck, fuck. I'm really scared now, what am I going to do? Shit, bollocks, wank, and I pissed on my fucking hand when I done it! Oh Pat, what am I gonna do?"

"First wash your bloody hands! Look Sis, go tell Dad, he's downstairs. Tell him first and see what he says. As for Mum, all I can say is good luck!" Patrice laughed as she walked away into her own bedroom.

Dreanna crouched on the bottom stair, knowing full well that she wasn't going to be able to keep this a secret. Why couldn't she get to grips with that bloody condom? Why didn't her contraceptive pill work? Why didn't she stop? She knew the consequences. She knew babies didn't get delivered by those poxy storks. Christ, she knew at the age of nine that having sex meant babies. Why couldn't she control those urges? Why didn't she just keep her bloody legs crossed! She took in a huge gasp of air, walked into the kitchen and sat next to her father at the dining room table.

"Dad, I, I need to tell you something."

"It's okay."

"What you mean, it's okay? I haven't told you yet."

Patrick put down his pen, lent back in his chair and crossed his arms.

"I 'spose you want me to tell your mother. You know she's not going to be happy, don't you? Don't worry – she'll come around sooner or later. Have you told Callum yet?

"No," she frowned. "How… you knew, I mean you know? I mean – oh shit, I don't know what I mean!"

Patrick stared at his daughter and gave one of his cheeky chappy smiles, his crystal blue eyes twinkled and danced. "There are certain things I know, okay? You're not the only one with secrets." He winked as he spoke.

Dreanna didn't feel much like socialising as her growing bump seemed to drain her energy – not that this bothered her as socialising was never really her thing anyway. She seemed to spend more time with Dawn, who had recently moved to live in a house opposite with her new husband, Andrew their eldest child, and Bernadette her two-year-old daughter. An added bonus was that Dawn was now pregnant with her third child.

Callum seemed happy enough. He continued doing all the things an unbri-dled teenager did at seventeen: sport, alcohol, experimentation with drugs… But he was always there for her, always supporting his young teenage pregnant girlfriend, taking her to her hospital appointments, holding her hair back when she was hurling up everything she ate. Dreanna often used the lame excuse that her feet ached and Callum would spend hours rubbing them for her, which was a lie, she just wanted a foot rub and was prepared to use the pregnancy to get what she wanted!

Most of the family were fine with the fact that another baby was joining their clan. Iris couldn't quite get to grips with the idea, but it was happening and there was nothing she could do about it.

Callum's mum was fine too but her mind was on other matters. Callum's dad was diagnosed with cancer a few years before Dreanna met him and in the last few months his father's health had started to fail. Dreanna could see the pain in his eyes whenever she went around his house and was desperate to tell him that there is somewhere we go after death, but this was one secret she still couldn't tell. She hid it well.

Dreanna and Callum were lying side by side on her bed discussing names for the baby growing inside her. Dreanna's head began to pound and for a brief second the world stopped. Dreanna lifted her pregnant clumsy frame from the bed. "We have to go see your Dad, now!"

Callum looked at her, his eyebrows joining together across his brow, "What? Mum's only just left him and visiting hours were over ten minutes ago."

Dreanna began putting on her boots, and grabbed her coat from the floor. She brushed her hair away from her face, looked in the mirror and wiped the smudgy bits of make up from around her eyes. "We need to go NOW! Sod the visiting times." Then she lowered her voice, "Trust me Callum, we need to do this. Please, please just put your trainers on and let's go. Don't ask me questions. Whatever happens – no questions okay?"

"Okay."

As the two young people entered the hospital, Dreanna sighed deeply, "Give me strength."

"What d'you say?" Callum asked.

"Nothing."

The ward was deadly quiet. Some soft lighting had been left on and the occasional cough could be heard. Callum's dad was in an all-male ward where the dying spent their final days. The air smelt of shit, piss and – there was no mistaking it – DEATH. You didn't have to be Dreanna to recognise the smell. It drifted and crawled through the air, its stubbornness was strong; it was there to remind everyone that death was a force of its own, and it would happen no matter what you wanted. Death would remain, death was life in reverse.

"Visiting time ended twenty minutes ago," the staff nurse said, looking over the rim of her glasses.

"Please," Dreanna insisted, "we just want to say, see, I mean speak briefly to one of your patients …please?"

Maybe it was because of Dreanna's pregnant form or that she was pleading with her eyes. Whatever the reason the icy glare changed into a sweet smile. "Alright, but be quiet, some patients are already asleep. You've got five minutes, no longer." She went back to her paperwork.

Dreanna and Callum sat down gently on his father's bed. He opened his eyes and his hand reached for her stomach. He smiled. He rubbed it gently. Dreanna smiled. No words were exchanged, just quietness, total silence.

The staff nurse tapped Callum on the shoulder.

"Come on you two, time to go, it's getting late. Time to say your goodbyes."

"There's no such thing as goodbyes," Dreanna said. "Only see-you-laters." Her eyes were fixed on those of Callum's father. She bent down so that her cheek touched him and whispered in his ear, "Go now. See you later, but don't forget to come back and see me. I love you." She placed a kiss tenderly on his cheek.

The phone call came just after they arrived back at Dreanna's house. Callum's father died a few seconds after they had left the hospital. She pulled Callum close to her, so desperate to tell him what she knew, but the words stuck in her throat. She couldn't even say she was sorry for his loss as she wasn't sorry. She wasn't sorry his father died because she knew the wonders that were yet to be seen by him; she knew the next stage of this thing we call life. She was happy that he would now experience an existence with no pain, no trauma, no anguish, just freedom.

"Don't ever leave me," Callum said. "If everyone and everything else in this world disappeared, I could survive as long as I had you by my side."

Dreanna kissed him tenderly on the cheek and pulled his head down on her shoulders. "I will never leave you, never."

The day of the funeral arrived. None of Dreanna's 'posh' clothes fitted her and she got highly frustrated as she tossed everything onto the floor. The only thing suitable for a funeral was a very tight very short black skirt, but there was no way a size eight skirt was going to go round her bulging bump! She sat on her bed looking at the mound of clothes on her floor-drobe. Iris was standing at her bedroom door.

"Well," Iris said acrimoniously, "If you will get pregnant!"

"Mum, really! I know you're not happy but please not today. I'm not arguing with you today." Dreanna rummaged through the piled up clothes again, hoping that by magic something would have stretched and grown in size.

Iris picked up the very short black skirt. "What's wrong with this then?"

"It's a size eight! And unless you've gone blind you should be able to see it won't go round this," Dreanna put her hands on either side of her bump and wobbled it.

"Kids today," Iris sighed. "Go get an elastic band from the kitchen drawer... well go on, don't just stand there looking at me!"

Dreanna sulked her way downstairs and back up again carrying a ball of elastic bands. Iris pulled Dreanna's dressing gown off her shoulders and for one brief second stared at the baby bump. She touched it with the palm of her hand and gave a wonky smile.

She does care, thought Dreanna, and smiled too.

Iris regained her stern attitude and attached an elastic band to the button hole, looping it through and back on itself. "C'mon, put your legs in."

Dreanna did as her mother ordered. The good thing about Dreanna's bump was that it was all out in front and she had gained no extra weight on her hips or backside. The skirt slid with ease over these places. Iris picked up the flapping end of the elastic band and hooked it over the button. "There you go, now all you need is a top that's baggy enough to cover the waistband and job done."

It was the first time Iris had come close to her daughter since Patrick had told her about their youngest daughter's pregnancy. Dreanna felt her mother's touch and knew deep down she loved her, even if she was too bloody stubborn to show it, even if she was too bloody stubborn to let go of her morals and her 'you should be married before having sex' beliefs. But Dreanna knew a secret. She had worked it out when she was going through the family's birth certificates and found her mother and father's marriage certificate. Iris was three months pregnant when she and Patrick married. Morals! Dreanna laughed as she pulled a white blouse off a hanger. She didn't care that the blouse wasn't black and that she would probably look like a waitress at the Beefeater, but it was all she had and she had to make do.

Dreanna stood awkwardly in the living room at Callum's house. There were so many faces she had never met before, so many eyes she had never looked into, so many people. Dreanna shuddered.

"Dreanna, do you want to come in our car to the crem?" Callum's mum asked.

Hospitals, churches, crematoriums... each brought with them the deep dark feelings Dreanna spent her life running away from. She hated these places even more than she hated school. "Er, no, not really, I don't do funerals – I mean I'm feeling a little bit sick today, you know morning sickness. Would you mind if I stayed at your house? I could prepare some food or something for you..."

"Only if you're sure Dreanna, that would be so helpful."

"Yep, I'm sure." She breathed a sigh of relief; the last thing she wanted right now was to stand in a packed crematorium with grief-stricken strangers.

Later, when the day was finally over, Dreanna mused that as the funeral was behind them and Callum's dad had been given a good send-off, life had to return to normal. After all, life goes on, and in Dreanna's case life grew bigger each day. Life was inside her and she was the vessel giving it everything it needed to survive.

July 1986

The months flew past, and Dreanna's belly grew big and round. It was the beginning of July and her baby was due at the end of August.

"Not long now, eeek!" she thought. She felt strange as she went to bed that night; there was a heaviness in her groin but also an ache in her heart that just wouldn't go away. She had become used to having peculiar feelings and never questioned them anymore, but these were different, strange and perplexing.

"What the hell!" She awoke with a start; water was gushing through her pyjamas,

"*Dreanna go and tell your mum. I will be with you, I promise.*" The voice was back.

Dreanna didn't hesitate. She ran into her mum and dad's bedroom. "Mum! Mum! I think my waters have just broken."

"Oh right, but you still have another four weeks left." Iris got out of bed and went over to her daughter. She stared at the huge wet patch on Dreanna's pajamas then placed a hand on her stomach. "Yep, you're in labour, contractions are strong – with any luck it will be over in about four hours, I'd say. Let's go find you a sanitary towel...have you packed your case?"

Iris ...no, Mum, was back! Back being a caring loving nurturing mother. She held Dreanna tight and cupped her face in her hands. "You've got plenty of time, now relax, everything is going to be fine, I promise."

Dreanna bent over as a contraction ripped its way through her body. "Shit, this hurts, she wants to come out!"

"Oh, a she is it? I hope you're wrong, I couldn't handle any more women in the house!" Patrick joked.

Dreanna was soon to be a mum. A very young, very youthful, very juvenile mother.

Callum and Dreanna were soon on their way to the hospital. The air outside the car was warm and still, the night sky was clear and full of stars, but the drive was uncomfortable and Dreanna could feel every bump in the road. "I don't mean to be funny Cal, but if you don't hurry I'm going to have this baby right here in the car!"

"Don't be stupid, Mum said first babies take ages."

"Yeah, your mum also said that I wasn't in labour as it was too soon, but I'm going to have to disagree with the both of you, so shut up and put your bloody foot down!"

The hospital was dark and eerie. 'The haunted hospital,' Dreanna said to herself. Then to Callum, "Ooh it's scary... I don't think I can go in there." She was holding her stomach with each new contraction. Dreanna had never attended any pre-natal care, much to the disgust of the midwife who checked her over every so often (or when she could be bothered to go). She had her sister to tell her what to expect and to answer any questions she may have and deep down she knew this baby was going to be fine.

"What? Well where else are you going to give birth? In the bloody car park?"

"People die in hospitals Callum; they are places of grief and fear and all sorts of emotions!"

"I really don't know what the hell you are on about, but you sound a bit cranky or is that just 'cos you're gonna give birth? Shall I get you a wheel-chair?"

With a deep breath Dreanna started walking forward. "I don't need a wheel-chair you prat; my legs aren't about to be amputated! It's just my lady bits that are going to be stretched and ripped and, oh my God, my vagina's just not gonna be the same again!"

"I hope it doesn't change too much, I quite like the way it looks at the mo-ment, and sssh, don't shout – you might wake the dead." Callum laughed as they entered the main corridor, then looked confused at the sight of the endless smaller corridors leading off in every direction. He headed towards one. "Do we go this way?"

Dreanna leaned up against the wall, her pelvis getting tighter and the pain in her back surging through her body like a wave hitting the shore. "How the fuck should I know? I've never been here before!" She tried to stay calm but she felt her cervix opening – there was now no break between contractions and fear was making its first appearance.

"Alright don't get stroppy, I only asked. In here – let's go in here."

"CALLUM!" Dreanna said sternly, "We're in the geriatric ward! What do you want me to do, jump in bed with some old geezer and ask if it's okay if I just give birth in his bed?"

They looked at each other, then suddenly burst into hysterics at just how ridiculous it all was.

"Shh!" A middle-aged woman appeared by their side "What are you two do-ing here?"

Callum was trying his hardest to stop sniggering. "We're looking for the labour ward, but think we may be a little lost."

"Down the corridor, turn left, first right. Now please be quiet and go." The nurse ushered the two teenagers out of her ward.

Dreanna slapped Callum hard on the shoulder, trying not to laugh. "You fucking rem!"

Dreanna was waiting in her cubicle to be examined. Ann, the midwife, knew Callum and his family well. She relaxed the worried 'father-to-be' quite easily. "Well Dreanna, I'm pleased to say you are 10 centimetres dilated, so push whenever you want. How long did you say it's been since your waters broke?"

"About forty minutes."

"Ooh I think we're in for a quickie then."

"That's what I said to Callum nine months ago!" Dreanna blushed.

The midwife grabbed Callum's arm and directed him to follow her to the kitchen area. His face was a picture. At eighteen he was still a 'Jack the lad'. Every Friday he was out on the town with his mates and his brother getting wasted on drink or stoned on a spliff. Tonight was a Friday night and you could see he was struggling with the after-effects of too much alcohol and wacky baccy. Ann wasn't stupid and could see she needed to sober him up a little before the arrival of the baby. They were lucky there had been no police on the road as he drove to the hospital. Things could have got a little awkward if there had.

"Come on honey," Ann said. "Come get a cup of tea before the drama starts."

Dreanna sat alone in her room, her heart pounding faster with every new contraction, her anticipation growing. Her eyes were fixed on the open door eagerly awaiting Callum's return.

A small woman in a dressing gown stood by the doorway. The light was dim and Dreanna was struggling to see her. "Good luck, hope you get what you want."

"Thanks," said Dreanna, curious as to why an old dear was allowed to walk freely in a labour ward. More and more people were sticking their heads around the door with good luck comments. "I hope it all goes well" was coming from the faces that peered into her room.

Callum and the midwife returned together, the midwife pinching the side of his cheeks as he sat down next to the bed.

"Can't believe you are actually gonna be a daddy. I remember when you was such a weenie little thing yourself. Still have such a cute little baby face don't ya?" she pinched his cheeks again. She turned to Dreanna. "How you doing anyway my darling, just going to have another little peek okay?" She lifted Dreanna's legs and inserted a finger inside.

"Ouch!" Dreanna winced.

"Sorry, gotta be done darling."

"I can't believe how busy this place is, all these people walking around out there." Dreanna was trying her hardest to take her mind off the examination.

"Sorry love, what did you say?"

"Busy. How busy it is here."

"I think you may have had a little too much gas and air. This is the quietest it's been in a while – we only have you and one other lady in tonight. That all looks fine, I'd say this is going to be all done in the next hour or so."

"I actually haven't had any drugs." Dreanna said quietly so no one could hear. The sound in the room had disappeared and all Dreanna could hear was her own breathing and the voice in her head.

"Dreanna, listen to my voice, concentrate on my voice. I am standing right by your side and we will do this together. Now breathe slowly my sweet and close your eyes. Can you see me?" The mystery lady was back again.

"Sort of, but I can't see your face." Dreanna answered.

"Don't worry about that, now push precious one, push and push hard."

Dreanna's eyes were still tightly closed as she bore down as hard as she could, the voice changed again, this time it was Callum's.

"Fuck Dreanna, you stink! You've just shit your pants!"

"Sorry I couldn't help it...do I smell that bad?"

"Er, yeah!"

The midwife could see Dreanna's embarrassment as she began clearing up the mess. "Don't worry darling it happens all the time, nothing to feel ashamed about... but now that's out of the way the next thing to come out will be your baby. You're doing amazing, you're a natural."

'Natural! It's really not natural to shit in front of your eighteen-year-old boyfriend. God this is going to be all over the rugby club before the week's out,' thought Dreanna. As another contraction pulsed its way through her body, she tucked her chin into her chest and pushed.

"Dreanna move onto your side...move onto your side sweet child."

She moved. Callum held Dreanna's leg tightly, high in the air. She pushed. "Oh my God you've done it! It's a girl! She's so beautiful!" Callum shouted.

This was the first time Dreanna had seen him cry. He'd never shed a tear at his father's funeral a few months back, but he was crying as he cradled his daughter in his arms.

"Good work Dreanna, and not a peep out of you either. One doesn't see that too often!" The midwife winked at Dreanna as she left the room, leaving the two new young parents alone, with Callum holding the brand new life in his arms.

August 1986

Rebecca's piercing screams shattered the silence in the house. It was three o'clock in the morning and daylight was just peeking through the curtains.

"Not again," mumbled Callum, trying to bury his head under the pillow.

"I'll take her downstairs, otherwise no one's gonna get any sleep," a tired

Dreanna replied. She was exhausted – it was the fifth time she had been up that night. Rebecca had been fed and changed but still she wouldn't settle down. As Dreanna sat nursing her daughter in her father's chair, the all too familiar voice of the lady with no name and no face came into her head.

"She is very pretty."

"Yes she is," Dreanna replied. *"But she just won't sleep, and I'm so tired."*

"She has spent nine months inside you, what do you expect? She needs to be close to you, you are her security."

Dreanna was tired but also curious and needed to know who this mystery lady was. *"Who are you? Do you have a name?"*

"My name is Jan."

"Will I ever get to see you? I have so many questions I don't know where to begin."

"We always knew you were too inquisitive. Your questions will be answered in time my sweet, in time... Close your eyes and search the darkness for me."

Dreanna closed her eyes tightly as Rebecca nestled into her breast, not really feeding but using her nipple as a comforter. Dreanna didn't mind because at least this way she wasn't crying. But her first-time-mother's nipples were quite sore.

"You're trying to concentrate. You don't need to concentrate, you just need to let it happen. Jan's voice was soft and calming."

Dreanna couldn't see her so she opened her eyes wide, blinked a few times, then shut them tightly again. She searched the darkness as ordered, starting with the place we all see when we first close our eyes. The backs of our eyelids.

"Over here, follow the sound of my voice."

Dreanna did as instructed and saw a glimmer of light and the outline of a woman's figure. Jan's voice got louder as Dreanna made her way closer to it. Within moments she was standing right next to the faceless woman.

"There, now you can see who you are talking to."

Jan had always been just a voice but now Dreanna could actually see her. Her body was encased in the same twinkling diamonds that she had seen in Susan as a child. Jan appeared to be old but with no lines or wrinkles, only smooth contours and a smile that melted Dreanna's heart.

"I have never left your side since you first heard me. I will be with you for some time yet, but I need you to know that you will be a mother again very soon."

Dreanna gazed at Jan, her eyebrows raised. She shook her head from left to right. *'No way, certainly not,'* she repeated to herself, *'No way, please not yet. I don't think I could handle another baby yet, there's no way I'm letting Callum anywhere near me, nope not a chance!'*

Jan stroked Dreanna's hair. Her touch was calming and it sent shivers down Dreanna's back, gently releasing all her anxiety. *"There is so much you need to learn. You cannot stand in the way of fate my darling child, and there is so much we need to teach you, but for now you have to look after her and nurture her well as soon there will be another baby to care for. I will leave you now, but will always be by your side."*

And then she was gone and Dreanna and her daughter sat motionless in her father's chair. They were sleeping… finally.

June 1998

Twenty three months later Dreanna's waters broke soaking the bed – and Callum.

"Shit! Callum, wake up, wake up!" Dreanna poked Callum in the ribs.

"What? God's sake is the bloody house on fire or summing! Why's the bloody bed wet?" He stared at Dreanna, "Oh fuck. Right, okay, erm I'll go and ring the midwife."

Dreanna felt the force of yet another contraction burn its way through her body. She breathed, she panted, she gasped, she pushed. Then Rebecca woke up and rubbed her eyes as she lay next to her mother in the amniotic-fluid-soaked bed.

"CALLUM!" screamed Dreanna.

Rebecca cried.

Callum returned to the bedroom after spending the last ten minutes on the phone to the midwife. Working shifts were changing and there was confusion over who was coming out to deliver the new baby. There were to be no hospitals this time – Dreanna had decided on a home delivery. She couldn't put herself through the mental torture she suffered last time. Giving birth was fine, it was the three days she had to spend in the ward that almost sent her into a mental breakdown. Mothers were supposed to stay in for at least a week but three days was all she could handle and she discharged herself at the first opportunity. Apart from a tiny graze which hurt like a bitch there were no other issues or concerns. At the end of the day Iris was on hand at home, and what better teacher could Dreanna have? Iris was a natural and Dreanna was learning fast.

Another quick phone call was made to Dawn to come and collect Rebecca. Giving birth and looking after a twenty-three-month old at the same time would have been impossible, and Dawn, who only lived down the road from Callum and Dreanna's new council house, was the obvious choice. Callum hoisted Rebecca into his arms, still in her nightie, and handed her over to Dawn.

"Good luck," Dawn shouted up the stairs as she headed out of the front door.

Dreanna screamed for Callum again. "This baby's coming right now!" She moved her hand away from her groin to reveal a head full of hair.

"Oh shit! What the fuck do I do? Erm… okay I can do this, I can." Callum placed his hands on top of his new baby's head. "Okay, so push, I think," his face was frowning with concentration.

As Dreanna turned to look in the mirrors of the wardrobe doors, Jan was there.

"You know how to do this – remember – turn onto your side, it will be less painful, trust me."

Dreanna turned onto her left side, grabbed hold of her leg at the knee and with the next contraction pushed, staring straight into Jan's eyes.

"Oh fuck, we've done it, we've done it!" Callum squealed. Cradling his second daughter in his arms, he reached for a pillow case and tucked her safely inside.

"Callum you've just put our daughter into a pillow case," said an exhausted Dreanna.

"Well what else am I suppose to use? I didn't exactly have time to get blankets or hot water... Why do you need hot water anyway?" he shrugged and continued to snuggle the pillow case around his child.

There was a loud rat-a-tat-tat on the front door.

"Can someone let me in please?" a muffled voice shouted through the letterbox.

"The midwife's here," mumbled Dreanna.

Callum was just about to hand the baby, pillowcase and all to her when Dreanna felt her stomach tighten again."Callum put her on the bed, I'm having another contraction."

"Eh, what? You're not having another one are you?"

Dreanna shock her head and breathed out through her mouth "No! The placenta's coming." She stared down at this new life as she pushed out the placenta Her daughter's face was bloody, but she was perfect. The look of the umbilical cord hanging over the top of the pillow case made Dreanna heave but her dry retching was soon dissolved by Callum as he kissed her and said thank you.

"Déja vu" laughed Jan.

The midwife entered the bedroom as Jan leaned over Dreanna.

"Well done!" the women's voices spoke in harmony. Then Jan was gone.

Be Mine Forever

"D'you fancy getting married Dree?"

"Why?"

"Well – we have two kids, we're living together and we're happy aren't we?"

"Yeah but… why do you wanna get married? It's a bit of paper and a piss up. Why can't we just continue the way we are?"

"Because I want a piss up," he sniggered. "Seriously though," he stared thoughtfully at her, "I love you, always have, and would like you to be mine forever."

Unsure of the seriousness in his voice Dreanna looked up. "Mmm… I don't know, I love you so much… but marriage, really? I just don't see the reason behind it… but… okay then, in for a penny in for a pound." She smiled and reached for her husband-to-be. "But… if I'm gonna get married, I'm wearing white. Let's pretend I'm a virgin shall we? Ha ha ha."

August 1989

For a long time now Dreanna hadn't left the boundaries of her home during her nocturnal wanderings; she usually spent the nights watching her growing daughters sleep. Occasionally she would take herself off to the field and her oak tree, to gather her thoughts and give herself some much needed time to recharge her batteries. It was her favourite place, a place that held no malice. It was her home.

The wedding nerves were beginning to build and she felt sick just think-ing about all the people who would be watching her. She knew she would be criticised for getting married in white, and she hated churches. Cold, dark, dingy places that would be filled with hypocrisy and bullshit. Her field was her church and her heaven, and she went there every night as the big day drew closer; before the big day came when she would say 'I do' and become Callum's wife.

Dreanna was sitting in her field, her knees bent, her chin resting on top of them. All around her was silence and peace. She stared across the mass of open space and saw a figure walking towards her. A man she knew. "Oh my God!"

"Hello Dreanna, long time no see." The figure grabbed hold of her tightly, his strong arms unwilling to let her go. "I'm so glad you're going to make an honest man of my son."

"Oh my God," Dreanna said again, tears forming in her eyes. "I never thought you would ever come and say hello."

"I'm sorry I, er, wasn't allowed, but I'm here now." He smiled the smile that Dreanna so loved to see when he was alive.

She pulled away, "What d'you mean you weren't allowed? Why wouldn't you be allowed?"

"There is so much you need to learn, but you know that anyway, don't you?" Callum's dad let go his firm grasp of his soon-to-be daughter-in-law and let his arms dangle by his side.

"Yep I know, or so I keep being told. It really does my head in, 'Dreanna not yet'... 'Dreanna in time'... 'Dreanna be patient'... on and on and on they go, but never telling me jack shit!" She hesitated and shrugged her shoulders, "What if I don't want to know? What if I don't actually care? What if I just want a life that's free of seeing and knowing and feeling? What if with all honesty and without a shadow of a doubt I don't actually give a fuck?"

"Oh honey, you are funny. You haven't changed have ya?" He laughed. "No wonder Callum loves you so much. Anyway look, the reason I'm here is the wedding, I'll be there I promise, look for me in the space between worlds, the same space Jan is... I have to go." He looked over his shoulder, then his energy faltered and he was gone.

Dreanna was alone again in the vast expanse of her field, her oak tree firmly and proudly towering high above her head.

The hired car pulled up outside the church, the white ribbons attached to the bonnet gently blowing in the summer breeze.

"Dad," Dreanna looked into her father's eyes, "I don't want to go in there; churches are such depressing miserable cold places and full of fucking hypocrites." She shivered. All she wanted was for her Dad to say "Let's go home then," like he always did when she was a kid. She wanted to go home and get out of that poxy dress and high heeled shoes, put the kettle on and watch shitty old snooker. Even in her adult years she had still never had the heart to tell Patrick she couldn't stand that sport. But she would have sat and watched paint dry with him. With the only man who made her world totally complete.

"Sorry kid, this time you've just gotta grin and bear it. It'll be over in next to no time; you never know, you might find God!"

Dreanna screwed up her face, looked at Patrick, and the pair of them squealed with endless laughter.

The organ began to play; Dreanna tentatively put one foot in front of another. Their arms were linked; she looked up at him, he winked.

"It's going to be okay. Eyes front and smile, for God's sake, smile!"

"Who gives this woman to this man?" the vicar asked.

"Give her?" Patrick said, "He can bloody have her."

Dreanna bowed her head trying to suppress her giggles. Only Patrick could turn a serious moment into a joking one.

"*Compose yourself Dreanna.*" Matilda was in her head.

Dreanna smiled, "Sorry Nana."

As Patrick let go of Dreanna's hand and gave it to the vicar, William broke the silence and shouted, "GET IN!... Fuck, sorry, Arsenal's just scored." His face went a slight crimson as he realised the whole congregation heard his every word.

Auntie Beatrice gave William a defiant stare. "Turn that bloody radio off, by God boy, or I'll slap your legs. Don't you know you're in the house of God!"

Dreanna peeked over her shoulder at her brother and giggled.

"Sorry" he said.

The vicar closed his book. "I now pronounce you man and wife."

The congregation clapped. Dreanna closed her eyes, searching for her husband's father, and there he was as promised, but not alone – rows and rows of faces smiled back at her. She gazed at each one in turn, every head lowering as she went from end to end.

Callum and his new wife walked arm in arm down the aisle of the church.

"What a hypocrite, dressed in white. A virgin, that's a joke."

She knew someone would say it and they didn't let her down. Dreanna just grinned up at her new husband.

Callum looked back at her. "Trust you to cause controversy."

"Yeah, but off-white just isn't my colour, I think some would have preferred me in black... can we hurry up and get out of this bloody church please?" Dreanna increased her pace and the brilliant summer sun beat down on them as they made their exit.

Jan was standing on the steps. "*Time to turn the page and begin a new chapter.*"

Then she was gone.

Three is the Magic Number

Dreanna was standing at the kitchen sink, staring out into the darkness. The shadowy outline of the trees in her garden were lit by the first full moon of summer. A warm breeze blew across her ankles from the open door and she gently squeezed out the dish cloth, folded it and placed it over the tap. Callum was standing right behind her and Dreanna smiled. "Callum… Callum I need another baby."

"Why?" He paused, frowning slightly. "We've already got two kids, you're back working and things are good. Why do you need another baby?"

"I don't know, I just don't feel complete."

"You're one crazy bitch, but if you really want one, I suppose there's no harm in trying; practice makes perfect." He reached out and took her by the waist, nuzzling her neck with his lips. Each kiss was tender and welcoming. Dreanna, eyes half open, turned her head to the clock on the wall. 'Fuck! It's nearly midnight and I really don't know if I can be bothered to do this now,' she thought. She was exhausted and had to be up at the crack of dawn. But each kiss made her sigh, each kiss made her yearn, each kiss made her body fill with a longing, a desire, a lust, a need.

She grabbed Callum's head and pulled it closer to her face. "I love you." Her lips were now on her husband's, their tongues gently dancing together. Her hands moved down, cupping his buttocks as she pulled him towards her, their groins touching, Callum sighed. He kissed her neck and moved his fingers through her hair. He took his hands away, lifted his arms and removed his top, and Dreanna became his mirror image and removed hers. He stared at her, his finger tips tracing her breasts down towards her navel. Dreanna shuddered. He undid the button of her jeans, his hands moving either side as he tugged them downward. Dreanna could not stop herself laughing inwardly at the sight of her husband trying to get the jeans over her thighs.

"How can anyone remove skin-tight jeans in a provocative manner?" she asked, knowing full well her jibes were not going to be welcomed. She couldn't contain her laughter as Callum fought the demon denim.

He looked up at her from the floor and tutted as he yanked them off her feet. "Don't ruin the moment, love." The look of 'shut up' was all too clear on his face.

Dreanna, still smiling, bent to her knees and kissed his neck. Their bodies slid down onto the laminate floor, the coldness taking her breath away. Callum kissed her breasts, his tongue like a snake, slithering with ease and precision as it moved down to her crotch. Her desire built stronger as he reached the moist opening between her legs and he paused to look up at her with eyes full of lust and desire. She grabbed his hair tightly in her hands and pushed his head back down to her warm, wet Garden of Eden. His tongue gently brushed against her swollen clitoris. He lifted his head, positioned his body above hers, and their mouths met again as both shared the sweet taste on his lips. The yearning in his groin pulsated onto her and with one tender movement their bodies became one.

Jan was back in her head. "*Dreanna, not yet! You can't have another baby yet, it's not the right time!*"

Dreanna ignored her; the passion was too deep inside her. Callum's body heaved against hers, droplets of sweat appeared on his face, and her skin was flushed and glowing.

"*Dreanna please, no!*" Jan pleaded.

'Too late,' Dreanna thought, as they reached their climax. She lifted her head in the direction of the open door, gasping for the breeze to cool her ardour. They lay there in each other's arms, and as Callum kissed his wife once more, she stared at him. "Well...'spose that saves us arguing over who's sleeping on the wet patch then."

"Dreanna, you're so romantic."

February 1990

Dreanna was once again waiting to see if the thin blue line would appear. Callum also eagerly awaited the result.

"We're pregnant."

"Let me see." He grabbed the test from his wife's hands. "Yep, I'd say we are definitely pregnant... Woo hoo! If possible can you make a boy this time? I'm getting a little bit pissed off with dolls and girly stuff."

"You decide the sex hun, not me...but we're having another baby! God, I'm sooo excited. Eek!" Dreanna wrapped the test in its packaging and threw it into the bin; she glared at herself in the bathroom mirror, "Warning, smorning".

Callum's head turned in her direction, "What d'you say?"

"Nothing, just talking to myself". Dreanna knew what she desired and what she needed, and now her dream of baby number three was on its way. She was happy, so very happy.

April 1990

Rebecca rushed to the phone, pushing her younger sister Leticia out of the way.

"Hello?"

"Hi Rebecca, it's Grandad, can you get your mum for me?"

Rebecca passed the phone to her mother.

"Hi Pops, what's up?"

"Dree – your Mum has had a bit of a fall at work, can you meet us at Casualty?"

"Erm... yep, sure, but is she okay?"

"Just get here as soon as you can, sorry pips about to go, b..."

By the time she arrived at the hospital with the girls, Dawn and Patrice were already there.

"Where's Mum? Is she okay?"

"She's inside the cubicle. Yeah, she seems to be, just got a nasty gash down the side of her head," Patrice explained.

Dreanna leaned over her mother's body and kissed her on the cheek. Iris, who had dried blood down her cheeks, pouted her mouth and kissed the air. Dreanna shook her head from side to side. "Why have you been bloody arguing with a concrete floor?"

"Just a little dizzy spell that's all. I'm okay now, promise." Iris forced a smile.

"You sure? You still look a bit shitty Mum."

"Dreanna, mind your language! I could do with a f..." Iris's sentence was interrupted by her retching.

"Bowl!" shouted Dreanna. She held her mother's hair back and watched her fill the cardboard bowl with the contents of her stomach. Dreanna turned her head away, the smell was too much for a pregnant woman to bear. She retched herself and tried to inhale the air behind her. Her mother's heaving ended; Dreanna picked up a tissue and wiped the vomit off her chin, and handed the bowl to Patrick, "Take it Dad, or I'm gonna puke too. Now Mum, what was it you wanted?" Dreanna pretended to scold her mother, "It began with 'f' as I recall, but please refrain from saying the 'fuck' word as we are in a hospital remember, and I will just have to wash your mouth out with carbolic if you insist on saying such a disgusting word."

"Dree," her mother paused, "What are we going to do with you?"

Dreanna smiled and a woozy sensation came over her. Her stomach began to cramp. "Sorry Mum, I've got to go outside. I think your dizziness is catching."

She stood out in the fresh air, taking in extra large gulps, hoping each one would make her a little steadier.

Patrice joined her and leaned against a 'No Parking' sign. She reached inside her jacket pocket and started toying with her fags. Are you alright Dree?"

"No not really. Feeling a bit light-headed and nauseous, not sure if it's Mum's puking or being pregnant, but I really don't feel good." A tightening soured its way through Dreanna's pelvis. "Fuck." She bent over, pushing her hands into her groin. "Pat, I've got to go home, something's not right, tell Mum I'll come back later."

Dreanna turned the key in the lock, leaning on the wall as she got inside her home. Her voice was low. "Girls take your shoes off, Mummy just needs to go to the loo."

"Mummy, what's the matter?" Rebecca asked, her words slightly jumbled with her thumb in her mouth.

"Nothing, my darling, Mummy just has a little pain in her tummy. Keep an eye on your sister for me for a minute, okay?"

Rebecca took hold of her sister's hand and both girls sat on the bottom stair as Dreanna slowly climbed the endless steps to the bathroom.

Callum came in the front door a while later to find his daughters sitting quietly on the stair waiting for their mother to come down.

"Hi squids, where's your Mum?"

"She's in the toilet, her tummy is sore."

Callum rubbed each of his daughter's heads and stepped over them to make his way to his wife, leaping up the stairs two at a time. When he pushed open the bathroom door, Dreanna was lying on the floor, her jeans stained with blood.

"Callum, please call the doctor." Her cheeks were soaked with tears.

One phone call later and they were on their way to the doctor's surgery.

"Up here, Dreanna." The doctor patted the couch, as she helped her patient lay down. "I know you don't want me to, but I really need to examine you. I'll be as gentle as I can."

Dreanna wept in pain as the doctor carefully explored her cervix. And then came the words she couldn't bear to hear. "I'm so sorry Dreanna, you're losing the baby. Go home and rest, then come see me in a couple of days. The chances are your body will disperse the fetus naturally but if the bleeding or pain doesn't ease in the next few hours, please give me a call." The doctor removed her gloves and threw them into a large bin lined with a yellow 'hazardous' plastic bag.

"Fetus?! It's a baby!" Dreanna sobbed.

Back home her crying eased but she was frozen, anesthetised with no emotion. She felt empty, alone and incomplete. She could hear Callum trying to cook dinner for their young children downstairs, the smell of burnt fish fingers circulating around the house. Suddenly a gripping contraction filled her pelvis and she rushed to the toilet, her head bent on her knees, her stomach absorbing the waves of convulsions pulsing through her body. She could feel her cervix open as it released its contents in the snow-coloured basin. "Callum!" she screamed in pain. "CALLUM!!!"

Callum rushed to her side and stroked her back. His eyes looked over her at the thick mucus glob that sat in the bottom of the toilet. Blood was running down the sides of the bowl as Dreanna's head leaned on his chest for support.

"It's gone isn't it?" She stared straight into her husband's eyes.

"I think so, I'm sorry love... It wasn't really a baby yet though was it?"

"What? It's a baby as soon as its heart's beating Callum, and my child had a heart and a soul... Please don't, don't talk about it like it wasn't real, it was growing inside me. It was part of me... it was my baby."

Dreanna lay on her bed, her eyes tightly closed, and memories of the day's events blended into one. As she drifted into an unconscious sleep, Jan met her.

"I'm sorry precious one, but I did try and warn you, it just isn't the right time for another life to grow inside you."

"What the fuck are you talking about?" Dreanna's voice was abrupt and cold.

Jan tried to reach out to comfort her, but she pulled away. "Dreanna, you will know in time the answers that you seek, but for now know that everything is written. Everything has a pattern, everything follows a path that leads to an end. We will look after him, and one day many years from now you will see him again, I promise you my sweet, I promise you."

"Why don't you just fuck off! You give me all this bullshit over and over again, 'Dreanna you will know in time, be patient, we love you!' You've told me what to do, you've told me what to think, you've controlled my life always, but for what? So I can feel pain, so I can lose something I want? TELL ME WHY! FOR FUCK'S SAKE, TELL ME WHY!"

"I cannot tell you yet, I'm sorry. I'm so sorry."

Jan faded and was gone and Dreanna was left alone again with her distressing thoughts, her confusion, and her secret.

With her mother resting at home and Dreanna on bed-rest for a couple of days, she knew that the warning she had been given was to protect her, but it felt like it was punishing her. All she wanted was another baby but instead of a baby all she had was pain and heartache.

May 1990

Dreanna was sitting at the dining room table in her parents' house. Iris sat next to her holding tightly onto her cup of tea. Dreanna was confused and looked at her mother. "Mum, you alright?"

"Yes, I'm fine, thank you my dear"

"Er... what? Thank you my dear'? Something's not right, is it? What is it? You seem different, a little strange."

Patrick looked over his shoulder; he had been busy scrubbing the oven, something Dreanna only ever saw him do when his thoughts were somewhere else.

"Dad, what's up with Mum? What are you hiding?"

"Nothing," he answered. "She's just tired."

"No she's not. Look at her! She's not even …"

"Dreanna enough! Your mother is fine, stop bloody nagging, child."

Dreanna angrily shoved her chair back under the table. "Fucking hell! I'm getting a little bit pissed off with people hiding stuff from me… Whatever, Dad, you know where I am if you need me."

She stopped in the hallway and glanced back at her mother, still holding her cup in the same position, her eyes still looking at its contents. She hadn't moved or flinched, she hadn't even told her to mind her language. Something was wrong, something was seriously wrong.

February 1992

"You know the procedure by now, when you're ready to push, go for it and push deep into your bottom. That's it, push, push, push! Well done, now pant for me sweetie. Well done, I think one final push will do it."

Dreanna looked around for Jan, but she wasn't there, in fact she hadn't been there since Dreanna had in no uncertain terms told her to fuck off. Had they really abandoned her? Had they really let her go? Was she now being left alone? She let her mind wander between the contractions; she hadn't even had any bad dreams in so many months. Did they listen to her? Did they really listen and take her seriously?

"Would you look at that? It's another beautiful daughter," cried the midwife delivering the baby straight onto Dreanna's chest.

Dreanna, still breathing rapidly, looked down at her new daughter. With joy in her heart, and a smile on her face, she sighed a simple sigh of satisfaction. "Three is a magic number. Now my family is complete."

She's Mine, Not Yours!

March 1992

Callum pulled up on the drive and gestured her to come outside and look at the new car he had just bought. He beckoned again and waved the keys in the air but Dreanna shook her head in disgust.

"It's so cool!" Callum said with a huge cheeky grin.

"It's a Capri!" Dreanna replied, sounding appalled and revolted. "How the hell am I going to get three kids in the back of a bloody Capri! You are a real numpty sometimes Callum, a real bloody numpty!"

Callum was walking up and down the length of his new prized possession, gently rubbing the body work as if it was a new baby. "All it needs is a bit of a wash, and it'll be fine. It goes like a bitch."

Dreanna threw her hands in the air and shook her head. "I give up."

Callum stayed outside washing his new toy and Dreanna looked at her watch. 3.45pm. She cupped her breasts which were getting extremely uncomfortable and full. She walked to Fawn's crib and stroked her back, "C'mon sweetness, wake up, you're an hour late for your feed." Fawn just lay there, her breathing shallow, her eyes closed. Dreanna lifted her into her arms, hoping that the manhandling would wake her. Fawn didn't wake, her eyes were still closed and her body limp in her mother's arms.

"Callum! Something's wrong with Fawn, she's not waking up!" Dreanna gently shook her baby. Her chest was still moving and she was alive, but her body was listless. Tiny bubbles of spit formed at the creases of her mouth, then she let out a whimper like a seagull being strangled. Then silence. Fawn hung in Dreanna's arm's breathing … just. But her body was lifeless. Dreanna looked up to the heavens and shouted from the bottom of her heart, "I WON'T LOSE HER!"

The Capri may have been an old rust-bucket, ugly and uncomfortable, but Callum drove it like a Formula One car, weaving in and out of the country lanes, ignoring the stop signs and not once stopping at the red traffic lights.

Dreanna held her daughter close. The whiteness around her lips was a sure sign the baby was dehydrating. Dreanna pressed lightly the soft spot on her baby's head; it was indented.

Callum looked in the mirror at his cargo on the back seat. "How's she doing?"

"Not good. She is so dehydrated. I'm so scared Callum, I'm so fucking scared!"

"Try and feed her again."

"What do you think I've been trying to do for the last hour! She won't open her mouth. She isn't even crying, she's just making a noise like an injured seagull. Please, hurry up!" Dreanna closed her eyes. 'Nanny please help her, please!' Her words echoed around inside her head, searching for someone to take hold of them, but they were alone, floating in the darkness of her mind until they disintegrated into nothingness.

Drips were inserted into Fawn's tiny body, each tube helping her fight for her life. One contained antibiotics, the other the fluid her body was craving. Fawn's hands looked so small, so delicate; each needle that penetrated her fragile skin looked like a spear piercing into her.

Two doctors stood over her, prodding and poking the weak little body. Dreanna, unable to do anything to help her child, sat still on the chair next to her cot. Callum stood beside his wife, his hand on her shoulder.

"We're going to give her a lumbar puncture; we think she may have meningitis, and to be honest with you, the way things are at the moment we can only give her around a 30 per cent chance of survival."

Dreanna just looked down at her feet. She was motionless and numb; she felt like she was the one that was going to die, not her baby.

Ten agonising days passed in the isolation room at the hospital, during which the young parents didn't even speak. They had eyes only for their tiny daughter as she fought for her life.

The room had no windows, just four blank walls all painted the same washed-out green colour, and the painted ceiling was blistering and peeling. A sink in the corner that should have been white was now off-grey, with limescale caked around the bottom of a tap that would cough and splutter when you turned it on. One solitary deep yellow chair sat in the corner, the fabric threadbare from many arms resting on it in the past.

Dreanna reached for the breast pump, positioned it over her nipple and squeezed. As she watched each droplet of milk filter into the plastic bottle her thoughts wandered. She desperately wanted to be in her field with both her nans by her side. She wanted to see the twinkling diamonds and for Jan and Susan to step out from them, but she couldn't concentrate – her mind was a disorganised mess of thoughts filled with nothing but the here and now.

A young doctor interrupted her with a cough. "She's going to be okay."

Callum, not paying any attention to his wife, jumped from his chair, his imprint still left behind, each spring only slowly returning to its original form. His arm was extended and his hand held taut. "I don't know what to say, but thank you. Thank you for all you have done, oh my God, thank you." Tears formed in his eyes and his hand tightly gripped that of this young doctor. "Can we go home now?"

"Tomorrow. You can go tomorrow." The doctor bowed his head and smiled at the disheveled Dreanna, who hadn't moved from her bed right next to her daughter's cot in over 240 hours. She couldn't even lift herself from it to shake this young man's hand, but mouthed 'thank you' and he nodded back at her.

Dreanna's bed was firm to the touch, covered by crisp white sheets and a blue blanket that she would wrap around herself as if for protection from the nightmare she had been living through. The stagnant air full of cleaning products hit the back of her throat. The dry heat in the room made it nearly impossible to swallow.

Jan entered her head. "Go to sleep, Dreanna. Go to sleep."

Dreanna was standing at the end of a long corridor, the walls as white as snow. Her body was being pulled forward, she couldn't fight it, she had no willpower, and she had no energy to resist where it was taking her. Jan stood engulfed in sparkling diamonds that seemed to shine brighter than ever, a light so dazzling appeared to be circling her.

"Why did you leave me so alone? I was so scared. Is it because I told you to fuck off? Is that why you left me?"

"No Dreanna, why would we leave you? We know you, we know your words are a little colourful at times, but these are just words. Think Dreanna, think, why would we leave you?"

"I don't know!" Dreanna fell on bended knees, a mist now surrounding her. "I'm tired, I can't think straight. Please just tell me, make me understand. Why did I lose my baby? Why did Fawn nearly die? Why did you want to take her from me? What have I done so wrong!"

"Some of what you need to know I just can't tell you, not yet, it's not the right time. Some things in nature we cannot control; we cannot control if a child is born with a disability or even if the child is born at all, but sometimes we can control if a new life is able to live. Let me explain."

Jan sat down and pulled Dreanna's head onto her shoulder, the mist slowly disappearing to reveal the softest of floors. Dreanna was unable to make out what she was sitting on. It wasn't grass or carpet or snow, it resembled cotton wool, but each time she ran her fingers through it, it glistened and then vanished. Confused by her surroundings she nestled into Jan, ready to listen. Jan held her tight and began to explain.

"Life is such a precious possession but it's Earthly time that is the most important here. The date of everyone's birth and their death is decided on many moons before it actually happens. We try, as the Keepers of Life, not to change these rules. The loss of a child in the womb will happen if the time is not right. A child whose life has been taken against the parents' wishes is not the way it should be and we have to re-write their day of birth, but their date of death remains the same. A life will also cease because of what

you know as nature. We cannot control the transit of nature or evolution, these things advance of their own accord. If a child is lost but it is their time to be born, another will be conceived as quickly as possible, and will be born on its intended date, even if this is weeks or months before the end of pregnancy.

The child you lost was a new soul, one that was formed of his own being. At the time of the first beating of the heart is when a kinetic appointment takes place, this is when life becomes a race against time. The beating of the heart is like the beating of a drum. It tells us that we have little time for an old soul to make its way down and seal itself into the new life. If we cannot get there in time then through the natural evolutionary process a new soul is made, this then blocks any other soul from entering the growing fetus. Every life has a purpose; every purpose will show itself in time.

Many times we do not try to reincarnate ourselves as it has already been decided to let a new soul be created. We cannot reproduce on our own, we are just energies, we have no sexual organs, and neither do we have the feelings of desire, and this is why so many of us choose to have a physical existence. We cannot feel like you do; we cannot experience life in its physical form with all the good and the bad that may come with it, because where we are is like no other place you will ever know. The only emotion we feel is love; we cannot feel anything else, and we have no need for anything else. This place, the place you have been visiting since you were a young child is what you call Heaven but what we call Home. It is the place where all living creations will eventually come. No matter what they have done in life, someday they will all come home.

Fawn got ill for a reason, but right now you do not need to know why, just know that someday in your future you will understand why it seems all these negative experiences have been felt by you. Very soon you will be left alone by us. Right now your purpose is to raise your children, nurture them, teach them well but more importantly, love them. Love them like you have never loved before.

You must return now. Your family – all your family – need you. Stay strong. You may not see us, but we will always be by your side. Awake my precious one."

Dreanna was awake, her head pounding, but this time she enjoyed its discomfort. She felt relieved that nobody had actually left her, and she was beginning to understand the 'whys'. She had had her first lesson in the truth behind life and felt honoured to have been given it.

Your Job is your Family

November 1992

The hot radiator burned into Dreanna's stomach as she held Fawn at the window-sill; they were looking out at the fireworks Callum was trying so hard to light. Dreanna, still holding Fawn, reached up and opened the metal catch of the window. The coldness of it made her shiver as Dreanna leaned out. "C'mon, what ya doing? You're taking ages!"

Callum's face was pink where he had been standing too close to the bonfire. "I can't get the bloody things to light, chuck us the matches."

"Well you did fire blanks for a few years so it's not surprising you can't ignite a few fireworks!"

Callum stuck his middle finger up in the direction of his wife.

It wasn't long before the sky was full of dazzling multi-coloured lights, each one making the children shriek with delight. Rebecca held her ears tightly, her eyes transfixed by the rockets that exploded over her head, Leticia screamed at Callum wanting more, and Fawn had her head pressed on the window from inside their home, not knowing whether to laugh or cry at the noise and merriment that was happening in the garden. Normality finally returned to her face when Dreanna lifted her into her arms to answer the phone.

"Dree, it's Dad." Her father's voice was dull. "Mum's fallen down the stairs, the ambulance has already been and she's on her way to the hospital. I've rung your sisters, can you meet them there?"

"What? How? It doesn't matter... I'll drop the girls off at Callum's Mum's and go straight there." Dreanna slammed the phone down so hard it missed its place on the receiver; the mist of tears hindered her vision. 'Be strong,' she told herself. 'Be strong.'

Dreanna was ushered by her sisters to talk to the rather large receptionist at the desk of the Accident and Emergency unit. The desk stood at the same level as Dreanna's waist, its edge covered in dust, with that god-awful smell of disinfectant that she remembered so well. A stained coffee cup that looked like it had never been washed was in the receptionist's hands.

Dreanna gulped. "My mother was bought in here a few minutes ago."

"Name?" The receptionist barked out the question as she put down her cup and shuffled a wad of paper.

"Iris D..."

The large woman interrupted her. "Cubicle 3."

Dreanna stood there staring at her.

"Anything else?"

"A smile maybe?" She turned and walked away murmering "Stupid bitch!" then beckoned her sisters to follow. The clip-clopping sound of Dawn's boots echoed through the corridor. Cockroach boxes were on the floor in every corner, and yellow bags full of soiled bandages and other hospital waste lay against the walls. Dawn gripped hold of the orange curtain that hung on metal railings around their mother's bed, her knuckles turning a pale white with the pressure. The sisters stared at each other longing for mutual support, their hearts pounding through their chests.

Dawn dragged back the material doorway. Their mother lay motionless, eyes closed, her arm in a sling and a blanket only just covering her dignity. Patrice pulled the blanket upwards making sure not to disturb the white cloth that held her arm in place. Iris opened her eyes, but they were rolling around inside their sockets unable to keep still.

"B... bbbb...." Iris's words didn't make sense, her head wobbled from side to side, and dribble appeared in the corner of her mouth. The stench of excrement enveloped them.

"What the fuck?" Patrice's hands shook. "I think Mum's shit herself, what the fucking hell is she doing? Is she fitting?"

Dawn gagged, "I'm sorry I've gotta get outta here, I think I'm gonna throw up." She hastily moved away from the cubicle.

"I'm sorry Dree, I can't do this either." Sheer panic spread across Patrice's face.

"Oh fucking bollocks!" Dreanna stepped closer to the bed. "Go then, but get a fucking nurse. I don't know what to do!"

Iris's head stopped shaking and she became strangely calm, seeming not to know or care that she had messed the bed. Dreanna tried to breathe deeply to settle herself down and stop the panic growing inside her, but she started to taste the air as the smell of the faeces entered her stomach. 'After all these years I finally know what "I can taste the air" means,' she thought, but forced her attention back to her mother and the nurse that had just arrived.

"I need to ask, how long has your mother been so vacant? We need to know if this was the fall or it's been going on a lot longer?"

"Vacant? I'm not sure what you mean. She's been a little out of sorts over the last few months, after a fall at work where she cut her head open, but she seemed ... well she wasn't herself, but seemed okay."

"So she's blacked out before then?"

"Erm yes," Dreanna replied, "But the doctors said it was just low blood pressure and she was going to be fine."

The nurse seemed bewildered by Dreanna's reply and began leafing through the notes in her hand. The pages were thumbed at the edges proving that many others had read them before her.

"Right. You were told this? Only her notes say she had a minor stroke, a few months ago." Curiosity halted her sentence.

"What!?" The words left Dreanna's mouth harshly and quickly. "No it wasn't the Doctor, it was my dad that said this. I had to leave the hospital quickly last time, I... erm, I was having a miscarriage... Sorry I don't know what to say, I'm confused, I... I... I...." She exited the cubicle in a rush. She glanced but did not speak to her sisters sitting in the waiting room, and sped outside to the fresh air and freedom from the lie Patrick had given her.

Dreanna searched her pockets looking for her cigarettes and lighter, her irritation growing. The November chill made her tremble and shudder as the wind ate its way through her clothes. She inhaled deeply, absorbed in her thoughts and paying no attention to her surroundings or the blue lights of the fast-approaching ambulance. As she began questioning her father's lies a man's voice interrupted her thinking.

"Sorry love, you can't smoke there!"

Dreanna lifted her head and carried on inhaling. "What?"

The porter pointed to her cigarette, "Can you not read? Look, 'No Smoking'"

"Oh whatever! I'd finished anyway." She threw her butt to the ground and stamped on it, waiting, hoping that the stumpy unshaven porter would again discipline her for leaving the dead fag in his vision. She was angry and ready for a confrontation and she didn't care with whom. But he just turned and walked away.

Dawn appeared behind her, wrapping her cardigan round her body as the chill filtered its way into her flesh. "What's up? Did it get too much for you too?"

"Actually no, but Dad lied to us. Did you know? Did you know Mum had a stroke all those months ago?"

Dawn leaned against the 'No Smoking' sign. "What you talking about? Of course I didn't know!"

Dreanna shook her cigarettes in her sister's direction and Dawn took one, both women cupping their hands so the flame didn't go out in the wind. Dreanna still hoped that someone, anyone, would return and tell her she couldn't smoke in this place again. She so needed to explode with the rage that was coursing through her body. Her stomach ached with anger and rage; her heart jerked with the deceit of the lie.

"But," Dawn said, her voice quiet as if hoping Dreanna couldn't hear her over the commotion of yet another ambulance.

"But what?"

Dawn sucked hard and heaved in as much nicotine as her cigarette could give her. "When you were in hospital with Fawn, Mum had a bit of an episode... We didn't want to tell you because of what you were going through. To say it was strange was really an understatement as it couldn't be explained by the doctors."

Dawn stopped and flicked her fag into the road right in the path of two burly ambulance drivers returning to their vehicle, laughing with each other about the size of the patient they had just taken inside.

"For God's sake Dawn, please just tell me – what did Mum do?" Dreanna's face was pleading with her sibling to at least tell her something that could explain why the lie.

Dawn sighed. "Dad phoned me two days after Fawn was admitted; he asked if I could come round. When I got there Mum was sitting in her chair and basically talking a load of old crap and laughing to herself. It was like she was there but it wasn't her." Dawn shifted her feet and rubbed her hands down her arms to try and warm her body. "Anyway we took her round to minor injuries and she was examined by the doctor, but like I said, he couldn't find anything wrong with her."

This still didn't answer Dreanna's original question and frustration was building in her gut. "What was Mum saying?"

"She kept saying it was her time to die and both her and Dad were going to die together. She was patting the bed and telling Dad to come and lay by her side so they could go... That's it really, but she was repeating it over and over again."

"But that doesn't explain about the stroke and why Dad didn't tell us?"

"I'm sorry Dree, I just don't know what else to say, but knowing Dad he had his reasons."

Dreanna was quiet. She didn't know what else to say or do. Her questions weren't being answered and she felt sick. Sick of the lies, sick of the rudeness of the hospital staff, sick of the smell of disinfectant, and sick of not knowing what it was that was wrong with her mother.

She went back to the ward and stood over her mother's body, brushing away a few straggly hairs that were stuck to her face. The sheets had been changed and her arm was now in a cast. She had also suffered a broken hip in the fall and the sisters were waiting for her to be transferred to a ward before leaving her alone. They didn't have long to wait before the same porter who moaned at Dreanna for smoking arrived to wheel her away.

Finally back home and completely exhausted by the day's events, Dreanna sank onto the settee and flicked through the television channels. Her mind was oblivious to what was on them but she needed something to distract her thoughts. She finally settled for the adverts as at least they were light-hearted.

Callum was out picking up their daughters from his mother and Dreanna knew he wouldn't be back for quite some time. She was so tired. The night feeds were draining her and now the added stress and worry about her mum was seeping throughout her whole being. She rubbed her temples, lifted her legs, and moved her body into the fetal position clutching a cushion close to her chest. Her eyes closed of their own accord and she fell into a deep slumber.

She found herself once again walking down the illuminated corridor. She was composed and serene and her head was held high. The quietness and tranquility made her relax and she knew soon that all her questions would be answered. How she yearned for Jan's voice to reassure her that everything was going to be alright.

"Dreanna." It wasn't Jan.

"Dreanna my darling, come unto me."

An unruffled Dreanna walked towards the warm voice of this mysterious speaker, wondering what awaited her when she reached her target.

A hand came out of the mist and behind it emerged the figure of a woman. A beautiful woman; her golden hair hung down over her shoulders to her waist, her skin was so pure, so white, unblemished and smooth, and her eyes were as black as coal. She signalled to Dreanna to sit down on the fluffy white ground. "My sweet, sweet, child I have waited so long to speak to you. I have missed you so very much." She held out her hand and stroked Dreanna's face. "You do not remember me and that's how it should be. My name is Seraphina. This will be the very last time for many years that you will be able to speak to me. You have responsibilities now to take care of your family, and this should not be hindered by us. Do you understand my child?"

"Erm I think so, but how... how can I cope without you ...all of you?"

Seraphina grasped her hand, caressed her fingers and placed a kiss on her forehead. "Oh my child, you will cope I promise. You have so many questions that you want answers to but for now I think the most important are the ones concerning your maternal mother. Listen Dreanna and listen well...

You have to remember that the body and mind have not yet evolved enough to sustain longevity to a point where health does not suffer. Your mother is already with us; her physical body is not at the point where it is due to die, this cannot happen for another few more years, but know that before she made the transition down for this life she was one of the many that decided to push the limits of what we already knew which enabled us and your fellow species to examine the boundaries of how the body can survive and function without the use of the mind. Look into her eyes Dreanna and see the void that has been left behind, see the empty space that held her soul, and know that she is safe, she is well and she is happy. Her body was and is just a vessel, because life, all of life is nothing more than an experiment in time."

Dreanna was awake; still curled up like a baby, her cushion clutched to her breast. Her mind was calm, her body relaxed, but she knew she was now alone, completely alone.

Another Time, Another Place

March 1994

The sun shone down brightly as Dreanna sat in her garden. She watched the ants busily scurrying around the patio and disappearing into a crack between the slabs. As one disappeared, three exited out of the tiny hole, none paying attention to Dreanna sitting crossed-legged, teasing them with the blades of grass that had grown through between each square block. She placed her hand in front of the ants but they were still not vexed and one crawled up her arm and down again. She lifted her hand and examined this tiny yet strong creation as it made its way to the tip of her finger. "How much time do you spend rushing around little ant, busily making burrows, collecting food and surviving the best way you know how? But then again. Don't we all do this, don't we all just try and survive? I suppose in many ways we are not really that different are we? Humans are like ants too, except a lot bigger, and a lot weirder." She replaced her finger on the ground and let the ant continue with his activities.

Her work for the day had finished and the events of the last long months still tugged at every nerve-ending in her brain. They had moved house in the last year, and had now joined the mortgage-paying sector of society. Both Rebecca and Leticia were happy and settled at school and Fawn was attending nursery three times a week. Dreanna took in other people's ironing during the day and her evenings were spent cleaning local offices. Not a job she actually liked that much but it gave them the ability to buy their house, and pay the bills without worrying.

Over the last few months Iris's health had deteriorated. Her children watched helplessly as their mother disappeared and a vacant vessel took over her faltering body. Dreanna too was beginning to feel the strain; endless pain from inside her womb, and tiredness seeped from every orifice, but she continued to plod wearily through life. She was happy, but at the same time lost, confused, and in so much pain. She shook her head, "C'mon kid," she said out loud, "You haven't got time to be melancholy. 'Time' again – what it is with time?"

"You need it." There was a pause. "Or do you?" A voice had appeared from nowhere; not one she recognised, but a man's voice, deep and kind.

"What?... I'm not going to ask who or why, as I think I may have outgrown all the questions I've put to you over the years, but please go on, please explain."

She sat motionless, with her eyes closed. Her head was full of auras and lights flashing around, and a pain like she had never felt before slowly ate its way through her. *Dreanna was used to pain but this one cut right through her core. She had to move away from it, she had to let her body go. She wasn't on the Earth, neither was she in her field or at the end of the corridor with the fluffy ground, but floating around above the Earth, floating around in space with the stars and the planets.*

"Are you ready?"

"Yep, but this is so different from before, this time it hurts... but I'm feeling all sort of floaty at the same time. Fire away, oh strange voice, but whatever you say please don't say 'beam me up Scotty'... Sorry, note to self, be more serious!"

"Hm, let's begin." The voice seemed a little agitated with her response, but Dreanna smirked anyway and smiled secretly to herself.

"Time is the one thing you on Earth concentrate on everyday of your existence. You rush around like the ants, you make appointments, you eat your food, you sleep, you wake, and you spend your lives being in many ways dictated to by time. Is time your friend Dreanna, or your foe? Do you need time or does time need you?

We have told you over and over again all your questions will be answered in time and in time you will know all what is needed. But how long is time? 24 hours, 48 hours or forever, because time only becomes an issue when you spend your TIME thinking about all the things you have to do and then you miss out on all the things you want to do.

Time is only essential for the survival of life. You see, each season can be seen as time, a time to grow food, a time to harvest, the daylight hours when you work and toil, when you live and learn, the night time hours when you rest and recuperate.

Indeed, it has to be said the physical world relies on time, every second of every minute, every minute of every hour, every hour of every day someone will rely on time, a gathering of people, a bad experience, a broken heart, all will remember that they had the time of their lives or this was the time their heart was destroyed. How you spend your time has to be down to you, you can utilise time or constantly complain that you don't have enough of it. Time is there to serve you; it is in the phenomenon of moving time that you have to make your life's decisions both the good and the bad. With the movement of time you will always have two choices, happiness or sadness, smiling or crying, and if you make the wrong choice then you have experienced for a brief period of time a tangible reality.

We have no need for time here, it neither moves forwards or backwards, we don't have a shortage of time nor do we worry about what time can bring, for us time is eternal, the same as life is.

Don't let time be your enemy sweet child. Make friends with it and listen with open ears and accept with an open heart all that time can offer you, because all that separates life from death and all that separates our worlds is a division of time."

Dreanna opened her eyes and blinked until her vision returned. She smiled. She was back. Then she turned her head in the direction of the opened patio doors where a very sleepy Fawn rubbing her eyes had awoken from her after-noon nap and was joining her mother in the sunshine.

"Hello poppet, d'you have a nice sleepy?"

Fawn, still dozey, replied, "Hm, yes, but I need a poo."

Dreanna giggled, "Nothing like a bit of natural bodily function to bring one back to reality!"

"Er...?"

"Doesn't matter Fawn. C'mon, I'll race you to the loo." Dreanna was back down to earth, back in her role as a mother, a carer, and a nurturer – all that was really important. She was physical, her children were physical, her world was physical, but every now and then she knew she was part of something bigger, something greater, that not even time could stop; where time did not matter, where life continued without the constant ticking of a clock or the need to worry about how much or how little time she had. Time was on her side.

The Hate Inside

October 1994

A very stroppy Dreanna walked into her father's house. She was in pain, and was so very tired; she felt like the time she had left was growing shorter and shorter each new day. She didn't feel it was on her side at all.

As she turned the key in the lock she could already hear her mother blathering on about something, speaking words that didn't mean anything to anyone but her. She knew her mother would be sitting in her chair, she knew exactly what position she would be in, she knew precisely what scene would greet her in the living room where Iris sat day after day and slept night after night. This room had become her prison; it was her cell where she was fed, where she slept and even where she used the commode to empty her bladder and bowels. This is how a mother of four and a grandmother to eleven would spend her days and nights; sitting, staring, rambling on and on, words escaping her mouth that made sense to no one but her.

Dreanna had never asked her father why he lied to her about her mother's health. After all, even if she'd questioned him it wouldn't have made a blind bit of difference to the outcome, and as Dawn said, he would have had his reasons. Maybe this was his way of protecting his offspring but the Alzheimer's was something he couldn't lie about or hide away. It stared them all in the face each time they entered the family home.

Dreanna had been up since 5 o'clock and had already stood for five hours doing other people's ironing. She had cleaned her house and prepared the Sunday roast, and now she had to roll and set her mother's hair. In reality Iris didn't care whether her hair looked nice or not, she didn't care about anything these days, but it seemed to make Patrick smile, and after spending every day of the week listening to his wife and her jumbled words he would at least be able to have some form of connection and proper conversation with someone else, even if for only a couple of hours. When all was said and done he needed a break too. He was exhausted and wasn't in the best of health, but, as he always told his children, Iris was his responsibility not theirs, and try as hard as they could he wouldn't let them help, no matter how tired he was.

Dreanna entered the kitchen and walked into a smog of cigarette smoke. Patrick was as usual sitting at the table, the massive magnifying glass he used for doing his daily crossword puzzles in one hand. He was so stubborn – he wouldn't get his eyes tested even though he was nearly blind. In the other hand was the obligatory fag. His cigarettes were compulsory, and who was she to tell him to stop smoking when she too was addicted to the foul-smelling, foul-tasting weed? She threw her bag of hair gadgets onto the floor and slumped herself down at the table. She stared for a long time at her dad, watching as he scratched his head with the biro, seeing imaginary light bulbs shine bright in the air when he worked out the answers to the conundrums before him. As he filled in the answers Dreanna poked the tip of his pen as it touched the paper.

Patrick glared at her. "Dreanna pack it in, I could win £500 if I finish this."

Dreanna, still staring, mouth turned downwards, bottom lip overlapping the top, carried on aggravating her father, flicking the pen from beneath his grasp.

"Oh you are such a bugger Dree! S'pose you want a cuppa don't you?"

Dreanna smiled, giving her father puppy dog eyes. "Yeah." She winked at her dad as he made a fresh cup of tea for them both.

A shout and a scream came from the living room, and the muffled words, "Itchy pops, itchy pops, they're coming to get me!"

"What the fuck?" Dreanna asked, a puzzled expression on her face. "What the fuck is an 'itchy pop'?"

"Don't ask me kid, it's Mum's new saying, but I wish the bloody itchy pops would hurry up and go, as this is what she talks about all day and night!"

Dreanna couldn't help herself, she looked at Patrick and tried not to smile, but was soon in total hysterics listening to her mother waffle on and on and on about these monsters known as the 'Itchy Pops'.

"Drink your bloody tea and shut up!" Patrick smiled that cheeky smile, winked and handed his daughter the tea. "You're looking tired kid, you okay?"

"Yep Pops. I'm okay," Dreanna reached for her father's cigarettes.

"Maybe you should go to the doctors, Dreanna."

"Maybe I should, but not just yet, okay Pops?" She finished her tea and made her way into the living room and the mop of hair she now had to roll up.

"Right, Mother dearest, what shall we do today? How about a skinhead, or maybe a Mohican, now wouldn't that be cool? You could be the first Alzheimer sufferer with a Moey."

"The itchy pops are coming, they're coming you know." Iris looked up at her youngest daughter.

"Don't worry Mum, I'm armed with a comb, a bag of curlers and my hormones; let them come and try to beat us down, we will have victory!" Dreanna laughed an evil mocking laugh.

"Shall we go to Australia? It's safe there," questioned Iris, "We can go on a plane... have I ever been on a plane?"

"No Mum, neither of us have ever been on a plane, but Australia sounds good, shall I drive the plane or you?"

"Erm... you can drive today as my hands don't seem to want to work."

Dreanna looked down at her mother's hands. They were the same hands that night after night would knit and crochet, they were the same hands that would bleed from scrubbing and cleaning, but more importantly they were the same hands that stroked her face, wiped her tears, and comforted her as a growing child. Now they lay contorted across her mother's lap, deformed beyond measure, each metacarpal, each phalange locked into the most awkward position, never to move, touch, or hold her again.

She could feel an overwhelming anger growing inside her. She felt it burn like a fire inside her stomach, felt the adrenalin flow to her legs and finger tips, felt her heart pound inside her chest. She was angry that her mother had lost her dignity and angry that there was absolutely nothing she could do about it. 'Shake it off,' she said inside her head. "Stop it!" this time out loud. And the feelings went as quickly as they had come. With Iris's hair finished and a bucket load of tea shared between her and Patrick, a wearisome Dreanna made her way home, to continue with her own life, her own children and her own pain.

Monday arrived. Dreanna started ironing at 5 o'clock. By 8 o'clock she had finished the first drop-off of washing for the day, the girls were ready for school and their bags packed, the dogs were fed, her housework was done and she began sorting out the paper work for her evening job as a supervisor for a cleaning firm. She sighed as she signed the order slip for more cleaning products to be delivered that week for her evening employment. She pressed hard into her groin, hoping that the twinges of the razor sharp pain she felt would just go away. But each day they got stronger and each day became more difficult to get through. She swallowed deeply and lifted herself from the chair.

Fawn was watching her from the doorway. "Mummy, what's the matter?"

"Nothing munchkin, c'mon let's get you lot to school."

"But Mummy, you are silly, I don't go to school, I go to nursery."

"Well, let's get you to nursery then." Dreanna tugged on Fawn's bunches before grabbing her coat and heading out the door with her children in tow.

Dreanna felt her rage building up through the day, as if she was about to give birth to a two-headed mega-beast with talons so sharp and poison so venomous it would kill its prey with one bite. These sensations were new to her. Yes, she had got angry before, after all, who hasn't? But this felt different, she felt like a warrior, a protector of the innocent, a soldier on a mission. Not understanding why, she took her anger out on a pair of jeans she was ironing, shaking her head as the iron glided over the denim. "Who the fuck irons bloody jeans?" she grimaced, "The things I do for money!" The hours ticked by and as the day progressed Dreanna felt her body falter. Her arms ached, her shoulders throbbed and her toes had beads of sweat oozing between them. By 4 o'clock she was dead on her feet. She'd finally finished ironing the endless shirts, duvet covers and the blasted jeans! Her children were sitting eating their dinner, and she now had to get herself ready for another few hours of scrubbing stains from toilet cubicles, emptying an endless supply of bins, and smiling sweetly at the office workers who looked down their noses at this small, heavily tattooed and pierced cleaner.

What always made the evening more bearable was that Dawn worked with her. They were two sisters on a mission. A mission of 'shall we hoover, polish, and scrub the loos or shall we do as little as we can actually get away with?' Both decided the latter most evenings. Both women worked tirelessly seven days a week, and natural survival instincts were what kept them going, especially in Dawn's case.

After years of mental and physical abuse Dawn had gathered enough strength to throw her husband out of their home. In the beginning he was an alright sort of bloke, quite happy-go-lucky and a good provider, but he had a side to him that turned sour and ugly; he was an alcoholic of the worst sort. Bottles of whisky were hidden in cupboards and alcohol was his only love and passion. His second love was his spiteful tongue and his fists.

On many occasions Dreanna and Callum had witnessed the controlling physical distress Kevin caused Dawn. They witnessed the pain and bruising he inflicted on her, but were helpless to do anything because Dawn had to make the decision to leave this abusive relationship herself, and neither could step over the line. No matter how many tears she shed, no matter how much torment he persecuted her with, she had to make her own journey through life.

"I'll do the toilets tonight Dree, your turn to empty bins okay?"

"Gee thanks Dawn....ooo how I love the bins," she answered sarcastically. Dreanna unlocked the cleaning cupboard and grabbed a handful of black bags, tucking some of them into her back pocket. Dawn filled a bucket of soapy disinfectant to wash the toilet floors and turned and walked away. The normal banter they shared on most evenings was not forthcoming, but Dreanna had learned over the years that if her sisters didn't want to talk then the best thing to do was leave them to it, not to question and never push for answers.

The office block was huge and on one floor there were over 100 bins. Each night more than twenty black sacks got filled and Dreanna always prayed that the lifts were in full working order, never wanting to think what would happen if they broke down. But she always said that if they did she would just launch the rubbish out of the nearest window!

All her bins were emptied, every desk was polished, but no hoovering this particular night as quite frankly she couldn't be bothered. So any rubbish found on the floor was either discreetly rubbed into the carpet, or if larger, picked up by hand. No one ever noticed or complained and she certainly wasn't going to kill herself for three pounds an hour. Dreanna searched the first two floors for her sister, but she wasn't there. They didn't clean the ground floor but her intuition was pulling her towards the managerial offices, four posh rooms which the head of the corporation used. No one was supposed to enter these and they had specialist cleaning staff that came in the early hours of the morning. Hidden away in the solid oak sideboards were individually wrapped chocolates that occasionally found themselves being swallowed down by Dawn and herself, when the chocolate fetish grabbed hold during their working hours.

Dreanna moved her feet around on the pile of the carpet, and with each circular step the carpet seemed to change colour and texture, which fascinated her. She walked towards the toilets, but as she did so the anger once again built inside her. Her hand reached out to push the door open and a surge of violent sensations overwhelmed every inch of her body. She felt dizzy, confused and not in control. Her body was swaying and her eyes couldn't focus. As hard as she tried she couldn't shake these feelings. She pushed the door open and saw Dawn crouched on the cold hard surface of the tiled floor, her arms gripping tightly to her body. She was rocking back and forth, endless tears streaming down her face. Still bowed, she spoke in a shaky quiet voice that sounded as if a vampire had sucked all the energy and life out of her.

"He hasn't paid the mortgage for nearly six months Dree, and refuses to sign the house over to me. If he doesn't sign, me and the kids are going to be repossessed. I can't lose my home Dree, I just can't… Hasn't he done enough to hurt me? Why is he being such a bastard?"

Dreanna couldn't speak. She felt such a wave of emotion overwhelm her, taking her to a place she had never been before. The woman in front of her was not her sister, but a scared child that she had to protect. She reached down and stroked Dawn's hair, then gripped the shoulder of her jumper and heaved her to her feet. She pulled her hastily to the door, out of the building and into the open space of the car park. Dawn was shaking but didn't speak another word as Dreanna beckoned her sister to get in the car. She hit the accelerator and they sped off in the direction of the house Kevin shared with his new girlfriend.

"Stay in the car," Dreanna told her sister when they arrived.

With one final look back at Dawn, Dreanna slammed the car door and made her way up the path to Kevin's new home. She could see movement through the glass front door and hammered it hard. A woman answered. Dreanna eyed her up and down.

"Can I help you?" the woman asked.

"Where's Kevin?" Dreanna asked sharply.

Kevin walked down the hallway, his arms opened to Dreanna. "Dree how the devil are you? It's been a while."

Dreanna looked at him with hatred in her eyes and loathing in her heart. Kevin went to hug her but as his hands touched her shoulder she clenched her fist and thumped his face over and over again. Blood flowed out of his mouth and Kevin tried to grab her arms, but moving fast, she turned and held his hair while throwing his body against the wall. Her arms swung ferociously in his face. He was unable to move. He was pinned, screams and yells of 'call the police' bellowed from his mouth. Then he slumped to the floor, his hands soaked with his own blood. His new girlfriend tugged at Dreanna's clothes but with one swift shove she was rammed into the wall opposite.

"What do you want, Dreanna?" His voice was begging her.

"Sign the house over, and do it by tomorrow or your life will be no more, d'you get me?" The words flowed from her as she banged his head against the wall one more time for good measure. Kevin didn't speak but nodded, his head lowered, blood dripping from his nose and lips.

As Dreanna turned and walked away she could see Kevin wiping blood from his face and his new woman leaning over him.

She was shaking, her stomach was turning, and her mind was full of all the years of pain he had given her sister. She climbed back into her car, her face and expressionless. Both women sat in silence on the journey home. It wasn't until they had reached their destination that Dreanna finally opened her mouth. "I love you Dawn."

Dreanna's body begun convulsing in the short distance left of her journey home. She parked up, unable to move for what seemed like hours. Her hands still trembled and her knuckles were raw and bruised as she reached for the door handle. The churning in her stomach climbed higher into her throat and she started to retch uncontrollably. She moved hastily up the garden path to the sanctuary of her home, and banged loudly on her front door as she started to vomit all over the door step. Callum appeared as the last mouthful came out.

"Woo, what's brought all this on?" he asked, rubbing her back and pulling her hair away from her face.

"Callum, I've done something terrible, and I never want to feel this way again!"

"What have you done that's so bad? Anyone would think you've just kicked five tons of shit out of someone."

Dreanna wiped her mouth with the back of her hand and said, "I have."

The rest of the evening was spent in near total silence after Dreanna explained the night's events. Callum was shocked that Dreanna could even do something like that but at the same time he was pleased she had. He had never liked Kevin and had seen what destruction he'd brought into Dawn's life. The only good thing he would ever say came out of that relationship was the two kids he had given her. Callum kissed his wife on the cheek as she lay in his arms. It wasn't long before he had drifted off to sleep, but Dreanna was still in total shock – she couldn't understand how she could do something like that.

The tranquil, composed voice of the man she remembered from the garden once again surrounded her. "This, my child, is hate. It's the one emotion that all men carry inside them. They use it as a weapon to destroy, to control, to reap revenge and to gain power. It comes in many forms and tonight you felt it in its most primitive form: you felt it as a protector, you felt it to right the wrongs that you have seen.

Hate is a cancer. It will destroy you, it will eat away, demolishing every inch of kindness you own, until you are left empty and destitute. Your world is full of people who do not think for themselves but live their lives following another. Many do not ask the right questions because fear stops them, but others gather their forces, they make armies full of hate.

Their reasons for this are vast. Some will lay blame with religion, some will say it's due to the colour of a person's skin, some will argue it's because of land or oil, or any amount of materialistic processions, but it's not. It's because of power. The more power you humans have the more control you desire, it's a drug to you, and what better way to feed a habit than to give it what it wants... anger and rage. Many innocent victims have perished in World Wars, men and women have led battles with their irrational hatred of other humans. They have wanted to destroy others that were not, in their eyes, equal to themselves. They thought they were superior and held rampant individualistic views that saw others as insufficient subordinates that were not perfect.

Sometimes these appalling hostilities happened and are still happening, because they were and are meant to happen, and they have occurred for a reason. When war strikes a divided world you humans manage to forget your differences and work side by side; you toil, you fight, you engage in battle to destroy whatever tyrant needs to be obliterated. You show each other the support you need for survival. The colour of a person's skin becomes irrelevant, their class status becomes null and void, their sexual preferences do not matter. As you unite, you become one with each other, until the disease of hate is exterminated. One day all will see that hate brings sadness, one day all will see that hate is the one disease that will destroy all human life, but for now my child remember the feelings of hate and anger that grew inside you today. Remember how they possessed you, for one day you will need to know what drives other people to hate and feel rage and you will know then exactly what you are up against; but rest assured Dreanna – you will be the victor as peace will end up conquering if only it's given a chance."

Dreanna, now slowly drifting off into the void of darkness that sleep brought, whispered as her eyes closed, "I will never allow myself to feel like this again, and I will never allow myself to be driven by the anger that took over every inch of my body today... never again, never..."

Find Me

May 1995

The days seemed to move so quickly, the hours and minutes ticking by in a relentless fashion. Each day rolled into the next, each tomorrow never somehow came, and every day was Groundhog Day.

Dreanna lay awake most nights in the darkness that seemed to swallow her up. It cradled her in its arms and she could feel its hot breath flowing over her skin. She showed it no fear, but its heaviness would pull her further and further down until they became one. Her weight began to drop considerably and when she looked at herself in the mirror she didn't recognise the reflection staring back. But life had to continue, she had to continue, but for how long? Even she was beginning to doubt how much strength she had left inside her. The love that had flowed so readily from her was beginning to disintegrate, and she was stuck an empty space in which she could move neither forwards nor backwards. She was hollow and lost.

June 1995

"Leave her alone!" Patrick shouted at his youngest daughter. "She's not your responsibility she's mine!"

"Oh Dad, for Christ sake, what is your bloody problem? You're sick too you know! You can't even get outta the chair and Mum stinks and needs a wash, so you have two choices. You can fight me off or let me get on with cleaning her up. I really don't need this right now so please let me just get on with it… please!"

Dreanna wrapped her arms around her mother's waist and lifted her out of the chair. Iris's body jerked as Dreanna forced her to try and put one foot in front of the other. Every day was becoming a battle and Iris's body was slowly seizing up. Dreanna gripped hold of her mother's nightdress and pulled it over her head. Her mother leaned on to her, her eyes expressionless and vacant. The nightdress was soaked in urine and excrement, and pressure sores were forming around her buttocks and on her back. Her legs had become unstable and taken on the same buckled shape as her hands and fingers.

Dreanna lay her on the bed, and grabbing hold of the creased sheet, wrapped it around her mother's naked body. Her mother's arms lay across her chest, locked in the same position as when the dead are laid out in the chapel of rest. In Dreanna's eyes Iris was already dead, and the image that lay in front of her simply confirmed that Iris wasn't there any more. She was dead and gone. She was no more.

Dreanna soaked a sponge in water and soap and cleaned her mother's body, embarrassment churning through her as she began washing her genitals. Seeing her mother naked wasn't the issue, she had seen her like that many times, but it just seemed wrong to touch her in such a personal area. She looked intently at the deformed body and wished she was a child again and her Mum was shouting at her for swearing, or not cleaning her bedroom. Memories of yesteryear played over and over. Dreanna winced, recalling the time when Iris overheard her call one of their neighbours a 'fucking twat', after they'd leaned over the garden fence waving their fingers and complaining about the loudness of the stereo. She had tried to explain that it was actually Patrick who was playing music but the neighbour was having none of 'her lip' and went into a full torrent of her having no consideration, no manners and the legal rights of being a council tenant. As her neighbour paused for breath, Dreanna just quietly exhaled the words 'shut up, you fucking twat', not realising she had said it so loud that Iris heard every word. Iris had stormed into the garden, dragged Dreanna by her jumper all the way up the stairs and shoved a bar of coal tar soap straight into her mouth, nearly touching the back of her tonsils. She grinned at the memory, and the taste of that god-awful soap filled her thoughts. Reminiscing will have to wait, she told herself as she placed the sponge back into the bowl of warm water and squeezed it out.

"Mum, say my name, please. I know a part of you is still in there somewhere, please I just want to hear you say my name one last time."

Iris opened her mouth, gargling in the back of her throat, saliva gathering in the corner of her lips. Dreanna took hold of her mother's cheeks, waiting, hoping, and praying for her to speak.

"Fucking cunt, fucking cunt, fucking cunt, I hate you, fucking cunt, cunt face cunt, cunt, cunt, cunt, cunt!"

Dreanna pleaded, "Mum! Stop it! Please don't! You're only saying those things because of the illness. The nurse said you would say things that hurt, that wasn't right, that just wasn't you... Mum don't do this to me please."

Iris stopped, her mouth tightly closed. Tears ran silently down Dreanna's face. She wouldn't ask again. It hurt so much to think she wouldn't hear her mother's mischievous laugh again, or hear the woman who gave her life say 'Dreanna'.

Dreanna shouted to her dad who was leaning on the door frame of the back door in the next room. "Dad, next time the district nurse calls, please can you mention the pressure sores on Mum's back? They're not looking too good."

Patrick didn't answer.

"Dad, did you hear me?" Dreanna shouted again as she cleaned up the wet towels and gathered up the soiled nightdress and sheets she had just stripped from the bed.

Patrick didn't answer. He was now sitting at the table, filling in yet another crossword, his fingers toying with the edge of the paper. He ignored the fact that his youngest was rinsing out the nightdress and sheets in the kitchen sink before putting them in the washing machine on a pre-soak setting.

"Dad, you're gonna need to put this on a normal wash once this cycle has finished."

Patrick didn't answer.

"Oh, suit your fucking self – don't bloody talk to me then! You know where I am if you need me." Dreanna grabbed her coat and made her way to the front door. "Love you Pops."

Patrick coughed but still didn't answer. Dreanna reached for the door handle still waiting for a 'Goodbye', but Patrick said nothing.

"Stubborn old git!" she shouted, as she exited her family home.

May 1995

Patrick didn't phone his daughter in over seven weeks and she made a point of staying away. She didn't even feel guilty about not helping him take care of Iris; she needed the break, and she needed the time to sort out her own family and life. But her life wasn't there and the dark feelings of the night now also circled her mind throughout the day. She hardly spoke to anyone, and avoided people whenever she could, often hiding in doorways or darting in shops when someone she knew was near. She made herself invisible, moving and darting away from the attention of everyone.

Her relationship with Callum had become strained and filled with awkward moments where neither husband nor wife spoke to each other for days on end. Always avoiding being left in the same room alone, never touching, never kissing, never showing an ounce of affection or fondness, they were ships in the night passing quietly through still, stagnant waters.

"Wish you'd fucking cheer up," Callum said as they waited at a set of traffic lights.

"Please Callum not now, I'm tired."

Callum changed gear and rubbed Dreanna on the leg. "Just cheer up then… please! I don't know how much more of all this shit I can take. Oh, and by the way, Patrice phoned. Your dad's not too good and she needs you to go and sort out your mum."

"Oh brilliant, and when was this exactly?"

"This morning. I forgot. Sorry."

"Well you better drop me off at dad's then, hadn't you?"

"Does that mean I've got to put the shopping away? I don't like putting the shopping away. Can't you go round your dad's after?"

"Oh for fuck's sake Callum. Grow up and stop being such a spoilt little shit!" Dreanna slammed the car door with as much force as she could muster, not looking in her husband's direction at all. The only thought going through her mind was what sort of mess Iris was going to be in.

She took a deep breath before opening the kitchen door. Dad and Patrice were drinking tea at the table; she could hear the wheezing of his chest and could see the endless tissues full of mucus in the bin.

She asked bluntly, "Have you called the doctor?"

Patrick ignored her but Patrice answered, "Yeah, Doctor's just left, Dad's got some sort of chest infection and a raised temperature. He also looked at Mum and is a little concerned about the sores on her back, but he's sending the district nurse out daily to change the dressings."

"So why do you need me here then, you seem to have got it all covered?"

"'Cos I really can't wash Mum, Dree. You're the only one that can. I've cut her toenails and fingernails, but you know I can't handle anything else. After all I'm the one that does their shopping, so someone else can do their bit!"

"Whatever," Dreanna sighed. Even she was shocked when she saw her mother sitting in the chair. She had ballooned into a woman that looked twenty stone. Dreanna shouted to her sister, "Why is Mum so fucking fat?"

"Doctor said it's something to do with fluid retention or summat like that, but he's put her on new tablets so hopefully it should all go away soon."

"Well there's no way on this earth I'm gonna be able to lift her out of this chair, she's fucking enormous! Can you help me please Patrice?"

"Not if she's shit."

"Of course she's shit. What do you think that god awful smell is?... Forget it, I'll manage."

Dreanna didn't have the energy to get herself out of bed most days let alone trying to move twenty stone of flesh that had no movement or elasticity left in it. There was physically no way she could have moved her. She grabbed hold of her mother's ankles and slid her downward until her backside rested on the edge of the seat, unbuttoned her skirt and began the arduous task of changing her mother's nappy. Dreanna wiped, washed and dried but didn't say a single word to Iris. She didn't stroke her hair, hold her close, or even tell her she loved her. Dreanna had nothing left to give.

With her mother now clean, she headed back to the kitchen. "I'm off," she said.

"That was a short visit." Patrice said.

"Well, there's no point in staying where I'm not wanted is there?" Dreanna stared straight at Patrick, and walked right out the door without even saying goodbye.

January 1996

The air was stale with the lingering smell of old cigarettes, last night's dinner and the faint odour of the morning's bathing. The noise from outside was un-bearable – the humming of cars speeding past, the sound of next door's stereo playing some old 'has been' country and western singer. Dreanna eyed the reflection of her pale sunken lifeless face. She slumped to the floor. With her arms folded across her chest she yearned for comfort, but there was none. She rocked, cradling her body, tears forming in her eyes. As the tears flowed, her mind grew darker. 'Why me? Why me..?' Still rocking, still crying, still numb, with snot dribbling down her face and mixing with the saltiness of tears, she felt empty, confused and alone. Loneliness engulfed her tiny form like never before.

The world outside didn't stop. It still moved and breathed and developed and materialised into a vast immeasurable globe of emotions, but the only emo-tions she could feel were the ones that were trapped inside her. They would squirm and contort, grip hold of her body and twist it from the inside out, pushing, tightening and contracting like a baby ready to leave the womb. Her head was filled with noise, disorientation and mayhem, like prisoners causing a riot, trying to escape their compounds. She got up and stared again at her own reflection. 'Where am I? Where have I gone?' she wondered. No one an-swered.

She looked at her naked shape. What was once a voluptuous woman with curves in all the right places had now been exchanged for skin and bone. Her breasts hung empty and shapeless, her skin was dry and desiccated, and the bony formation of her rib cage was her most prominent feature. "Where am I, where have I gone?" This time out loud. No answer.

At the end of every day the house that has lain silent is filled with the com-motion of her children all demanding food, demanding attention, demanding HER. Her husband arrives home, demanding food, demanding attention, de-manding HER. The phone rings, her stubborn father is demanding help, de-manding attention, demanding HER. The people she works for knock on her door demanding her time, demanding her attention, demanding HER.

Her body is in pain, her womb crippled in agony, her body is demanding her attention, and Dreanna ignores it. Her tormented mind begs her over and over again, "Help me, help me." Dreanna ignores it. She soaks up the silence as her daily chores are completed, the children now sleeping, the husband now sleeping, the world now sleeping. She once again is alone, alone with her pain, and the disorganised mess that's nestled inside her brain.

Dreanna pulled open the curtains and stared out into the darkness. One lone star shone down. She stared and wondered if a star could ever feel as isolated and separated as she felt in her own body, in her own life? For that brief moment she didn't feel alone any more. Her body wasn't hurting and her mind felt calm. It only lasted for one brief moment, then the all-too-familiar stabbing pain filled her pelvis. She bowed, clutching her groin. 'No more. I can't take any more!'

She grabbed the car keys and unbolted the door. Only when she had left the sanctuary of her garden did she realise she was without shoes, without coat, and almost certainly without any dignity. The icy January wind ripped through her tee-shirt. Dreanna shuddered and shivered but was not going to allow a bitter wintry night to stop her from achieving her goal. Her hands were shaking from cold and from the fear of what she was about to do.

She heaved up the garage door and forced her frozen body inside. The only light shone from the moon and that one lonely star. Her trembling hands searched the dark for the garden hose and continued feeling the shadowy structure for the exhaust of her car, then rammed the hosepipe into it. With her arms outstretched she grabbed hold of the garage door, stared one last time at her familiar surroundings, and yanked it downward. Total darkness now filled her world.

She felt her way round her car and settled into the driver's seat. Tears again filled her eyes as so many memories cascaded over her like the torrent of a waterfall: her childhood, her parents, her siblings, her husband, her children, her life, her pain, her mixed-up mind, her children... My children. She began arguing with herself.

 'Do it! Turn the key!'
'Stop, don't! Your children – who would look after your children?'
'What have you got to lose? They'd be so much better off without you.'
'They need you, they love you! Get out of the car!'
Her tears had turned to uncontrollable sobbing. The feelings and emotions that had overwhelmed her for twenty-seven years filled every inch of her frozen body. She wrapped her arms around herself for some form of comfort. The tears eventually stopped and a void of nothingness encircled her. She stared into the darkness and her hand moved down to grab hold of the keys once again...

"Dreanna, it's not your time. You know we won't let you die, don't you? You have too much to do. Do you really want to die?"

Dreanna let go of the keys and closed her eyes. "Nanny! I can't take any more. I'm so tired, the pain, Mum, the kids, Callum, work... I'm not strong any more. Please Nan – I want to be with you, I want to come home."

Matilda was having none of it. "Now c'mon, listen to me. Get your backside out of this car, get indoors, warm yourself up, go to the bloody doctor, and for god's sake child, pull yourself together! Okay you're in pain, big deal, so is half the bloody human race. Okay you work hard – your choice – nobody else's. Yes you've had to look after my daughter, well she looked after you for 18 years, so show a bit of respect. Nobody said life was going to be easy and in your case I'm afraid it has to be hard. You chose this life Dreanna, and you need to go through all what you are. Do you not see what they are trying to teach you? Do you not get it? Do you not remember what you screamed at the heavens when you were a kid?... Hark at me, I've nearly let the cat out of the bag! Please, get out of this car, get indoors and rest. Find yourself Dreanna, find yourself!"

"But Nan... I...."

But Matilda had gone, and Dreanna, well, she felt like a scolded child, and if it was her choice to have this life then she had to cope – didn't she?

The Darkness

Dreanna's frozen hands clicked the button of the gas fire to ignite its life-giving warmth. As she sat in front of it the warmth from the flames penetrated her cold body, her toes cramping as the blood started to circulate more quickly through her veins. Her common sense questioned just what she had nearly done. She knew it was wrong, she knew that it wasn't her time, but she couldn't help wishing she had had the courage and the nerve to have succeeded in her mission. She rubbed her skin rapidly in the hope that the prickling feeling would soon disappear and her body would resume some sense of normality. Her words echoed around the room, "Why do I feel like a prisoner in my own body, a prisoner in my own life?" She reached down and stroked her legs. "Why do I have to spend my life asking questions? Why can't I just be like everyone else?" Despite the questions her eyes felt heavy, and they weren't responding to her wish to stay awake. Soon she was in her field.

"*You are so afraid, are you not?*" The translucent figure of a man stood before her.

"*I'm tired,*" was all Dreanna the energy to say.

"*Hm I see… You also do not speak the truth.*"

"*Please – just leave me alone.*"

"*I'm afraid I cannot leave. You are here and so am I. Even when we plan to have no communication with you we are wrenched to your side in times of need and turbulence. We are attached to you and you to us; we feel what you feel because we are one.*"

"*Well if we are one, why the hell am I feeling so detached from you, and so detached from who I am? Why the hell do I feel so abandoned? Please, I can't do this now, who-ever you are please just leave me alone, go away, fuck off and get out of my life!*"

"*If that's what you wish I will leave, but I will never be too far away.*"

He was gone.

The sound of Fawn's giggles woke Dreanna from her rest. She rubbed her eyes only to find two pieces of Lego stuck to them.

"Mummy is a Lego head, Mummy is a Lego head!"

Dreanna reached out and hauled Fawn to the floor and nestled her into her arms. Fawn shoved one finger inside her nose and wiped the slimy contents down Dreanna's face.

"Fawn, why have you just wiped a bogie on my face? That's so disgusting."

Fawn squirmed her way out of Dreanna's clasp. "Well, Mummy, *Drop Dread Fred* does it… I love *Drop Dread Fred.*" She jumped up, her feet twisting round on the carpet. "Lovely smelly dogs muck, lovely smelly dogs muck!" she shouted as she ran the entire length of the lounge.

Dreanna couldn't help but smile. "I knew we shouldn't have let you watch that film. You are crazy! Are your sisters awake yet?"

"Nope. Can I watch *Drop Dread Fred*? Pleeease let's watch *Drop Dread Fred*."

"It's *Drop Dead Fred*, not Dread."

"Dat's what I said silly, *Drop Dread Fred*."

Dreanna shook her head, grinned and beckoned her daughter to sit with her, wrapping her arms tightly around this tiny package of merriment. "Let's watch it together shall we?"

February 1996

The doctor's surgery was heaving. Wet soggy bodies were squashed uncomfortably side by side, their coats sodden from the driving rain outside. She had given in and was here in the one place that she dreaded more than anywhere else. Dreanna stood in the queue, her feet fidgeting as she waited to give the receptionist her name. She fixed her eyes on the 'full stop' on a poster stuck to the wall behind the receptionist and concentrated hard as she erected barriers up in her brain, steel frames to shield herself from others' emotions.

"Name?"

An old man poked Dreanna in the ribs to get her attention. Dreanna hastily blinked as the old man pointed his finger in the direction of the receptionist. "Sorry, erm Dreanna, to see Dr James."

"He's running a bit late, but take a seat and he'll be with you soon."

Dreanna took the seat nearest the window so she could look out at the pouring rain instead of having to make eye contact with the restless, dripping bodies only inches away.

Callum soon joined his wife. "Sorry, couldn't get a space. Ooo, glad to see everyone's happy," he grinned.

"Shut up! It's a doctor's surgery, sick people and all that!"

"And? That stops their mouths from smiling, does it?"

"Shhh!" Dreanna picked up a magazine that had been thrown on the floor and whacked it hard in Callum's lap.

"What am I supposed to do with this?"

"Look at the bloody pictures!" Dreanna answered and smiled at a lady opposite who looked irritated that she and Callum had the impertinence to speak. Dreanna returned to looking out the window.

"Somewhere over the rainbow, way up high, in a land that I've heard of once in a lullaby..."

Dreanna inhaled. 'Go away!' she screamed inside her head.

"Someday I'll wish upon a star..."

'Enough!' Dreanna interrupted the lone voice.

"Go tell my wife over there I'm okay, please," the voice begged.

'NO, go away, and leave me alone.'

"You can't avoid us forever you know."

'I can! Go away.' As Dreanna fidgeted in her seat, her head was pulled in the direction of a young child. The boy was trying to build a tower of bricks but his tiny fingers couldn't quite get the bricks to stay together.

"He's going to be sick," Dreanna whispered to Callum.

"Er what?" Callum looked up from his magazine.

"Five, four, three, two, there she blows."

The child hoisted himself up from the floor and began violently retching; his mother tried to cover his mouth with her hands as they ran through the surgery to the toilets.

"How d'you know he was gonna puke?"

"Mother's intuition. See..." Dreanna tried halting her sentence but her mouth carried on, no matter what her brain did or did not want her to say. "See that woman over there? She's next to be seen and has a limp, right foot."

"What the hell are you talking about?"

"Sorry gotta get out of here – I need some fresh air. Can you come and get me when my name is called?"

"But Dree!...Wait up, what's going on?"

Dreanna couldn't answer him. Her head pounded and throbbed as the intense feelings inside started to take hold. Her ears vibrated with the noise of the emotional angst being broadcast in the waiting room; she was trapped in their fear, their pain and trauma. She wanted to run and hide and curl up in a ball, hold herself tight and die. She had failed herself. She had let her barriers fall.

The outcome of the doctor's visit was what Dreanna had expected, and she now had to sit and wait for the appointment for the gynecologist to arrive. The doctor armed Dreanna with a prescription of iron tablets and anti-depressants. Dreanna questioned the doctor as to why she needed anti-depressants.

"To help you sleep. You'll drop off that little bit easier, that's all. Don't worry, they're not addictive and you'll feel so much better taking them."

"I doubt that," Dreanna replied. But who was she to argue? After all, doctors know best. Something had to control the emotions building inside that were slowly destroying her very being.

Dreanna made some limp excuse to Callum and took herself off to bed early. So many questions ran through her brain as she tossed and turned, and in the end she just couldn't find a position that would bring sleep so she just lay staring at the ceiling, her mind jumping from one question to another. 'Am I really depressed? Have I let myself get so low that others can see something I can't?

Am I so close to losing my mind that I've forgotten who I am? Am I losing it to the point of being a clone of my Mum? Am I crazy? Is everything I've been through a dream, an over-active imagination?' She squeezed her head hard as thought after thought hit her. 'Maybe I am crazy; maybe I need the drugs; maybe all these years I've been someone I'm not; maybe I'm just a fucking loony twat that needs the tablets to stop the voices, the pain, the heartache inside.' Dreanna reached for the packet of unopened pills, tugged at the silver paper and popped one of the tablets into her mouth, then lay back down on the bed and closed her eyes.

"The pills will help you sleep, but they are going to make you so very sick my sweet child. Please do not take them."

Dreanna was in a nothingness – she heard Seraphina but could not see or feel her. She knew she was there with her but where was there? Where was she?

Seraphina's words flowed on in their usual composed manner. "Life is undoubtedly one of the hardest adventures we will ever have to deal with. A tide of emotions fill us every day, some are euphoric that give us reason to live, others poignant, miserable and wretched. Depression grabs you and never wants to let you go; it eats away at you slowly, consuming you like a spider slowly sucking the life out of its prey. It rips out your heart, and saturates your every thought like the rain drenching an arid plain. Its talons bury themselves into your flesh and grasp you, pulling you closer and closer until the day arrives when depression stands victorious and you bow beneath its feet an empty vessel, too tired to fight any more, too scared to run; you become a blank, vacant, person unwilling to care, to wash, to laugh, to live.

The causes of depression are vast and immeasurable. It can be looked upon like a Hydra, the mythological beast with many heads. Each head is a reason behind why depression is felt. Each reason gathers strength as long as it has all the others to rely on. Each head you defeat seems to be replaced by another. The head of grief, the head of ill health, the head of loneliness, the head of self loathing, the head of fear, the head of stress, the head of abuse, the head of hate. All these heads give strength and force to the central head that has more intensity, more muscle, and more power than any of the others alone – 'The Head of Depression'.

There are many weapons that can be used to help defeat this beast of destruction. Each in turn can aid, support and give us the courage needed to place it back into Pandora's Box, but the one item that is required more than anything else is the exact same thing that never flew off when Pandora's box was opened and that is HOPE.

Never lose Hope my sweet child, never lose Hope."

Dreanna's mind became empty as she drifted off to a sleep filled with fear and the sinister feelings that began sucking her life away. Gloomy shadowy figures of herself floated around her. Each figure was her, but her eyes had disappeared into holes in her face that showed no meaning. Her limbs were so heavy she could not move away; she couldn't run and even if she could she had nowhere to hide. She had to face these demons that looked like her, that were her, and defeat them with every last bit of strength she had. She somehow had to fight them to the death, to free herself from the chains they imprisoned her in. The darkness swallowed her up and overwhelmed her very essence. She was powerless, she was hopeless, she was gone...

Imagination is Everything

February 1996

The sun shone through the gap in the bedroom curtains and flecks of dust drifted and glided in the rays that trailed their way across the room in a beam of
weightless illumination. Dreanna tried to lift her legs to get out of bed but they
didn't want to move. As she raised her head a woozy giddy sensation overwhelmed her; she could feel her stomach churn and the acid move up to her
throat. With a big heave she gagged and vomited on the bed sheets that covered
her. The yellowy-green liquid soaked through onto her skin, and she called out
for Callum but her voice was squeaky and dry. She tried again, but her voice
did not have enough strength to be heard. Dreanna turned her head to look at
the clock by the bed, it flashed 2.45pm. "Bollocks! I've been asleep for nearly
eighteen hours! God I feel weird."

As she reached for the glass of water by the clock, her hands began to shake.
She blinked. Her arm seemed to be moving of its own accord. Her breathing
was shallow, she felt like she was floating in water. As she stared again at the
clock, the numbers drifted away from it and headed straight for her, glisten-
ing above her face in vibrant red and orange hues. She reached out again for
the glass of water but which one? She now had three glasses in her peripheral
vision. She leant over the edge of the bed and gawked at the floor but the floor
wasn't there – in its place was a vivid moving flow of 'goo', swirling around in
a circular motion. She reached down to touch it, it was sticky, and she smiled in
total awe of its beauty. Each droplet clung to her fingers and slowly fell back
into the pool with a euphoric splash. She dropped her head back onto the pillow and looked up at the hypnotic dust particles. Each one had quadrupled in
size and an acid smiley face had emerged on each grain. Her bedroom walls
started to breathe, in a superficial way.

"Wow, this is so cool," she laughed.

Jan was with her.

*"Oh look, it's my wonderful dead birthing partner! You look one hot mumma! And
you're all shiny," Dreanna giggled childishly.*

Jan shook her head. "Dreanna, what are we going to do with you?"

"Hey Jan, come sit with me in the goo, its so amazing!"

"There is no 'goo', you are hallucinating!"

*"Hmm, this is so totally radical," Dreanna reached out to touch Jan. "Wow, look at
my hand. It's all twinklerly like yours. Am I dead too?"*

"Dreanna, firstly you are not dead and secondly there is no such word as twink-erly!" Jan heaved a sigh. "Now please don't be afraid but I am going to place my hand up on your head. You will feel a powerful tug inside your mind; it will feel like you are detached from everything, then my child you will sleep. When you awaken you will feel extremely queasy, but whatever you do, do not take the tablets any more, they will not help. Only you can change the darkness you are feeling inside. You have the strength."

Dreanna still sat with a pathetic grin on her face in her imaginary pool of goo and nodded, totally oblivious to her instructions. As Jan reached out to touch her, Dreanna couldn't help but fall into another fit of giggles.

"Hey Janny, my floaty friend, when you were alive did you ever... You know, did you ever do sexy things? Did you ever... ever take it from behind?"

"Now that is enough... But yes, of course I did sexy things, I haven't always been who I am here! Now please, lay back, stop your giggling and close your eyes."

Jan once again reached out and laid her translucent hand on top of Dreanna's head. A searing pain shot through her brain. The smarting tenderness heaved its way throughout the abyss of her rational and irrational thoughts, her mind went dark, and she fell into a deep sleep.

Dreanna didn't move for three long days and nights. She awoke only briefly to drink and then fell straight back into an undisturbed and peaceful slumber. Her mind did not have any sense of reality, nor did it think of pain and darkness. It held no demons of contortion and fear; it only brought the one thing her body needed – respite from her physical existence.

She opened her eyes wide and her three children stood before her, their faces glowing. Each one was smiling the sort of smile to melt the coldest of hearts.

Leticia was the first to speak. "Mummy, are you getting up yet, 'cos we think you need a bath as you're a bit stinky, and Daddy really can't cook and he keeps getting stroppy with us 'cos we can't do our homework, and we are bored of you being in bed."

Callum entered the room looking tired and stressed. "Finally awake are we?"

"Take the girls downstairs Callum, give me five minutes and I'll get up."

"Yep, and don't forget to take your pill." He handed her the anti-depressants. Dreanna stared at the packet, she knew she had to remember something but was struggling to think what. Words floated about in her brain not making any sense. Tablets, tablets, tablets... *Don't take the tablets!*

"Thanks. I will take them, don't worry." She popped the pill from its silver foil and put it in her mouth. Callum left the room with the children following.

Dreanna watched as they headed down the hall, waited till they were out of sight, then spat the white pill back into her hand.

She hauled her feeble frame out of bed and felt the blood rush to every part of her body. Her head was beating as if a huge bass drum was playing inside it, and she felt unsteady. The consequences of no food and laying in bed for such a long time made her feel worse than ever. She surveyed her frail form and realised that Leticia was right, she stank!

'One step at a time,' she told herself, and made her way into the bathroom, the pill still between her fingers. She stood in front of the bathroom mirror and was shocked at what she saw. Her eyes were drawn with dark circles around them, her cheek bones protruded from her face and her lips were white and blistered. She shook her head and let the tablet fall from her fingers down the plug hole.

'Okay kid, clean your goddamn teeth, jump in that bath and for god's sake pull yourself together. This is gonna be so fucking hard but you can do this, I know you can!'

She ran the taps of the bath and climbed with shaky legs into the surge of flowing water, watching as it got deeper and deeper around her. "I'm not alone in this bathroom, am I?" Her words echoed around the room.

"No Dreanna, you are not alone. Do you feel different?"

"I feel fucked!"

"We had hoped that what just happened to you wouldn't have happened for a few more years. You are just too curious, in many ways too demanding of answers. People always want to know the 'whys', 'ifs' and 'hows' but what they don't want is what has to happen to them in order for the answers to be given. The pain, the confusion and the sickness is all needed for your mind to evolve. Sadly, people expect that their minds can change with no trauma, they expect they can just tune in and become what you are. What you are is not what a physical life should be; you see, you are alive, your body is alive because you breathe, you eat, you touch, you feel. But you are one of us, you are the closest thing to what we are like in a physical form.

Please do not worry, but this will happen to you a few more times in your life. Each time it happens you will learn more so that you have the knowledge to help others. It is nothing more than a transitional moment in time. Many people believe they have the power to talk to us in the manner you are, but sadly they are mistaken. It is not that we cannot or will not converse with them, it is that their minds are different to yours, their approach, to life is different to yours. They want to be the best, the greatest, the most convincing. You my child, well, let's just say you are so very special, your future will show you. Your future will make you into what our hearts know is the real you."

"But who and what are you? I'm sorry, more questions..."

"You can call me Qulib, I am a Keeper of Life. There are forty of us in total.

Dreanna interrupted her teacher. "Are you... a god?"

"We go by many names and many guises, it is only you on Earth that make these names, we have tried over the eons to interpret who we are in a simple way so it is easy for all to understand, but as time has moved forward more names have been fashioned, more beliefs have been formed and more humans have become led by others' thoughts. Life is a simple adventure with simple equations but these have become lost and more difficult denominations have filled the minds of many. You have now met two of us and over time will meet many more..."

"But," Dreanna paused, "surely there must be one that is in charge, one that says what can or cannot happen?"

"We all take charge of our own position. You must ask the right questions Dreanna. What you really want to know is who was the first. Am I right?"

"Yes... Who was the first, there always has to be a first, doesn't there"?

"The first Keeper to have a physical life was Cia, and she is watching you intently. You will work out soon who she is, just as you will work out who I am and who the others are. I cannot give you the answers so please do not ask – it is your job to find them."

"But why me?" There was pleading in Dreanna's voice.

"It is not just you my child. There have been many and are many: scientists, artists, musicians, princesses, nurses, religious men; each have been given a task to do, each of them were and are able to have the connection we have. The point in the altered state of your imagination is where the answers are, where the communication with us lies. Everything we give, every word that is chosen, can describe all of what we are. All will be explained, the coming years will bring the answers. A little bit of homework for you my child. Study the pyramids, not the history behind them, but the pyramids themselves, and remember - everything is simple."

Dreanna ducked her head back into the bath so the water streamed over her face and her hair floated in the warm stillness. After a moment of pure peace she sat back up and opened her eyes; on the shelf by the sink stood a purple pyramid-shaped candle that Rebecca had bought her last Christmas. She looked intently at its shape before lifting herself out of the water. She dried her undernourished body and made her way down stairs to the chaos of family life – her children, her husband and the physical tribulations that lay ahead of her. She knew that the only person that could help her now was herself. 'It's only a thought,' she told herself, and all thoughts can be changed. 'Today I choose to be happy.'

The Move

September 1998

Dreanna stood watching as the blossom from the trees floated in abundance around their garden. Callum stood behind her, his arm around her waist, his head on her shoulder. They were admiring their new home.

"That's all ours," he said.

"Well actually it's the building society's," she corrected him, "But I know what you mean. We've come a long way since the shitty old halfway–house the council first gave us. But as Mum always said, if you work hard, you can get what you want, and fuck me we have worked hard haven't we?"

Callum kissed her neck. "Yep we have, but I'm still wondering about something."

"What"?

"Why did everyone we told about moving to this place tell us not to buy it, even the bloody woman in the post office kept asking if I was sure about it?"

Dreanna turned to face him. "Hm, I know, that is a bit strange isn't it? The funniest thing is, I used to pretend when I was a kid that I lived in one of these houses, even used to dream about running up and down the garden. But I wonder why people keep saying it to us? It's not like we don't know the area. Christ, I was born around the corner, and we know all the neighbours." They made their way up the garden into the conservatory and Dreanna continued, "Don't you think the people we bought it off were a little odd though? Whenever we asked about living here they always seemed to change the subject. Anyway I've got to go round Dad's and see how Mum is. Those sores on her back haven't improved, and some of them nurses don't know their arses from their elbows. I'll see you in a bit." She leaned over and kissed Callum on the forehead.

He just stood still admiring their new home. "Dree," he called, "remember what the gyno said, no overdoing things."

"Whatever," she shouted as she slammed the front door.

Patrick was in the garden hanging out yet another load of soiled bed sheets. He was looking shattered and jaded. Dreanna couldn't help but hope that all this would end soon. She wasn't used to seeing him looking so worried: he always hid his feelings well, but it was inevitable that sooner or later Iris's condition would need extra medical intervention. As she sat down on the back doorstep and stared down the garden, so many memories flooded into her mind.

"Dad?"

Patrick turned.

"Why do you think people keep telling us we were stupid buying our house?"

"Maybe it's got something to do with the neighbours, not the house itself."

"But I know all the people; I grew up with some of them."

"Do you? Do you really know them Dree? You know better than anyone people aren't always what they seem. My advice is trust no one and stop thinking everyone is nice 'cos the chances are you'll be the one getting hurt."

Dreanna watched as the sun shone down on her father. Even though he was old and his body was slowing down, he was still such a handsome man. His crystal blue eyes were like pools of water that had seen so much during his life. His long white nicotine–stained beard hung down his face, the beard that as a child she used to run her fingers through and try and plait. He was her very own Father Christmas and her best friend, but she could see the pain he was feeling; the tiredness, the fear, and the lack of fight had begun to show. His body ached and his heart hurt that he was slowly losing the wife he had loved and cherished since early manhood.

"Dad I love you," Dreanna said, admiring her father.

The normal response she was expecting came back, "And me, I love me too, and what is there not to love?" He winked at her, and picking up the laundry basket he moved back inside the house.

Dreanna soon followed and began filling a bowl to wash her mother. As she entered her mother's downstairs room the smell hit her full force. She heaved. "Dad, what is that disgusting smell?"

"I can't smell a bloody thing," he answered.

Dreanna stood over Iris; the smell was certainly coming from her. "Mum smells like she's going bad. Just out of curiosity, when was the last time the nurses came to change her dressings?"

Patrick stroked his beard. "Erm – last Tuesday, I think. The one that's been coming in said she was off on holiday but would send a replacement."

Dreanna leaned her mother's body forward and lifted her jumper; her eyes watered as the disgusting odour hit her at full pelt. The dressings were soaked through, oozing a gluey greyish–green liquid. She peeled away the gauze. "Mum seriously needs a doctor. Have you had a look at these?" She pointed to a fist–sized hole at the bottom of Iris's back. What was once pink skin was now red and black, ripped, torn and eaten away by infection. "I have to go to a meeting in a bit, but I'll call a doctor to come for a visit before I go. I'm also gonna call the district nurses and ask why the hell they haven't been back in over a week." She paused, "I hate to say this Pops but I think it's time you let Mum go. We just can't take care of her needs. She doesn't eat, she doesn't talk, she pisses herself at every opportunity and in all honesty you are so tired. You just can't cope anymore."

Patrick looked down at the floor as he turned and walked away. His voice held nothing but sadness; in his mind he had failed his wife. "Do what you have to do."

Dreanna reached for the telephone, arranged a visit from the GP, and moved into the kitchen where Patrick was sitting staring out of the back door.

"They're coming round after morning surgery has finished. I've got to go now but I'll call later to see what they said. I'm sorry Dad." She kissed his head, and left.

Dreanna hated the monthly meetings she had to attend in her supervisory position of 'head cleaner'. They bored her senseless and it was always the same, 'we need this done', 'that isn't good enough', yawn, yawn, yawn. But she always nodded her head in the correct places, smiled attentively, and was on her best behaviour, for after all, no matter how much she hated this job it had to be done to pay for her new home and higher mortgage.

The boardroom smelt of stale coffee and soggy biscuits, but the curtains had been drawn back in a very precise fashion with every pleat falling in line with its partner. The pristine white paint gleamed from each wall and every skirting board so they looked like soldiers standing to attention. The highly-polished table where many an influential business type had leant their elbows was only inches from her. Dreanna swivelled in the leather armchair sniffing the air deeply. With each movement the odour and freshness from the seat overwhelmed her senses. She turned round and round, pushing until her head span. Then she stopped abruptly. Any moment now her boss and the head of the company would join her in this vast space of importance. She could no longer play – her adult, 'sensible' head had to be put firmly on her shoulders.

The head of the company entered the room and took his seat at the head of the table. He was a tall lanky man, clean–shaven, suited and booted, with thick bushy eyebrows that crept across his forehead like a hairy slug. He always squinted and his face had more lines on it than a road map, but he was pleasant enough to talk to. A little too bold for her liking, but in many ways he had to be as he ran this sizeable company. Her boss followed him in. He, on the other hand, looked like he badly needed a bath and always stank of body odour. His face didn't look like it had seen a razor in years, his trousers always seemed to be closer to his knees than his ankles, and he only ever wore a scummy old pair of Reebok trainers.

Mr Scrutton, the head of the firm, flicked his way through some paper work and turned to Dreanna, "We actually had a complaint about you." He didn't make eye contact. "Jo Cheesman said you were rude to her the other night, which in all honesty I find hard to believe as I've never had any complaints about you or any of your staff… Could you explain please?"

"Yep." Dreanna stared at him. "We had two people off that night with a stomach bug and I was rushing around trying my hardest to do their work as we had no one else to cover. I asked Jo if I could empty her bin, she told me to come back in an hour when she'd finished, and to be honest I didn't have time, so I just said I'm sorry but that won't be possible. She then looked me up and down and told me I will do as she asks, as I'm the cleaner and beneath her. I'm not going to lie, I turned to her and blatantly asked her what she had achieved in her life, as picking out staples from bits of paper in my opinion wasn't really anything to shout about."

"So you did argue with her?"

"No, an argument is when voices are raised, my voice was not raised."

"What else did you say?"

"I carried on saying that I had left school with a total of nine passes in my exam results, had over seven poems published in books around the world, won the Editor's Choice award for one of them, owned my own home, have been with the same man since I was fifteen, and my greatest achievement was to have three amazing daughters. I finished by saying I may be tattooed and pierced in various places but some of us are not shallow jumped–up bitches who think that a person is beneath them just because they are doing a job that they see has no importance. And without insignificant people like me you wouldn't have a job as Health and Safety would shut you down."

Mr Scrutton put his hand over his mouth as if he was in thinking mode. "So tell me young lady, what do you think of me?"

"In all honesty, you're an alright sort of chap. You've built this company from scratch, and you've worked your backside off to get where you are. You employ over one hundred people including me – without our jobs we wouldn't be able to pay for the roofs over our heads or put food on our tables – and I respect you for all you've achieved. But you are still a human being and shit the same as me and in some very strange way we all need each other to survive. So as much as I respect you I still see you as my equal; you're not better than me, you're just different."

He laughed openly. "At last, a person who doesn't kiss my arse! Thank you for your honesty Dreanna, and take it from me, Jo will be put in her place. Whatever it is that pulls you along and keeps you who you are, don't ever change. The world needs more people like you." He rubbed her arm, gathered his papers and left. Her scruffy middle–aged boss followed him through the door like a puppy dog, brown–nosing him at every opportunity and being the 'yes man' he had always been.

Dreanna shook her head and smirked, "People are fucking weird!" She left the plush meeting room and walked to the car park. Safely back in her car, she opened the window and lit a cigarette. She wasn't sure if it was the brightness of the sun that made her vision distorted or if she was coming down with a migraine; it only took her seconds to realise it was the latter. By the time she reached home her head was throbbing and her stomach churning. The slightest movement crippled her head and the mass of grey matter that lay beneath. She poured a glass of water in the kitchen, popped some tablets into her mouth, and took herself off to bed. The searing pain in her head and the nauseous feeling that heaved its way up from her abdomen pulled her in and out of consciousness. Her two dogs began barking furiously in the kitchen but she didn't have the energy or will–power to get up and see what was making them so frantic.

There were heavy footsteps on the stairs and the sound of creaking as they stopped on the landing outside her bedroom door. Dreanna knew Callum had hurt his back the day before and assumed the dogs' barking and the sound of clumsy feet approaching must have been him. She turned to face the door hoping he had bought up a cup of tea for her and a much–needed hug. The door opened. Dreanna peered out from half–closed eyes, her vision still blurred from the migraine. The figure entered her bedroom, paid no attention to her still form, and reached out to open the wardrobe door. Dreanna bolted upright, the figure froze and so did she – it wasn't Callum!

Trying her hardest to bring back her full sight, she threw off her bedclothes and kicked the door with her feet as the stranger tried to escape. She reached for his sweatshirt, but he slapped her arm hard and forced his way past her. She still couldn't see his face fully, but chased him down the hallway as he headed for the bedroom at the back of the house, its window already open. She knew she had closed that window before leaving for her meeting but he jumped out onto the flat roof of the outside toilet,threw his agile body to the ground, hoisted himself over the garden fence into the neighbours' garden and was gone.

Her body was in a state of total shock; with her hands trembling and her head exploding, she ran downstairs to pick up the phone and dial her sister. "Dawn please come round, some fucking cunt has just broken in! Please Dawn, I'm really scared." Her voice was stuttering, each breath hurting as she tried to breathe.

"Call Callum, call the police, I'm leaving now!"

Both Dawn and two police officers arrived at the exact same moment. Dreanna was standing in her garden still shaking and confused, and holding onto some stranger's arm begging her, asking her, if she saw or heard anything. The woman was pulling herself away from Dreanna's grasp, looking at her as if she was a woman possessed.

Dawn cradled her sister in her arms and led her inside the house, followed by the men in uniform. Dreanna sat with one of the officers as he wrote down all she was saying. The younger–looking policeman searched the house.

Once he was sure the assailant had well and truly gone he joined his partner at the table. "Looks like he entered through the downstairs window. The top window has been forced open so it would've been easy to stick an arm in and open the catch on the larger of the two. His footprints are on the ledge and on the flat roof at the back. Got some smudged finger prints too and dirty trainer prints on the bedroom carpet... Did you recognize this man?"

Dreanna held tight to the cup of sweet strong tea Dawn had made. "No, he was young, wearing a blue sweatshirt and jeans, and a shaved head – that's all I can say about him. It could have been James my nephew, or even one of my neighbours' sons. All teenagers look the same nowadays."

"Would you stand in a court of law and say that?"

"What, say what?" Dreanna's frowned.

"Say it was one of your neighbours' sons?"

"What? Of course I wouldn't, I don't know who it was... I just said all teen..."

"Has anything else that you can think of happened that is a little odd?"

"No I don't think so, we've misplaced a few items since we moved but..."

"But what?"

"Underwear has gone missing from our washing line, and Rebecca has lost her gold chain... do you think whoever this is has been here before?"

"Well we don't want to speculate, but we do have to examine all the facts. Anything else?"

"Not really. We don't really speak to next door – we did but don't now," Dreanna sighed, "You see one of their sons had a bit of a crush on Rebecca, he asked her out, she said no, she's only twelve and he's sixteen, so end of story really. We haven't argued or anything, just don't take much notice of them anymore. But it's not him, if that's what you think. I grew up with his mother, she's a lovely lady."

The policeman slid a piece of paper along the table in her direction. "Sign this please." He pointed to the dotted line and Dreanna signed.

An hour passed and finally Callum arrived home. Dreanna and Dawn were still sat at the dining room table.

"You're not going to believe this," Callum said as he sat down. "I've just seen that copper who you gave the statement to. They've arrested Shawn next door – they've just put him in handcuffs and thrown him in the back of their car."

"What d'you mean, arrested Shawn?" Dreanna looked confused.

"He was wearing a blue sweatshirt and jeans, and they said that's enough to arrest him."

"But it couldn't be him surely?

"Well that's not the end of it, I've just been talking to hairy Mick, you know, the mechanic. He just said the reason the people left and sold cheaply was because of all the shit they got from next door. Apparently the woman, what was her name? Oh yeah Helen, had a nervous breakdown so that's why they uprooted and moved to France. She couldn't take any more. He said that Glenda is a nasty piece of work and a bit of a psycho."

"No – I don't believe it. Are you sure?"

"Well it would explain why people kept telling us not to buy this place wouldn't it?"

Dawn pushed her chair under the table and shook her head. "It would make sense Dree, and I hate to say this but Glenda was a strange one when we were growing up. I'm off now. Don't worry about work tonight – I'll cover you. Give you a bell later, love you."

"Thanks sis, love you too."

As Dreanna pulled onto the drive after the school run she could see Glenda, the neighbour, leaning out of her bedroom window, her eyes penetrating right through every molecule of Dreanna's body.

"You fucking little whore. Have my boy arrested would you? Well you haven't heard the last of this, you cheap little slut, I'm gonna make your fucking life hell, total fucking hell you little bitch!"

"But I never said it was him! I said all teenagers looked the same, I never said it was him! I wasn't the one who arrested him, that was the copper. I even asked a lady that was waiting outside the house if she saw anything…"

"I've seen the statement you little cow, it plainly says you said it was him."

"But I didn't. I couldn't even see the person's face properly, I don't know who it was."

"Well you're gonna get it now, and your fucking sluts of daughters!" Glenda slammed shut the window.

Dreanna made her way into her house and poured boiling water from the kettle into her cup as her mind rummaged around for the words she supposedly told the policeman. 'Did I actually blame him?'

"*No Dreanna you didn't.*" Jan was with her. "*But did you read the statement the officer took?*"

"No, I couldn't see properly to read, I had a migraine, remember?"

"*So he could have written that a beast with hairy hands and six heads could have done it, and you would have signed it wouldn't you?*"

"Yes I suppose I would have. What are you saying?"

"*I'm saying you cannot step in the way of fate. Everything happens for a reason. Take care of yourself little one.*"

Moving On

November 1998
The glass doors of the hospital gleamed brightly in the morning sun. The over–
flowing steel ashtrays on either side were like smelly, grotesque statues. As
Dreanna got closer the doors opened automatically and she walked through
them towards her mother's ward. Her head was flustered and confused and an
uncomfortable feeling of fullness was trapped inside her mind. Death and dying was all around her; she could feel it, she could see it, and she could taste it.
Black emotions entered her body, and a strong pain ate its way into her core. It
wasn't the transition of death but the grief that it left behind that was using her
body like a sponge, soaking up every piece of life she had left.

She stood still, closed her eyes and used her words as her weapons: sharp,
angled spears that tried hard to defeat the emotions that whirled around in her
head. Each word she spoke grew louder until in her own mind she inwardly
screamed: 'Look straight in front of you. Don't look at the patients, don't look at
the relatives. These people are not important to you, they don't care about you
and you don't care about them. All they are is just more of your own species
that are sick and dying. IGNORE THEM, IGNORE THEM!'

Her eyes were fixed on the door of the ward sister's office. She tapped on it
gently.

"Come in," a woman's voice replied.

"Hi," Dreanna entered the room. "I'm here to see my mother, she was brought
in yesterday – Iris…"

"Oh yes, please take a seat," the skinny but perfectly groomed woman
answered. "Your mother is very sick you know. Her sores are badly infected
and she has contracted septicaemia." She shuffled some paper. "Your father
wants you to sign the 'do not resuscitate' forms. To be honest with you we
were expecting you yesterday, but I suppose you were too busy?" Her tone was
sarcastic and she frowned at Dreanna.

Dreanna looked at her and the energy she was generating in the room. Sarcastic, often thinks highly of herself, self–absorbed, controlling, hiding a secret
that's kept her prisoner all her life, arse–kisser, likes being tied up in sexual
games… hmm. Dreanna's thoughts made her smile. "I don't have to explain
anything to you as to my whereabouts yesterday, and yes, we as a family do understand how sick our mother is, and excuse my candour but your nurses – or
should I say the district nurses – have been coming in daily for the last couple

of months, so in all honesty the fault lies with them as they should have known the severity of my mother's wounds and sores. So please pass me the forms so I can sign them." Dreanna returned the same sarcastic smile she received and signed the papers that were passed over the desk to her.

"Now may I please see my mother?" Dreanna's eyes never left the gaze of the Sister.

"Did your mother never tell you it's rude to stare?" the ward sister asked.

"Did yours never tell you to be careful about getting tied to the bed? One day you might lose the keys to your handcuffs – now that would be a reason to stare wouldn't it?" Dreanna pulled her gaze away and smiled as the Sister's cheeks began to glow a bright crimson. "Bay four isn't it?"

The Sister stuttered, "Yes, but how did you know? I haven't told you yet, and how...?"

"It's on the board behind you, derr!" Dreanna sucked in her lips in a bid to contain her smile. "Thank you so much for all your help. It's been such a pleasure meeting you, keep up the good work."

Iris lay alone in a four–bedded cubical, highly sedated. Her breathing was deep and shallow, her weightless, child–like body covered by a white sheet and a bright pink duvet. A drip had been inserted into one of the frail veins in her hand, and she had a vacuous expression on her face. Dreanna moved a plastic orange chair from the corner and placed it next to her mother's bed. She held her hand in hers and stroked each finger in turn, examining their deformity and the tautness of the thin pale skin that encased each bone. She could find no words to say to her. She had no words in her mind, even her thoughts had disappeared. The darkness in her mind moved around her body and before long all she could see was the obscurity of blackness. The whole ward and hospital had disappeared from her sight. Was she now in her mother's head?

Dreanna blinked and rubbed her eyes, but the dim shadows of obscurity didn't leave her. She was in nowhere–land; a state of total limbo where she could move neither forward nor backward. There was no fear, no happiness, no movement; everything was at a standstill, everything was stagnant and halted. Iris's mind was immobile like the pathetic vessel her body had become. She was paralyzed from the neck down, wearing nappies like a newborn baby, and now her body, her vessel, was fighting for life against a rampant infection eating its way through her like maggots feeding on necrotic tissue. How strong was her mother's body to keep fighting in this way? Dreanna knew she would have to be the stalwart figure here, she would have to be robust and resilient. Whatever was to come, whatever was to happen, there had to be a reason. There is always a reason, isn't there? She was brought back to earth by her mother shouting one solitary word.

"Glenda!" Iris was clearly incensed.

Dreanna gazed, astonished that her mother had actually said something, but why 'Glenda', her neighbour?

"She sees all that is going on, Dreanna." A voice came from nowhere.

Dreanna repeated, "She sees all that is going on? So she really is split between the distance of time and the transition of death. She really is stuck in limbo, isn't she?"

"Yes my child she is."

Dreanna shook her head like a dog shaking water from its fur; reality had returned and so had the ward, the bed and her mother's unnatural state. She kissed Iris's hand and left the hospital, knowing wherever and whatever was going on in her life, her mother somehow observed it all from afar.

May 1999

"Mummy!" Fawn screamed as she run straight into her parent's bedroom. "What's that noise? I'm scared!" Fawn was soon joined by her sisters, both screaming and crying and wondering what was happening. The windows of their house were rattling in their frames, the walls were vibrating and the whole house was moving and pulsating. Callum and Dreanna jumped out of bed and Dreanna pulled all three daughters close to her while Callum reached out and turned on the bedroom light.

"This is a fucking joke!" he shouted. "If it isn't enough that they've fucking pissed up our front door, fucking threatened a seven-year-old, hung a fucking blown–up alien by the neck with your name on it in their garden, they now have to fucking use a whacker plate at gone midnight in their fucking house! Sorry Dree but I've had a fucking belly full." Callum paused to catch his breath. "Why the fucking hell didn't you let the family sort out all this crap before it got to this stage? They wouldn't have had any fucking knee-caps left by now. This is your fault it's got this far!"

Dreanna held on tight to her daughters, stroking each of their faces and wiping the tears from them as they fell. "Callum shut up, you're scaring the girls even more. You can't fight violence with violence, just call Geoff and then call the police. Please, I'm begging you, don't do anything. Everything happens for a reason – everything!"

Callum glared at his wife. "You're fucking mental woman, you really are!" his voice bellowing as loud as it could above the exaggerated din of the machinery next door.

Geoff, a neighbour from two doors away, stood in their lounge with his fingers pressed tight into his ears as the deafening sound hit the back of his ear drums. He walked to the window and pulled back the curtains as a police car pulled onto the drive. As the police got out of their their vehicle the noise stopped, the house fell silent.

"Thanks for coming," Callum said as the officers entered the house. He continued to explain the events of the last hour.

A young female officer who had been writing all the information down shut her note book. "Well it looks like they've got bored now and as it's gone silent I think it's best if we just record this and leave it be. Any more problems, then give us another call."

"Sorry?" Dreanna asked. "Every bloody thing they've done in the last few months we've recorded. How much more crap do we have to put up with and fucking record before you actually do something? My children are petrified. They get escorted to and from their lessons at school because one of their sons put his hands round my daughter's neck and pinned her to a locker – we've called you each time they do something. Surely enough is enough now?"

"But you see, they haven't actually threatened anybody have they?" The second officer spoke.

"Not threatened? What do you call shouting at a seven-year-old child 'I'm gonna kill you', then? I'm sorry I just can't be bothered with all this crap right now. My advice to you, young PC Plod, is to start to ask some questions, like how the hell they manage to run a youth club when the husband has a record for grievous bodily harm, or why the sergeant in charge of your nick seems to spend an awful lot of time around their house drinking beer. Sorry but this is all bollocks. I think you should just leave, go please! Just get out of my house."

Dreanna held open the front door, shaking her head from side to side and biting her bottom lip. The anger had built up in her stomach and she looked with disgust at the officers as they walked back to their car. Within minutes of their leaving the thunderous sound started again.

Dreanna looked at Callum. "I'm taking the kids to sleep in the back room, and if you really wanna go and kick ten bails of shit out of them, be my guest. Just be prepared for the fact you'll be the one going down, not them!"

A cold breeze was blowing through the open window in the bedroom at the back of the house, and the stars that had filled the clear night sky slowly disappeared as dawn broke. The early morning sunshine fell across her children's faces as finally they lay sleeping curled up in one bed, the covers pulled tight around their young bodies. She stared lovingly at them as she sat on the window sill; all was quiet and still, the noise from next door had stopped. Dreanna pulled the tiny window closed as a shiver went down her spine. Her fingers tingled and every nerve and muscle contracted as an electric shock travelled through her body.

"One more week Dreanna; they will be gone in one more week. You know everything happens for a reason; even the bad things we experience have to happen to make us be

where we are supposed to be. You blame yourself for all this but please stop. This isn't because of you; this is not a lesson that you have needed to learn as some would tell you. This is not about making your children afraid or hurting them. This has happened for no other reason than to move your neighbours to the place they need to be. If this never occurred then they would not meet the people they are destined to meet, they would not do the things they are supposed to do in this life. They would never have come up with the idea of moving far away from here and starting again.

Please my child, please know that wherever you are you are protected as we will guard you and shelter you from harm."

Dreanna's body jolted as she gasped a sharp intake of breath. Her startled response knocked an ornament off the ledge she had been sitting on and woke up Rebecca. Within minutes all three girls were wide awake so they made their way downstairs to the living room where Callum and Geoff had spent the night. Dreanna, her body still prickling from the high voltage that had scorched its way through her system, followed them downstairs.

Callum shouted from the living room, "Now you can fucking stop! One more thing and I promise I will rip your fucking heads off!"

Dreanna ran into the living room to see Glenda leaning over the fence a broken broom stick in her hand, a look of trepidation across her face. Callum still stared in her direction; in one hand he held the curtain and in the other his fist was clenched. Glenda pulled away and disappeared from sight.

"What the hell has happened now?" Dreanna asked.

Geoff spoke, "I think she thought the girls had come down and turned on the telly, Glenda obviously heard them and started hitting the glass of the door with that broken broom, calling them sluts and saying she's going to get them. I think she got a bit of a surprise when your old man was the one that actually opened the curtains, she's been caught well and truly in the act."

Callum's face was distorted with rage and he didn't hesitate as he flung open the door. He wedged his feet on the wooden slats of the fence, hoisted himself upwards so he could see into their garden, and roared with anger at the family that had caused his children so much distress, "I fucking mean it – one more thing and I promise you, you'll know what it's like to spend the rest of your sad pathetic little lives in a wheelchair. You wanna play the hard man, you little cunts, come on then let's see who has the biggest bollocks shall we?"

Dreanna walked outside and grabbed Callum, her hand gently stroking his leg. "Leave it Callum, they'll be gone soon. Come inside, forget them, they're not worth it. Please, they'll be gone soon I promise."

He looked down at his wife and glared once more at the faces of Glenda and her sons staring at him from an upstairs window. Then he jumped to the ground.

Dreanna watched the slow passage of each day – even the hands of the clock seemed to move more slowly than usual. Every day she woke up hoping that the neighbours from hell would be finally gone, but each morning they were still there and in the evenings they set fire to old car tyres, the rubber burning ferociously, choking the environment with thick black smoke. But they had become silent; no more two–fingered gestures, no more abuse, and every evening there was peace.

She sat in the stillness and tranquility of her garden enjoying the last of the autumn sunshine. Glenda and her family had left early that morning and had still not returned. It was mid–afternoon. There was no black smoke, no crackling of flames, and no fear from what might be next in store for her. She inhaled and tasted the fresh flavor of the air as if for the first time, looked upwards to the heavens and sighed a huge sigh of relief. The clouds were gently floating above her head as her body relaxed for the first time in months. The silence and her serenity was interrupted by a knock on her front door.

"Hi, I just thought I would introduce myself. I'm Sandy and am going to be your new neighbour. We're moving in on Friday but I thought I'd come and introduce myself now."

The biggest smile spread across Dreanna's face, "Oh right! Okay, well it's lovely to meet you and I so hope you're really happy in your new home." Dreanna couldn't help but laugh out loud; this day was just getting better and better.

"Sorry, did I say something to amuse you?"

Dreanna flung her arms around this stranger's neck. "No, not amuse me, but you've just made my day. Thank you! Thank you so very, very, much."

Till Death do us Part

December 2001

Each step made the ladder creak louder as Dreanna reached the opening to the loft. Leaning against the ladder for support, she wiped away the silky cobwebs that hung above her and winced as the trapped cold air surrounded her body like a wedding ring around a finger. She had always hated the dark and even now at thirty-three years old she slept with a light on. The hairs on the back of her neck stood up and her breathing became rapid as her fingers searched for the light to guard her against the depressing darkness. The light flickered and shone brightly and for one moment her vision was completely distorted. She sighed with relief as the yellow tinge of the light bulb lit up the murky room.

Hands on hips, she looked at the extreme amount of clutter they had gathered over the years. All she wanted was to find the Christmas decorations that were concealed somewhere in this mountain of chaos. She heaved out the way the copious amounts of junk that lay in her path and searched for the baubles, tinsel and tree that every year stood proudly in the lounge with bundles of presents beneath it. She placed her hand instead on the edge of a plastic box and pulled it towards her. It had been filled with many photographs through the years and was now a box full of memories that made up her life.

As with most people, she couldn't help but pick up a handful and look at each one in turn, some making her smile, others reminding her of times she'd spent her life trying to forget. Pictures of her school days that haunted her, pictures of her nana that made her smile, pictures of Callum's dad and his last dying days... her body was overwhelmed with a tide of emotions. Her reminiscing was halted by Callum shouting up from the floor below.

"What you doing up there? Have you found the decorations yet?"

"Erm no...sorry, was looking at other stuff. Hold on, I'll look in another place."

"Well bloody hurry up, the kids are driving me insane. They wanna decorate the tree... Shit, there's someone at the door, be back in a min."

Dreanna threw the pictures back in the box and was about to close it when she noticed one of her mum and dad. It was taken over thirty years ago and they looked so happy, so young, so healthy. Their arms were around each other's waists, and they were holding and squeezing each other tightly.

The soothing tones of Maltilda were with her. *"They'll be together soon. A love like theirs never dies but grows stronger after death. Soon Dreanna, soon."*

Dreanna was about to speak when Callum called out to her once again.

"Dree, you really need to come and see this."

"But I'm looking for the decorations. Can't do both at once you know."

"Leave it, you really, really, need to come and see this."

Dreanna didn't realise she had been kneeling for so long as pins and needles shot through her legs and feet, making standing uncomfortable. Climbing down the ladder, she called out, "This better be important!"

"Oh you're going to love this, I promise." He grabbed her hand and led her in to the next-door neighbours' house. She was greeted on the landing by Sandy and Brian, the new neighbours.

"We didn't know whether to show you this or not," Brian explained, "but thought in the end you should see it." He moved out of the way to reveal a wall full of pictures and words all written in indelible black marker-pen.

Dreanna's mouth fell open as she read out loud all that was written.

'Callum is a fucking poo-pushing cunt, Dreanna takes it up the arse and is nothing more than a prostitute, a low life whore. Fawn is the Devil's child who will rot and burn in a fire of shit, Leticia is a cunt of a child, Rebecca is a slut prick-teasing bastard, Geoff is a back-stabbing arse-licker who fucks his own children…'

On and on it went, each person that had lived on the estate that they hated was abused in some manner either with words or pictures.

"I, I, I really don't know what to say," Dreanna stuttered.

"That's not all of it." Sandy ushered them into another bedroom where another wall of abuse stared straight at her, then grabbed hold of her hand and led her into the final bedroom and yet another wall.

"That's still not quite it," Sandy said as she led the way downstairs into the kitchen.

Dreanna and Callum looked around.

"There's nothing written in here," Callum said.

"Not on the walls, but pull out the drawers of the kitchen units."

Callum pulled out one drawer then another and another, the same insensitive, dull-witted insults that had filled the bedroom walls upstairs were written on the sides of each drawer in turn.

"How long did you endure all this?" Sandy asked him.

"Too long, but it wasn't just us. It was the people that lived here before and some of the other residents on the estate. The police were told about everything but nothing was ever done. Imagine our relief when you moved in."

"Well we'll take pictures of everything for the record of course, and please don't worry. We really are nothing like these people – if people is the right word to use."

Dreanna looked at Sandy. "They're in the past now. Time to forget and move on." She rubbed Sandy's arm and left.

January 25th 2002

With the decorations finally taken down and the excitement of Christmas nothing more than a distant memory, Dreanna's household seemed strangely calm. For the first time in months Fawn overcame her fear of heading to the bathroom upstairs alone, Leticia was once again enjoying school and Rebecca seemed to have taken on a whole new approach to life. The end of the horrible abuse from their old neighbours had given the girls a new spring in their step, but in the back of her mind Dreanna wondered whether any of them would be able to trust another person again. At the end of the day she didn't trust anyone either, as every person she came across that she'd given a special part of herself to had sooner or later decided to leave her. But she would always smile and be polite and laugh to herself in the knowledge that no matter what they said, she had the ability to know what they were really thinking and what they were saying behind her back. 'A new year, a new start,' she told herself as she started getting ready for work that evening.

She had just finished washing up the last of the dinner plates when the phone rang.

It was Patrice. "Hey Dree, erm... I've just come round to Dad's with his shopping and he's not looking too good. I've actually phoned the Doctor and he's on his way now. Can you come round too... please?" She sounded really worried.

"Can you really not handle it Sis? I'm just about to go to work."

"No I don't think I can. He really does look rough and doesn't seem to be breathing properly."

Dreanna left for her father's house. The door was wide open as she walked down the garden path and he was already being examined by the doctor. His shirt was opened at the chest and the doctor's was concentrating on the sounds coming through his stethoscope. He held up Patrick's hands and looked intently at each finger. Dreanna and Patrice just stood and stared. Patrick's fingernails were blue.

"Patrick... may I call you Patrick?" the doctor asked.

Patrick nodded.

"I'd like you to go into hospital for a few tests. I can arrange for an ambulance to pick you up as soon as you're ready. There's a possibility that they will keep you in for a few days, but I really think we need to get you there sooner rather than later."

Patrick shook his head and stared at Dreanna.

"Dad doesn't want to go to hospital – he wants to stay here. We'll look after him... Maybe Monday, eh Dad?" She looked back at her father. He nodded.

"Well I can't force you Patrick. I'll arrange the tests for Monday then, but if you need us in the meantime please don't hesitate to call." The doctor returned his stethoscope to his bag and walked towards the door, followed by Dreanna. He turned on the doorstep to face her. "Your father is a very sick man and I would really advise you to try and persuade him to go into hospital as soon as possible. I'll arrange the tests for first thing on Monday morning. Can you get him to the hospital?"

"Monday, hm, yes," Dreanna answered. The word Monday floated around in her mind, changing colour and stopping at the space at the inside of her forehead, huge capital letters shining brightly MONDAY.

After work that evening the three sisters met up in the local pub. They sat around a table, none of them knowing how to approach the subject of their father's health. Dawn and Patrice's heads were bent low as they fingered the edges of their glasses and Dreanna looked hopelessly into space, the word MONDAY still shining inside her brain. As usual on a Friday night the pub was relatively busy, the familiar faces from the estate sat in their favourite places, chatting to their friends and laughing at the right moments. The jukebox blared out dated songs that were only suitable for a room full of middle-aged people and their memories.

Dreanna stared at some old photographs that hung lop-sidedly on the wall. All were of soldiers that had been burnt in the Second World War. They were the guinea pigs of Sir Archibald Mcindoe, a pioneer of plastic surgery, hence the name of the pub 'The Guinea Pig'. So many times as a child these disfigured faces had haunted her dreams, and each time she entered the pub as an adult she would be drawn to the pain they had suffered, the heartache of their families who knew that their proud sons, who had once stood tall in uniform would now have to walk through society with heads bent afraid that their disfigured features would scare some child. They were not ashamed of their scars, far from it. They just had to learn to live in a society that had trouble accepting them as they were. She admired their courage and bravery and she admired the way they risked their lives so their families at home could have the freedom they needed. But she could never understand why a human being would want to maim another, or disfigure them in such a manner. But then again she had felt the hate that drove men to this. Why would anyone want hate to have precedence over love?

Dawn was the first to break the silence. "What are we going to do?"

Patrice and Dreanna looked at each other.

"We're gonna look after him," Patrice said.

Dawn's next question hit all three right in the heart. "But what if he dies?"

"We're all gonna die someday, and maybe soon it's Dad's time," Dreanna looked down at the table knowing the words she had spoken put fear in her sisters' hearts. Patrick was the pin that held their family together. None of them wanted to lose him. "We'll take it in shifts. Dawn you can do the first shift of the day."

"I ...I can't Dree. What if he dies in the night? I couldn't cope with that." Dawn answered.

Patrice agreed, "Nor can I. You'll have to do it."

Both sisters stared at Dreanna, who still looked at the table.

Dawn said, "I'll do his dinners and lunch and washing, and Patrice can do the shopping and other stuff, but we can't do all that personal stuff. You did it for Mum, so please can you do it for Dad too?"

"Dawn... I don't know. Washing Mum was horrible, but at least she had the same as me," Dreanna pointed to her pelvic region. "I just don't know if... if I could wash Dad's private parts."

"Dad wouldn't let you anyway," Patrice said, lifting the remnants of her drink to her mouth. "Let's just take each day as it comes shall we?"

The sisters nodded.

Dreanna slid her key into the lock, letting herself into the family home. Patrick was sitting in his chair in the living room. His breathing was laboured and his hand lay across his chest. For the first time in her life she saw an old man staring back at her. The strong man who had looked after her was nowhere to be seen and all that was left was a wrinkly, slightly chubby, bearded, crumbling old man. His fingers were stained with nicotine, his shirt was buttoned up wrongly so that it gaped at his chest and his big toe poked through the end of his sock. God, he was a scruffy old bugger.

"Cup of tea Pops?"

Patrick nodded.

She squatted down on the floor at his feet, picking fluff from the carpet.

"Shall I do a bit of cleaning?" She didn't really know what to say to him.

Patrick nodded.

She lifted herself from the floor. "Are you in pain, does it hurt?"

Patrick nodded

"Promise me one thing – that I'm with you when it happens. Please don't die alone."

Patrick spoke. "You come into this world alone, you leave this world alone. Tell me Dreanna," he gasped for breath, "would you watch me having a shit?"

"Ooo Dad, course I wouldn't... well not if I could help it."

"Dying is a personal thing," he gasped, "just like going to the loo, some things are best done alone okay?"

"Understood... but I still want to be with you. I think we ought to bring a bed downstairs too for you, and have you still got Mum's commode lying around? 'I doubt you'll make it upstairs to the loo."

"It's in the shed and broken... I can manage." He glared back at her.

"Yep, course you can! Well you'll have to piss in a bucket then till I can sort a new one out Monday." MONDAY lit up inside her head again.

"Whatever you say Dreanna," Patrick's eyes met hers.

"Monday it is then Dad."

With her house cleaned, school uniforms washed and ironed, and a chicken roasting slowly in the oven, Dreanna left to check on her father. The day before, Callum and the sisters had brought a bed down from upstairs and Dreanna had cleaned out a bucket for him to urinate in, hoping that his ill health would finally win over his stubbornness.

Patrick was lying fully clothed on the bed. The room was dark, the curtains tightly closed. He didn't speak but nodded his head as she bent down to pick up the half full bucket he had used through the night. When she reached the toilet and began pouring out its contents, it was the colour of fresh blood with crimson red droplets dribbling down the sides of the pan. She hastily pulled the chain. Her heart was burning and her eyes began to fill with tears. She leant on the wall for strength; she was so scared, her world was crumbling. By the time she had composed herself and returned downstairs Patrick had somehow managed to sit up on the bed with his legs awkwardly positioned on the floor.

She wasn't going to let him see her upset, so she smiled brightly at him. "Bloody lazy old sod, what time do you call this? I don't know what the older generation's coming to. Cuppa?"

He looked at her, slowly nodding his head.

"Dad, I don't really wanna do this, but I think you need a wash. I've brought some clean clothes down from upstairs, socks and pants. Will you allow me to wash you?"

Patrick gasped in a gigantic amount of air, "Not on your bloody nelly! Leave me a bowl of water, I'll do it myself."

"I'm not going to argue with you, but if you can't do it I will."

"Dreanna." Patrick paused to inhale deeply, "go home... Go home to your kids." He touched her arm and she felt instantly cold, as if her heart was being ripped in two.

Her head felt as if razor blades were being forced through her skull. She wanted to run, to hide, to curl into a fetal ball and grip herself tight till the world disappeared. But she took hold of Patrick's hand. "On one condition. I want to be with you."

Patrick made no movement. "Go home."

So Dreanna obeyed.

Later at home, she played with the roast dinner on her plate, pushing it around, the food not touching her lips. Her body felt numb, her head still full of razor blades. She took her plate into the kitchen, ran the tap and washed up, paying no attention to whether things were clean or not. She didn't care. She felt hopeless and numb, without any physical sensation at all.

"Mum," Rebecca stood watching her mother, "is Grandad going to be okay?"

"Granddad is..."

Leticia was standing next to her sister, their eyes waiting for her response.

"Granddad is ...is going to be happy again."

She walked past her children and took herself upstairs. She lay on her bed and stared at the ceiling. Her body shivered and she reached for the duvet and wrapped it around herself. Her eyes closed and she slept. In her dream state her mind filled with the sound of ticking. She was standing in the kitchen of her family home, staring at the clock on the wall. Every second ticked by, every minute got slower and slower, until it stopped, at 12:04am. Then she was awake, but her house was dark and quiet. She reached for the alarm clock, 11:45pm. She looked at Callum sleeping, mouth open wide and snoring, then stared down at herself, realising she was still in her clothes. She got out of bed, walked across the landing to the bathroom and began to get undressed, the cutting-edged blade still piercing through her head. Filling the sink she soaked a flannel to wash her face. She froze. The pain was gone. 'Why am I washing in the middle of the night?' She walked back to her bedroom; the alarm clock read 12:04am. The rest of that night she lay unable to sleep, but unable to move.

Matilda was in her mind. *"Be brave my little one, be brave."*

The girls' school bags were packed and all three were waiting for Dawn to pick them up and take them to school. Dreanna sat at the breakfast bar trying to gather her thoughts. The sound of Dawn's car horn made her jump and brought her back to reality. She hugged and kissed each of her children in turn and waved to her sister from the front door. With all the children safely buckled into the car Dawn drove off. There was a bitter chill in the air although the ground barely showed any of the previous night's frost. Dreanna breathed in deeply. The phone rang.

"Hey Dree, how's your dad today?" Callum asked.

"I think he's dead." Her voice sounded pathetic and stuttering.

"Are you sure?"

"No, I, er, haven't been round..."

"How the fuck do you know he's dead then?"

"Callum... I... I'm scared; I don't know if I can do this."

"Don't be such a tit. Pull yourself together and go sort out your dad, and I'll call you later okay?" He hung up.

Dreanna pulled up and parked on the grass verge outside her family home. Unable to move out of the car, she felt her hands shaking, and that sick panicky fear eating away at her. 'Be brave,' she told herself, 'Be strong'. She took a deep breath and opened the car door. She reached inside her jacket for the front door key, but her hand wouldn't stop shaking and she couldn't get the key into the lock. She stamped her feet, getting angry for not being strong and tried again. The front door opened. The house was silent. She held the handle of the living room door but couldn't pull it down. For five minutes she stood still, not moving. Then she closed her eyes, gulped in another deep breath and pulled the handle downwards. Patrick was sitting in his chair in his pants and vest, a flannel in one hand, a bowl of water by his feet. His eyes were tightly closed.

Dreanna whispered his name, "Dad?"

No one answered.

"Dad, wake up." Her bottom lip began to quiver. "Dad please, please wake up."

No one answered.

The tears flowed down her face but she swallowed them back. "Fancy sitting here in your pants and vest in the middle of winter, you'll catch your death of cold!" She reached for a blanket and covered her father. His body was a block of ice, his skin a bluish grey. She kissed him tenderly on the forehead and collapsed at his feet. "I wanted to be with you. Don't leave me… Dad, please don't leave me. I can't live without you, you're the only one that understands me, you're my only friend… Dad! Please wake up!" She cried until she had nothing left inside, and she was frozen just like her father's body.

Finally she stood up. She had to be strong, she had to be strong! "Cup of tea Pops? Yep, cup of tea …always makes you feel better, isn't that what you always say?" She fought with the broken catch on the kettle forcing it to stay on. Once it had boiled she poured the water into her cup and watched the bag slowly releasing its flavour. Her eyes took in the clock on the wall; 12:04. It had stopped dead. It wasn't ticking; the hands were no longer moving.

Dreanna sat alone at the table drinking her tea and playing with an unopened packet of her father's cigarettes. Her body was strangely composed even though the house was freezing. So many questions poured into her mind: 'What was last night about? Was I doing what Dad was doing? Was the pain I was feeling his? Is death really so infinite? Why is he not here to say goodbye? Why did you take him from me? Why did I have to find him?'

With both hands around her cup she blew in it and sipped it slowly. The house had never been so silent. Even with Patrick living there alone and Iris in the nursing home, there was always noise, always music, always the ticking of that bastard clock hanging on the wall. But now nothing, not even the stupid bird in the dining room was squawking, it was just sitting on its perch admiring itself in the mirror.

"Fucking stupid bird!" Dreanna spoke aloud. "You really are an ugly bird, and why do you do that stupid thing with your beak? Why is no one answering me, telling me what to do next, telling me Dad is okay? Where are you all? Where have you gone?" Her questions remained unanswered.

Her eyes began to well up again, the tears fell and her cheeks glowed red as the apprehension of telling her family built up inside her. She didn't want to go back in the living room with the body of her dead father sitting in the chair, but if she didn't, who would? The phone was on the table next to his chair and she paused at the doorway staring at the man, his dignity covered by the blanket. She moved over to stroke his bald head, stroking his white hair back into place, hoping the warmth from the blanket would have reached his frozen body. It hadn't. Dreanna pulled open the curtains just enough to be able to see the numbers in his telephone book. She lifted the phone.

"Appointments," the lady on the other end said.

"Erm, Doctor... Doctor, I'm sorry I can't remember who it was," she began to ramble, "Saw my father on Friday and he's, er, sleeping now."

"He's sleeping?" the woman questioned her.

"Sorry... I mean... I mean," she forced the words out of her mouth. "He's died, my dad is dead."

February 2002

The day of the funeral arrived soon enough and the last few days seemed to go so quickly, but Dreanna couldn't remember them. Dawn and Patrice took it upon themselves to visit Iris in the nursing home and tell her that her husband had died. Callum tried to persuade Dreanna to go too, and didn't understand when she said her Mum died years ago. Dreanna had sorted out the funeral, the hymns, the order of service, and now had to sort out herself and be strong enough to get through this day.

Patrick's will stated no black, and no flowers. The 'no black' suited her but no-one listened to the 'no flowers' and his coffin overflowed with wreaths from well-wishers and family.

The hearse pulled up outside the family home. Dreanna was sitting on the window sill in the upstairs bedroom, her legs dangling outside just like in her childhood.

Leticia tapped her mother on the back. "Mummy, Daddy says it's time to go now."

Dreanna nodded in her direction.

The family and friends stood outside the crematorium waiting for the coffin to arrive. Dreanna smiled as each person in turn told her how sorry they were for her loss or how wonderful Patrick was. She wondered why so many had turned out to say their goodbyes. Patrick hadn't seen many of them in months or even years, but here they were hovering like flies around excrement giving their condolences to his children.

"Where were they when Dad needed a friend?" Dreanna whispered in Patrice's ear.

"Er what?"

"All these busy-bodies, look at them. Pretending they care, pretending they loved Dad. Half of them wouldn't know what love is, fucking hypocrites!"

"Dreanna, that's a bit unfair."

"Is it? Is it really?... So tell me, when Dad needed a friend or someone to talk to when Mum lost the plot, tell me which one of these fuckwits actually came to see him or Mum?... Come on Sis, which one?"

Patrice's eyes scanned the crematorium. "Point taken."

"Pisses me right off. Can't be there for someone in life then don't fucking be there when they die, 'cos they don't need your help then do they?"

The congregation took their seats and waited for the coffin to be positioned in front of them. The vicar stood at the front of the altar, waffling on and on about this man he never knew, telling the audience his body was soon to be resurrected and he would be held safe for eternity in the hands of God.

Dreanna stared at Callum and mouthed, "What a load of bollocks."

"Shh Dree."

She felt frustrated and angry. Angry that Patrick had died, angry that all these so-called friends and family turned out to say goodbye, angry at their complete ignorance, and angry at the stupid vicar who talked endless words of religion about this high and almighty powerful God that loves all his children – all the children that in Dreanna's mind were killing each other every day. This wonderful father who watched as his children were starving to death because of the lack of food, because of disease and hatred. Innocent children that each day were abused by some kiddie-fiddling pudenda that got his kicks out of pleasuring himself while stealing the innocence of a child. Oh this father, this God is such a wonderful man! Her anger was turning into a fire in her stomach. She breathed deeply to calm herself, her attention pulled to the piece of paper in her hands. It was a poem Patrick had written many years before his death, and William and Dreanna would soon read it aloud. She calmed her thoughts and turned to the job in hand as the vicar announced, "Patrick's children would like to talk about their father."

They stood in front of the waiting congregation. Dreanna unfolded the poem and ushered William to come closer.

He shook his head. "I can't."

Dreanna sighed and stared at the words on the page. She began reading.

> "I went to bed, not feeling well,
> My eyes slowly closed, and darkness fell.
> Into a deep sleep, vivid dreams I had...
> And there in a circle of pure white light,
> Stood Mum and Dad.
> Arms outstretched, reaching out for me..."

She choked. She couldn't hold it in as the tears ran down her face and she couldn't breathe. She missed him, she needed him and she wanted him back.

The vicar reached out and tapped her on the shoulder, "Give it to me, I'll read it."

Dreanna stared at him, the tears flowing like a flooded river from her eyes, "No...! He's *my* dad!"

> "Smiles on their faces, their souls are free.
> They come closer and clutched my hand,
> To know they are there is something grand.
> I leave my bed and hand in hand we go,
> On a journey, to where, I shall not know.
> Travelling through the cold night air,
> We reach golden gates, I can only stare.
> The gates slowly open and inside I'm led,
> Dad on one side and Mum strokes my head.
> The colours I see, I've not seen before,
> A calm, calm sea, runs by the shore.
>
> No noise, no wind, but peace is there,
> People I see, but they do not stare.
> Joyful, happy children playing there,
> No houses I see, but they don't care.
>
> My worried face, my mother sees,
> She comes and then she cradles me.
> She smiles and clutches, at her heart,
> And slowly tells me, that from Earth I have to depart.
>
> We are together now, you're not alone,
> This land my son is your new home..."

The vicar caught Dreanna as they were about to leave and make their way to the wake. "God gave you the strength to read today – he gave you courage."

Dreanna blinked slowly and lifted her gaze to his. "God gave me nothing."

"But God is your father."

"God is not my father. My father is now being burnt, soon to be nothing more than a pile of ash and dust." Her words were brusque and curt.

"You do not believe in God?"

"I'm beginning to not believe in anything."

"But you must believe in something. You have a tattoo of a pentagram on your neck. Are you a pagan?"

Dreanna repeated, "I believe in nothing." And she turned and walked away.

May 16th 2002

Dreanna was standing at the ironing board, her legs aching, her arms hurting and her body feeling like it had been kicked by a horse. She was tired and weak and beginning to lose all hope that life actually did have a good side. Since losing Patrick she had become so angry and incensed, nothing seemed to matter anymore. She believed in nothing, she had no faith, and she wouldn't answer any of the voices in her head. Everything was now just a figment of her imagination; an imagination that at times would run away with her. She was trying hard to re-build her life without the one man she loved more than anyone else. Patrick was her rock, her friend, and her father. Each day that passed she thought of him, the pain building up inside. It cut her to the core that he was no longer in her life. His stupid bloody crosswords, his stupid bloody parrot, his stupid, often rude, sense of humour, she missed it all, even his stubbornness.

She wasn't the only one who was suffering. She could also see it in the eyes of her daughters, her siblings and their children, but life had to go on, and they all were trying hard to continue theirs in the best way they knew how. The children were playing outside in the late spring sunshine. Dreanna watched as Fawn tried to hit a shuttlecock back to her sister. Fawn threw it up in the air, swung her racket and missed. Over and over again she tried and each time she missed it. Fawn stared at her racket.

"Fawn," Dreanna called, "I think you've got a hole in your racket."

Fawn looked up from the bottom of the garden in her mother's direction. She lifted the racket, poking her finger through the tiny holes, then she picked up the shuttlecock and tried squeezing it through one of them.

She shouted to Dreanna, "But it doesn't fit through the holes."

Dreanna smirked.

"It's my go anyway," an impatient Rebecca said, as she grabbed the racket out of Fawn's hands.

With a disgruntled look at her sister, Fawn began walking up the garden.

"You're shit anyway," Leticia said as she passed her.

"Leticia, language!" Dreanna gave Leticia a defiant stare.

"Well you swear, and Granddad used to let me say it."

"Yeah well I'm older than you, and Granddad isn't here anymore is he?"

Fawn sat down on the step that separated the patio from the edge of the lawn and Dreanna joined her. Both watched the other two children, the shuttlecock never quite going where it was supposed to, but each one doing their best to run and hit it back over the net. Dreanna propped her elbows on her knees and leaned her head into the palm of her hands. Fawn copied. Dreanna scratched her head. Fawn copied. Dreanna stuck her finger up her nose. Fawn copied. Dreanna turned her head and looked at Fawn. Fawn looked back at her, both of them still with their fingers up their noses.

"I think," Dreanna said, "it's time to make a mud pie."

"I think," Fawn answered, "we should."

They chased each other into the shed and came out with a plastic bucket and spade, made their way to a corner of the garden and began filling their buckets. The mud in the garden had already dried from the last few warm spring days and its dusty appearance made them cough as it mixed with the air. Dreanna threw the spade to the ground, knelt down and used her hands like claws. Dragging the sod towards her, Fawn scooped it up and filled her bucket. "Mummy, where is Granddad? My teacher said he's in Heaven."

Dreanna could feel the tears coming but continued digging the ground with her hands. "There's no such place, Fawn. When you die you just die, you become just like this mud, you're nothing but dust."

"But she said you carry on living in Heaven."

"No Fawn, there's no such place as Heaven, the only way you are kept alive is in someone's head. You become nothing more than a memory... that's all you are, a memory." Dreanna swallowed. "Right, we need water, lots and lots of water."

The hose pipe flowed into the buckets as both began squelching the mud between their fingers. They were giggling, a childish giggle, as each finger nail in turn filled with the brown mess. Dreanna lifted a handful and dolloped it on Fawn's head.

"Hey, that's not fair," Fawn squealed. Her hands now full of mud and she hurled a load at her mother. Each now armed with a bucket of wet soggy mud they darted around the garden, trying to land it on anything that moved including Rebecca and Leticia. The mud-flinging contest had began, and before long all the family were filling their hands and lobbing wet soil at each other.

Callum, not wanting to be outdone by the females, lifted the badminton racket and tried using his wife and daughters as moving targets, his weapon the shuttlecock. With one hit the shuttlecock went flying through the air, all of them watching and waiting to see if they had to move out the way as it soared high in the sky. They didn't. It landed in the next-door neighbour's garden.

"Dad, jump the fence like they do on *Jackass!*" Leticia screamed.

Callum launched himself at the fence, charging like a bull at a red rag. The family chortled loudly. Callum, undefeated by this six foot high wooden boundary, walked backwards and charged again, but his foot caught in a pot-hole in the grass and he fell to the ground clutching his ankle. Their chortles got louder and louder as they joined Callum on the grass, holding their stomachs as their muscles hurt, not one of them asking if he was okay. Their laughter turned into hysterics as they rolled around, faces covered in mud, bellies aching, and for the first time in ages tears fell from their eyes through happiness not grief.

June 2002

The gravel crunched as Dreanna walked across it. In front of her was the old stone building of her mother's nursing home. The grounds surrounding it were truly amazing, well-kept grass and trees further than the eye could see, rabbits running freely and an array of different birds in the air above. It was quiet and peaceful, a place she would love to have lived in herself if only she had the money to buy such a property. But the inside was dark, cold and depressing. Ill-fitting carpets frayed at the edges, paper and paint peeled off the walls, dark wooden furniture showed every speck of dust, and that god-awful smell of vegetables and urine spread through the whole building. There were shouts from residents suffering some form of dementia or just the boredom of old age. The old, the sick and the dying sat in every spare corner as you walked through the corridors. Occasionally one of them would greet you, shaking your hand not willing to let it go, their endless chatter making it impossible to move away. Dreanna's heart always sank each time she arrived. How she hated the sadness she felt. She hated the look on their faces, she hated seeing them all herded together in one room, forced to sit in chairs and watch some crap on the television... but more importantly she hated the fact that her Mum was in this place.

The office manager had called her the day before, complaining that Iris's bill hadn't been paid, and that they now owed over three thousand pounds and if it wasn't paid the home would take legal action. Iris's pension from her hospital job paid her £7 a week and both this and her state pension were paid straight to the nursing home for her upkeep. The rest of the money they had to pay came from what was left of Patrick's life insurance and Callum and Dreanna's combined savings. Dreanna had always been good at paying her bills and couldn't understand why the nursing home were demanding more money. She had paid them in full every month since Patrick died and had never once forgotten.

She knocked on the door that read 'Manager' and was asked to take a seat outside the office as the owner of the establishment wanted to speak to her personally. Dreanna watched as some frail old lady still dressed in her nightdress was escorted out of the lift opposite her. Her hair lay limp on her shoulders, un-brushed and dirty. Her hands held tight to the care home assistant who was busily talking to her colleague. Neither had noticed that this poor old lady's backside was hanging out for all to see. Dreanna got up out of the chair and pulled her nightgown down to cover her bare arse. Their eyes met.

"I want to die, when can I go?"

The care assistant nudged Dreanna, "Wish they would all fucking die, make my life a bit easier," she laughed with her friend.

"Soon," Dreanna reassured the old lady, stroking her arm. Then she looked at the care assistant with disgust. 'We treat prisoners better than we treat the elderly,' she said to herself as tears gathered in the corners of her eyes.

She was called into the office where two women sat in front of a large teak veneered table. One was the owner of the home, the other her lackey. The owner was a tall well-dressed female with long dark hair, gold chains hanging around her neck, and a large diamond ring on her finger. She spoke first.

"Thank you for coming to see us, I won't beat around the bush. You owe us a lot of money and we'd like it very much if you paid your debt." Her candour confused Dreanna who was still unsure as to why she owed them money.

"I've paid you in full every month, so to be honest I really don't understand how I could owe you anything else. You have Mum's pension paid directly to you and I pay the extra via cheque each month. I have all my paper work here." Dreanna reached inside her bag.

"Not needed, not needed," the owner announced. "It's not that we are questioning you haven't paid, but we've had to increase your mother's fees. She's one of our most demanding patients you know."

"What?" Dreanna's tone changed, her voice slightly higher pitched than normal. "Mum, demanding, how? She stays in her bed 24 hours a day, you wash her, you turn on the machine that feeds her and you change her nappies when needed. Apart from that you don't have to do anything else with her, so how can you say she's demanding?"

The woman stuttered, "Well, I'm sorry but we don't see it that way, and anyway it's not as if you can't pay for the increase is it? Didn't your father die a few months ago and did they not own their own home?"

"Ah, so that's it," Dreanna said. "You want my parents' home to pay for this dump."

The owner fidgeted in her seat and pushed her hair behind her ears. "We are in our legal rights to obtain property to pay fees for our services. We are one of the best care homes in the area, and if you didn't want your mother to come here, then why did you put her here in the first place!"

"My father had no choice. The decision was made by the social workers as to which home Mum was put into." Dreanna paused "Is that your Jag outside?"

"Yes."

"Brand new isn't it? Top of the range?"

"Yes actually it is."

"You like the finer things in life don't you?"

"I like nice things, yes."

"Take a look around this place, don't you think some of these people would like nice things too, including their dignity remaining intact?"

"They are old people, many of whom do not even know what day it is," the owner stuck her nose in the air and sat rigid on her seat. She looked at Dreanna as if she were not worthy and beneath her greatness.

Dreanna rose and stood proudly, glaring down at this outrageous woman, this woman who repulsed her to her very core. Dreanna's bewitching eyes held her gaze. "But they are still people, and one day you will be old too. One day when you're old and infirm all your nice processions won't mean a thing, so enjoy them now 'cos sooner or later you too will be a sad lonely woman who pisses herself." Dreanna turned and walked to the door, knowing full well if she didn't leave the room soon she wouldn't be able to control the vicious anger building up inside her. She slammed the door and made her way to Iris's room. Her mum lay on the bed, eyes closed, a single blanket covering her body. A thin layer of skin stretched tight over her face, the bony skeletal structure her most prominent feature. Dreanna stroked her hair, her dark brown baby-fine hair.

Iris opened her eyes.

"Mum please die. I can't see you like this much longer." Dreanna's head began to ache but she ignored it. "I know you can hear me. I'm struggling Mum, I've lost all my belief, I'm starting to think my life has been one great big dream, one huge nightmare.

"Dreanna!" The voice seemed to surround her.

"Go away! I don't want to hear you any more. You, your world, your lies, you are nothing more than my imagination! Leave me alone."

"You must listen, please Dreanna, listen to me."

"No. Fuck off!" Dreanna stuck her fingers in her ears.

"Dreanna please listen, we don't mean you any harm or pain."

"You don't mean a thing to me anymore. I don't trust you, I don't need you and I don't want to hear your constant bullshit. You are not real! Leave me alone!"

Silence.

August 2002

Thunder was rumbling through the air outside and the raindrops were getting bigger as the storm moved closer. Dreanna opened the patio door and sat on the step waiting for the flashes of lightning and counting the seconds like she used to as a child to see how many miles away the storm was, but never really knowing if there was any truth to it. The raindrops splashed on the patio and the warm musky scent of parched ground being moistened by the rain filled the air. She stretched out her legs, watching as the water dripped down her skin. After the dry heat of the day the liquid was welcoming and she enjoyed the feeling as it trickled through her toes.

Fawn was on the sofa talking to her imaginary friends, not paying any attention to the strident thunder and strobes of lightning outside. Dreanna often wondered if these imaginary friends really only existed in her daughter's mind or if they were as real to her as the voices, images and people she had met throughout her life? Fawn had always been so fixated on the film *Drop Dead Fred* that Dreanna wondered if the reason she loved it so much was because it made her feel that these little people she played with day after day weren't just her over-active brain but reality. And anyway Fawn hadn't watched the film since she was four and her friends first appeared to her when she was two. How Dreanna hoped and prayed that none of her daughters would have to experience the things she had; she wanted them to be free, to travel the world and live life without the constant restrictions she'd had to endure.

Rebecca and Leticia were sitting on the window sill watching the storm from the dryness of their home, shoving biscuits in their mouths, chatting to each other and counting in the same way as Dreanna had. They all counted together, "1, 2..." Boom! The rumbles of thunder moved closer, within minutes another lightning strike and their voices in unison again. "1..."

A colossal crash filled the air. Rebecca and Leticia jumped so high their backsides left the window sill, their biscuits hurtling through the air as each child screamed. Dreanna couldn't help but laugh.

"That was a bit scary," announced Leticia, covered in biscuit crumbs.

"My heart's really beating fast," Rebecca answered, trying her hardest to stay frightened, but the giggles couldn't be held in any longer and the girls soon fell about laughing. Apart from Fawn who merrily carried on playing with Max, her favorite imaginary being.

The fun and frolics were soon to be terminated by Callum announcing it was bedtime. "It's gone ten and it's school tomorrow," he said, to his daughters' disgust. Callum looked at Dreanna, "These kids really should have a proper bedtime you know."

"Why?"

"'Cos they should, they need more sleep than us, and anyway everyone puts their kids to bed early don't they?"

"I never had a set bedtime, don't see the point in it. If kids wanna sleep they sleep – why have them if you spend most of your time arguing when they should go to bed and forcing them to go to sleep when they're not tired? Makes no sense to me." Dreanna continued sitting on the step, her legs drenched by the falling rain.

"Well maybe I would like to spend some quality time with my wife then," Callum winked.

"Why don't you just be honest and say you want to play hide the sausage?"

A bemused Fawn gawped at her parents. "What's hide the sausage?"

Both parents smiled, eyebrows raised. Well that could have been one of those awkward moments couldn't it?

"Bedtime Fawn," Callum said, hoisting his youngest into his arms and taking the precious cargo up to bed. Rebecca and Leticia followed behind and soon all three children were in the place where inspiration is found and dreams are made.

By the time Callum returned downstairs Dreanna was standing in the garden, clothes removed and arms outstretched, her head leaning back as the unrelenting rain soaked her naked form. He watched as the moisture ran down her tanned body. Dreanna let her arms fall to her side and their eyes met. Callum walked towards her, reaching out his hand to caress her skin, his finger tips barely touching her. The downy hair on her body stood up and she sighed. With their lips now touching he lifted Dreanna in his arms and carried her to a corner of the garden. With her body pressed against the fence Callum kissed and licked every droplet of fresh rain from her body, their desire building.

The razor-sharp piercing pain filled Dreanna's head. "Stop!" she shouted.

"What's wrong?" Callum pulled away from her.

Dreanna clutched her head, "Leave me alone..."

"What? What have I done?"

"It's not you, it's..." Dreanna didn't have the courage to tell Callum what or who was causing her pain. "I love you. Please... just hold me?" The pain in her head soared through her body and she looked at her husband, her heart racing not with lust but with agony. She began to cry.

Callum pulled her towards him and Dreanna kissed him frantically. He drew back. "You are so confusing, Dreanna."

Dreanna stared into his eyes and swallowed back more tears, her mind fighting the energies from the other side. "I know....but...please make love to me, just make love to me..."

Their love-making session was brief, but at least it gave Dreanna respite from her pain. She lay on top of the bedcovers, the bedroom still hot and muggy from the day's excessive heat. Her head was still being attacked by rods of fire cutting through her brain, ripping, shredding, burning it. She didn't want sleep to take hold of her; she was forcing it away. The barriers she carefully erected in her mind would not protect her from what was to come, but she didn't want to see, feel or know what was about to happen. She fell asleep.

Windows appeared on both sides of her, a mist outside them. She touched the glass but could not feel it, tried to see in front of her but there was nothing there.

Matilda was by her side. "You shouldn't be here Dreanna."

"I don't want to be here Nana."

"Go back."

Dreanna tried to move. "I can't, my feet are stuck." She looked past her grandmother as two plastic swing doors appeared. She saw her mother's bed in the nursing home, surrounded by many people. "What, why… that's my granddad, your husband, isn't it? I've never met him, Can I go see him?" Dreanna's feet were freed and she walked onward.

Matilda hurled her body forward to grab hold of Dreanna's arm. "Dreanna – no! You cannot see this."

"But Nana I want to meet Granddad." Dreanna stopped "Why is he round Mum's bed, why are all these people round Mum's bed?" Understanding dawned in her mind and she understood. "Nan please, no, please I can't lose Mum too, don't take what's left of her. I didn't mean it, I don't want her to die … please Nan, please," Dreanna spoke in a whisper as the tears started to fall. She sank to her knees.

Matilda reached out and laid her hand on Dreanna's head, partly to give comfort and partly to make her wake up. "Please, you must go back. We have to prepare the body, you can't see this. Please my little one go back, Go back!

Dreanna gasped as the air hit her lungs with such force that her eyes opened. She nudged Callum, then, agitated, she shook her husband to wake him up. "Callum please wake up, please wake up!"

"What the fuck…what's the matter?"

"Mum's dying, she's being taken tonight. I told her I wanted her to die… I didn't mean it… I don't want her to die… I don't want her to go!" Dreanna spoke fast, the days of verbal diarrhoea had returned. Tears streamed down her face. Callum looked at her, confused and angry that she had woken him.

"Dree please! Your mum is fine. She will most probably outlive the rest of us… now go back to bloody sleep, woman!"

Dreanna fell back onto her pillow, tears cascading down her face. She wasn't going to let sleep take hold again. She forced herself to stay awake. She didn't want to see her mother taking her final breath. She could do nothing but cry and hope this was just her imagination, nothing more nothing less.

Callum's alarm clock buzzed as the time hit 5am. Dreanna was still wide awake; she nudged him in the side and he reached over and turned it off. It buzzed again, he turned it off again.

"Are you awake?"

"No,"

"Do you remember me telling you last night that Mum is dead?"

"No. Shut up, I'm asleep."

"But Callum..."

"Dreanna please, you said this about your Dad remember?"

"And if you remember he did actually die," her words left her mouth, but her brain was trying to forget every second of that day.

Callum left for work and Dreanna stayed in bed. Her thoughts were only concerned with last night's trip to the place in her mind that only she could see. The phone rang. Nobody could get to it in time and the call was collected by the answer-phone. Dreanna still lay in her bed. She could hear the sound of her daughter's feet running up the stairs.

Leticia ran into her room. "Mummy?" There was fear in her voice. "The message was from Patrice... Nanny died last night. She wants you to call her back." Leticia threw herself into her mother's arms. Within minutes the other children joined them on the bed, each one crying, each one knowing that they would have to relive the same awful emotions of a few months ago.

"My children are too young to see so much death," Dreanna said aloud. And as she held them close, she closed her eyes, and knew that the razor-sharp pain, the visit to the other side, was not her imagination but painful reality.

It was another hot summer's day, another day when other children were running unbridled through the estate, and another day when Dreanna, Callum and their daughters, her siblings and their families were gathered at the parents' home following the same procedure as just months before, waiting silently for the hearse to arrive.

One member followed another into the building where bodies were burnt every hour of the day. Their mother's coffin was positioned in the exact same place as their father's. Each grandchild held a yellow rose, their parents a red one. Silence fell as each in turn placed the perfectly formed flowers on the box that held Iris's corpse. The room was nearly empty, but then why would it have been full? Most people had forgotten Iris the day she fell ill, all those years ago. Even her own brother didn't trouble to come and say his 'see you laters'. Her sister had turned up but Iris and her sister were like chalk and cheese. You always get one snob in the family and Phyllis was theirs. She looked down on her working class roots and had nothing to do with Iris's delinquent offspring. But here she was sitting bold as brass with her nose sticking up in the air.

"I wonder if she'll cry," Dreanna murmured to Rebecca.

"Doubt it… don't think she's got a sensitive bone in her body."

After all Dreanna had been through, she was struggling with her own faith and belief. Her heart told her there was more than just a physical existaence, but the anger she felt at losing the two people who had given her life and nurtured her was erupting like a volvano inside her body. She was a hypocrite. She had told her children that life after death did not exist, that there is no heaven, just a dead body that turns to dust, but she knew better than anybody that the afterlife was real. She could only hope and pray that she would come to accept their deaths and that her anger would burn itself out.

Dreanna stood once again in front of the mourners, this time composed and unruffled, and once again unfolded a piece of paper from her pocket. She stared at the faces glaring back at her. "I didn't know how or what to say about Mum, so I decided to write my own poem for her."

My life maybe over now
But do not cry nor shed a tear
As I am now without any fear
Remember my hair and the colour of my eyes
But do not sit there and begin to cry
Remember my mouth my lips my face
Remember the times I moved with such grace
Remember my hands my feet my heart
And know that we will never be apart
I may not stand there by your side
But know that I will always be there to guide
Remember the good times and not the bad
This is not a time to feel sad
This is a time to be happy and full of glee
As now my soul is eternally free
Life is given and taken away
So please be grateful for each new day
Remember my clothes or my favorite song
And remember life really isn't that long
When the sun rises up from the East
Know this is your time on life you must feast
When the sun sets and goes down in the West
Rejoice in life and always do your best
So wipe your tears and hold your head up high
This is just see you later and not goodbye.

She finished with one final sentence … "Till death us do part."

The Truth is Out

October 2002

Time stands still for no-one and the grief ate slowly away at her, tearing Dreanna's heart in two. An argument with her sisters ripped her family apart when they were all struggling to come to terms with not only losing one parent but two. To make the whole situation worse, Patrice's husband had been diagnosed with cancer. Their relationship was different in that they didn't share unconditional love but more of a companionship between two consenting adults – but Patrice's anguish and fear was just as high as anyone's knowing that sooner rather than later she would become a widow. Her way of coping was by drinking vast amounts of alcohol until her body became accustomed to the relaxation that 'just that one more' vodka could bring. Dreanna had given up telling her to stop; this was her body to use and abuse any way she saw fit. In Dreanna's mind Patrice had the right to use whatever coping strategy she could, the right to find strength in any method even if it was making her ill. We all have to find ways to cope even if someone doesn't agree with our actions … don't we?

Every year for the past four years Dreanna and Callum had held a Halloween party at their home, and plans were being made for this year's. With all that had recently happened it was the first time Dreanna really didn't fancy her home full of guests, and she couldn't be bothered with the preparation or to be jovial and welcoming. Plus her home was like a building site as they had just started building an extension with the money they had received from the sale of Patrick and Iris's house. The rest of her family nagged her constantly and as always she backed down and agreed, but they knew she wasn't happy as her distant expression and quiet manner was a complete giveaway as to how much interest she actually had in holding this social gathering. Today would have been Patrick's seventy-fourth birthday and she couldn't stop thinking about him. How she would have loved to stop all the clocks and jump off this world, even if it meant that for eternity she could do nothing but float around in a place that held no emotions, no pain, no grief and no other person telling her what she should do or who she should be. She wanted time to freeze.

The guests began to arrive, dressed up in the usual Halloween costumes, fake blood carefully painted on their faces, bodies and clothes. The half-built living room was strewn with decorations, decomposing plastic heads, and strategically placed cobwebs. The table was laden with treats and goodies and the worktop and fridge filled to bursting point with alcohol and soft drinks.

Dreanna spent most of her time trying to keep busy, fluffing around, filling up the crisp bowls and asking if people wanted their glass refilled. She had already planned not to stand still for too long and have to make idle chit chat to her guests. The last thing she wanted was to be asked, "How are you coping? Are you and your sisters talking again yet?" or the too-familiar question, "How the hell can you afford an extension this size?" She had been a bit too forthcoming with an old family friend a few days previously who had asked the same question and her frank response of "cos my parents fucking died" didn't go down too well. So tonight she wasn't going to allow any futile question-and-answer sessions to take place.

One of their guests was a young girl called Marisa, with long flowing blonde hair, an engaging smile and an infectious sense of humour. Dreanna liked her – she was fun to be around, and there was never an awkward silence. The two women were sat outside in the garden, bottoms perched on the edge of an old wooden bench, each of them holding a cigarette between their fingers. Marisa held a plastic glass full of red bull and vodka.

Dreanna was listening intently to her rambling on about her husband's family not understanding her, then lost her concentration and her mouth opened before she could think of the consequences. "Lillian loves you. She wants to tell you she has your baby and will look after her always. She says you must be true to yourself and not be what they want you to be. She also says 'Take care, my sweet princess.'"

Marisa's mouth opened but nothing came out.

Dreanna's attention returned. "Shit! I'm… I'm sorry, please take no notice, ignore me, really I'm so sorry," she shook her head and looked down at the ground.

"But," Marisa looked straight at her, "my Nan's name was Lillian. She died in February, and no one knows about my baby as I had a termination six weeks ago. Dreanna, please explain to me how you know all this?"

"I can't, I'm sorry. Please just ignore what I just said. Pretend it never happened and please, please don't tell anyone… please!"

But a persistent Marisa would not stop. "My God – how can I ignore it? You have to tell me, can you see…?" she paused, "can you see dead people? Can you hear them? Are you some sort of psychic or, what are they called, a medium?"

Dreanna was confused. All her life she had kept her secret and the last thing she wanted was for this to become public knowledge. She didn't want people looking at her differently; she didn't want their curious stares, and she didn't want to be different from them. But how was she going to dig herself out of this mess? If she lied, how could she cover her tracks and give a decent reason for the words that had just escaped her mouth of their own accord? If she told the truth, was she strong enough to accept the questions that would follow?

Lillian was back in her mind. *"Tell the truth Dreanna, be honest."*

Dreanna looked up from the ground. "Yes I see dead people. I see them, I hear them and I feel them. I also feel people's pain and see it inside my head. I'm not proud of it, I don't like it but I can't make it go away."

Her secret life was now out in the open.

When the party finished everyone went up to bed but Dreanna stayed downstairs. She spent the whole night sitting at the dining room table, full of fear and an uncontrollable urge to run away. Her mind was somersaulting through a multitude of thoughts, wondering what was going to happen if the truth came out and everybody knew just what she was capable of. This was her secret, this was the 'thing' she had learnt to live with alone and deal with alone. If she ran away she could save herself from being interrogated and bombarded with questions, she could save her family from the ridicule that their mother was some sort of weird fucked-up witch, some sort of sub-normal human being. She lay her head on the table; she had no idea what to say or do. Could she lie her way out of this or should she, for the first time ever, tell the truth? Tell the people she loved that she sees and feels more than the physical body should? She rested her head on her hands and drifted off into sleep.

"Why not just tell the truth? You have been born with a unique ability that can heal many people's hearts and bring hope back into their lives. If we didn't think you could use it wisely we would not allow it to happen. You know only too well that for this to evolve you must change, you must accept and you must believe. Can you believe, Dreanna?"

Dreanna wasn't sure. *"No, I don't think I'd ever have enough belief inside me. My life is a prison and will continue to be until I die. I want to have the faith that you're talking about, but I don't know if it's ever going to happen, no matter what you show, give or tell me. I will always question. I'm sorry, I'm so sorry. I think you may have chosen the wrong person here."*

"We have not chosen the wrong person, Dreanna. Your life's experiences to date have given you the knowledge to heal the pain of others. More will happen, this is not meant to cause you harm but teach you. Not everything can be taught from a book, no matter who the author is. Your heart is ready to burst with love, you are like a flower ready to bloom and its beauty is not with the transparency of the visual effect but with what is held close inside you.

Prisons come in many shapes and sizes; bars, walls, emotions, even love, all can be viewed as a prison, a cell, a secure unit.

As rational, free-thinking human beings that would never admit to being anything but the most evolved species on this planet, you have the brain power to build machines that can teach, that can communicate, that can speculate on certain problems before they arise, you have a brain that can control, condition, influence; a dominant machine that is filled with strength, force, vigour and energy; a computerised blob filled with electronic currents, an abundance of wires all joining, stimulating, energising and mo-tivating you in every hour, every minute every second of your lives. Even when you are in the deepest throes of sleep your subconscious continues to stimulate your mind. Your brain is a computer that never rests.

But your brain can also be your own worst enemy, your own built-in prison with bars, locks, barriers hindering and blocking you, stopping you moving forward and evolving. Could it be that you are not the free-thinking machines that many believe, but a mammal like any other that gathers strength in numbers, that feels by following oth-ers' thought patterns they too can have the sanctuary and security that many desire?

By filling your lives with love and the need to be committed to another of your spe-cies, does it really give you the hope and freedom to enjoy whatever time you have, or does this one emotion, Love, build yet more obstructions? You all see love as the be all and end all of your existence but when love breaks down you find yourselves lost in a void of broken emotions, a void of nothingness, a void that can somehow never quite be filled. The physical emotion you choose to call love is yet another prison with added bonuses; with this emotion comes passion, desire, lust, sexual fulfillment, companion-ship, and like your naturalistic evolutionary reality it brings with it the security that you work better as a team. It gives you a refuge and the self-assurance that you have a better chance of survival, whether this is down to being able to procreate, or just down to the fact that with the help of others you have a greater chance of surviving this jour-ney called life.

The prison of a conditioned mind neither helps nor hinders. Who can argue that a certain amount of conditioning is needed for you to fulfill and learn, for you to see objectionable arguments which inevitably can help with the continuation of mankind? The prison of a conditioned mind comes in many forms – you are conditioned by par-ents, siblings, teachers, friends, acquaintances as to what is the correct way to think, what is sociably acceptable behaviour, but yet again an incarceration of solitary confine-ment can follow. Why? Because you conform so as not to hurt another, you conform because you do not want to upset people that are close to you, you conform to keep your species alive and flourishing. You become an imprisoned mind, an imprisoned vessel too scared to challenge, too frightened that your actions may upset, offend or displease. You suffocate your own conscious and natural instincts in order to be accepted by your fellow homo sapiens.

An urge, a desire, a thought, a need, an emotion, a transitional move forward to aid another, all begins and ends in the computer you call the brain, the one machine that can set you free or imprison you for days, weeks, months or years for as long as you live.

They say your eyes are the doorway to your souls, but they are also the window of the detention centre that encases itself in the skeletal bony structure you call the skull. How much of each day can you really see? Do you take a little peep, a long stare or like many are you too alarmed by what reality is outside the security bars and fences you have built around yourselves? The world is a big place, but you all only observe a tiny percentage. You all know to a certain level the truth that makes up this world, the pain, the trauma the suffering, but 'hey, if it's not happening to you, then why worry? Why be alarmed? Why care?' Because, Dreanna, if you all didn't care then mankind would sooner rather than later become just another physical apparition that once inhabited this planet.

But then again if you did all show some sort of compassion for your fellow species there wouldn't be any need to try and re-condition others into seeing new ways, forming new ideas. There would be no need to evolve as each one of you would have reached a level of acceptance. The bars, barriers, chains, locks, cells and prisons would indeed become null and void. Both arguments can be understood, but also can be used to help prolong, nurture and develop human beings.

So quite honestly what is the point in trying to be honest, to have faith and believe Dreanna, if your mistrust in us is always in question? Then what are you going to do? You can build your life and a hypothesis as to what has happened throughout it or you can build yet more prisons of varied degrees. Both will hold an equal amount of distress, both will hold pleasure and pain. You can allow us to help you evolve and be the person we believe you can be, or you can hide away like many humans do, too frightened to change, too scared to move forward. Make the right choice Dreanna. We love you."

December 6th 2002

The continuous questioning began: the hows, the whys, and the since-whens all being asked time and time again. The attention she so didn't want was building up and it wasn't long before nearly every person she met became curious about her ability to communicate with the dead. Even though Callum was still a non-believer he was now at least beginning to understand why Dreanna hated being surrounded by people, and was slowly coming to terms with the fact that his wife was just a little bit different. But he still found it a challenge to believe. How could he accept it when Dreanna still struggled with her own self, her own faith and her own belief?

Dreanna was celebrating her 34th birthday and the family were gathered at the dining-room table filling their faces with a meal of her choice. The endless banter and the not-very-funny jokes flew across the table. As Dreanna reached for a pot of noodles, the smarting intense pain shot through her head. She blinked and blinked again, for a split second her reality was still with her, then another abrupt twinge soared through her conscious mind and her surroundings disappeared from her vision. Everyone and everything had vanished.

The soldier she had once met as a young girl was back standing by her side. He looked at her, his face blackened and dirty, his eyes swollen and red. "Watch and observe," he said as he jumped into the trench below her feet.

Dreanna stood still. Gunfire surrounded her, the air was cold, and she didn't even know if it was day or night. She looked down at the men standing in the earth below, their bodies pressed tight to the walls of their make-shift barricades. One young man sat crying, he was no older than 17, his hands were shaking, he stared right into Dreanna's eyes,

"I don't want to die, I'm so scared," his voice was one of a frightened youth, a child so afraid.

She wanted to hold him, tell him everything was going to be okay, but she couldn't move. Another soldier brushed past her, and kicked the feet of the younger one.

"You are a soldier, this is your job! Get your arse into gear; load your weapon boy!" The words bellowed from the sergeant's throat.

The young soldier reached down for his gun, and erratically began man-handling it; he looked up in Dreanna's direction again before vomiting all over himself. "I am a man; I will fight to the death."

The sergeant nodded. "Good lad, good lad."

Dreanna gazed at her surroundings, the sound of the huge guns echoed around her, the shells whistled through the air splitting their target's bodies in two. She looked back down into the trench; men were falling to the ground, some with their stomachs blown away, others with limbs missing. The able-bodied were sleeping, eating, urinating and defecating on or near each dead body that surrounded them. There was not time to mourn, there was not time to cry, and there was no time to care. Each soldier had to forget the present, forget the pain, and dig deep to find their courage and become the victors over this raging battle. The sound and smell of the firepower and artillery pervaded throughout the atmosphere.

The sergeant's booming voice hit the air, "Over we go boys!"

A tirade of angry words filled the air as each man and youth in turn clambered over the sunken, wet, boggy sod, and every dead body that stood in their way. Dreanna watched as her Unknown Soldier ran forward, his face full of anger, his body weak, his weapon firing blankly into space. He fell to the ground, blood surging from a gaping hole in his chest. He moved his head to face Dreanna and pulled from his pocket a photograph of a small child. "I will never hold him in my arms, I will never hold my wife again. Stop the wars Dreanna, stop the pain, the heartache, and tell the world the real truth." The Unknown Soldier closed his eyes.

Dreanna was back sitting at her table. She looked around at her family, each one staring straight at her, watching as the tears fell from her swollen eyes; she could do no more than shake her head and leave the room.

A World Suffused with Pain

March 10th 2004

Dreanna's life had changed beyond measure; her house was constantly full of strangers, her head full of the deceased. Every evening and weekend her house was inundated with one person after another. Her heart was slowly being rung dry of any emotion and she felt no pity as people sat in front of her crying openly and speaking about the loss of a loved one; she had no compassion for the folk who sat at her table telling her they wanted to take their own lives, or people begging her to tell them their future. The more people she saw or spoke to the less sympathy she had to give. Every question was the same: "Does he love me? W ill he leave his wife for me? Will I be rich? Will I be famous? Give me the lottery numbers, blah blah blah blah!" People called at her house day in, day out, and every day the frustration built up inside her. In her curiosity to find others like her she went to many 'psychic' events. She watched one medium after another live on stage, but she struggled to understand why these so-called psychics copied each others' words as to the real truth behind life and existence – they didn't seem to have an original thought amongst them – and their egos! By God, how she hated their egos! Each one claiming they were the best, the UK's finest spirit whisperer, but it was their stories of how they became psychic that she never could understand. They were the same in every case.

"I have had my gift since the death of my nan, my dad, my uncle, my aunt... Since then I have had the ability to communicate with the other side. I was taught my gift by a psychic college and hold a qualification to prove it. This is my destiny."

Dreanna's logical mind couldn't understand how you can be taught to be psychic, it was like trying to teach a dog to be a dog, then giving them a certificate to prove they could bark and piss up the nearest lamppost!

She could sense their dislike of her when she asked them questions they couldn't answer. They disliked the fact that she thought differently from them and she disliked their nonchalant attitude about things they should care about. She was resentful that she hadn't chosen her 'gift' and that it affected her life in a way that it didn't seem to affect theirs.

August 4th 2004

Dreanna had decided that a day in the garden was what she needed more than anything else. Just as she reached to disconnect the phone, it rung. A woman's voice was on the other end.

"May I see you?"

Dreanna heaved a sigh. Why, when she needed time to herself, to recharge her batteries and not think, did someone always want to see her?

As her mouth was about to say no, the voice inside her head said, *"You must see her, Dreanna, you must!"*

Dreanna sighed again. "Yes, when would you like to come?"

"I'm standing outside your house now, may we please speak?"

Dreanna hung up and walked to the front door. A woman smaller than her own 5-foot frame was staring through the stained glass window. Her skin was dark, her hair pulled back and hidden under a vibrant head scarf, her clothes were old fashioned and too big for her tiny body. She held out her hand. "I is sorry to interrupt you, my name is Grace, and I feel I need to talk with you."

Dreanna beckoned her inside. Both women sat at the dining room table.

"I have to ask how or who gave you my number and address?" Dreanna was curious.

"I did bad thing, I took your address and number from a lady I work with, she was saying you helped her. I do not think I need help but feel I need to tell you my story, may this be okay with you?"

Dreanna nodded.

"My name is Grace and I come from Rwanda, and I is what many of your people call an illegal immigrant. I travelled for many days and nights in the back of a van to get to your country. I is a nurse and trained here. I love my job." Grace smiled. Her brilliant white teeth and childlike expression grabbed hold of Dreanna's soul.

"Why did you leave your country?" Dreanna asked.

"I was married and had two children. My husband worked doing many jobs and I stayed home looking after my babies. Sometimes he was gone for many days and weeks, trying to find any paid work. We lived in a small village and were very close to the people who lived near us, we helped each other, you understand, yes?"

"Yes… But you are talking in the past tense?"

Grace bowed her head. "I will explain why. My husband had been away and had just returned when our village was attacked, we hid ourselves inside hoping that in some way God would protect us and keep us safe. I was sat crouched down holding my babies close to me, my son was three years old and my daughter was six. They were so precious. My husband stood by the door, he had a hook in his hand that he used for his work, to turn the soil to grow food. The door was pushed open and my babies were crying, I tried to stop them making a noise but they felt frightened." Grace lowered her head again.

"They saw my husband and pushed him to the floor. They kicked him, they did not stop. They picked up the hook he had and forced it through his throat, it came out the other side, my husband cried in pain and his blood covered us all. The hook slid easily into the walls. My husband's body hung like a piece of meat dying in front of me and my babies.

One man took my son from my arms, and threw him to another. He did not catch him and he fell to the ground. He picked him up and began poking him with a knife, he cut his skin here," She pointed to the inner part of her arm.

"The other man took my son and ripped the clothes from his body. One man took hold of his head, they turned him so he was facing the ground, the other man took out his penis and forced it inside my son. My baby screamed, he bled, there was so much blood... after he had finished, they swapped and did it again. My baby cried no more.

My daughter was next, they punched her face they ....they held her throat with their hands so she could not breathe, they raped her again and again, forcing her body to take more of them inside her. My daughter was very brave; she did not cry she just stared at me. I could not help her, I could not stop them. She died looking into my eyes.

Then it was my turn. They hit my face, they held a knife to my throat as they pushed their penis into my mouth, they forced my legs to part and took me over and over and over again. They cut my stomach." Grace lifted her top to reveal a scar that was around nine inches long.

"I cannot remember any more. I woke up and my family all lay dead around me, my blood soaked on the ground mixed with that of my husband and my children. Only a few in my village survived this attack and we travelled many days and came to England. I is not a bad person, but people here now know that I travelled here illegally, they abuse me verbally every day, they put dog excrement through my letterbox, they threaten to kill me. I do not take your government's money. I work hard, I look after sick people, I look after these men who abuse me after they get drunk and fight each other. I mend and sew their skin together, I clean up their vomit, I care for their parents who are old, I wipe their backsides yet still they threaten me, still they try and hurt me further. So I am going back home, because I would rather die at the hands of my own people than the hands of people who know nothing about me." Grace stopped and stared at Dreanna, who had silent tears falling down her cheeks.

"I... I'm so sorry. I don't know what you want me to say... I don't know what to do." Dreanna cried.

Grace leaned forward. "You tell my story, you make people realise that just because my skin is black it does not mean I am a bad person, you tell them the pain I've suffered. I ask no more of you than that."

Grace got up from the table, rubbed Dreanna's arm and left. Dreanna sat motionless. She was numb, stunned and completely bewildered as to what she was supposed to do next.

Thou Shalt not Judge

September 20th 2004

Dreanna was unloading the shopping from the boot of her car when she noticed the figure of a man standing at the top of her drive staring straight at her. She stood still looking back in his direction. "Can I help you?"

The man walked towards her. "No, but I can help you," He spoke while taking a hankerchief out of his pocket and blew his nose. He was dressed in a pair of brown slacks, a stripy shirt and a dark blue blazer that was far too short for the length of his arms. His eyes were squinty and twitched and he had the infamous comb-over as the predominant feature of his balding head. It lifted as a gust of wind carried it in a vertical direction. Dreanna bit her bottom lip to suppress her laughter.

"My name is Norman and I'm a pastor in a local church, and I'm doing the rounds to tell people about God."

Dreanna sighed, "Not again."

"Sorry, what do you mean 'again'?"

"Over the last few weeks, I've spoken to Jehovah's Witnesses, Mormons, more Jehovah's Witnesses, more Christians, all telling me the same thing, and I suppose you are going to tell me the same too. 'The end is nigh'." Dreanna laughed in an evil mocking sort of way.

"You do not like religion, you are not religious?"

"Am I religious? Er let me think… No. But if you're asking me, do I believe in religion the answer is Yes – but I do not believe in man's interpretation of religion, nor do I believe in the constant hypocrisy behind it, nor do I believe that any person, yourself included, has the physical right to try and get others to conform to your way of thinking."

"But I am God's chosen messenger and you lady are …are blasphemous, and when the end comes you will burn in hell for your sins."

"Pray tell, what do you know about me and what are my sins?"

"You have a pentagram tattooed on your neck, and one at your front door, which means you are a pagan. God hates pagans!"

"It may interest you to know, I wear a cross around my neck, and I am also wearing a Buddha necklace too. I believe in all religions, as all were given to bring hope and faith – no particular one is right or wrong – but it's people like you who make it hard for others to have faith, or have belief. You constantly try and belittle each other, you all have to be right! You never accept that just because someone thinks differently from you, they in fact may be the ones who know more than you. And please don't tell me I'll burn in hell. My life is a hell on Earth each day!"

The self-confessed pastor walked closer to Dreanna and poked her in the shoulder. "You …you are nothing more than Satan's spawn! You hold no right to walk on this Earth and God will judge you for your sins!"

"What the fuck? Will you wind your bloody neck in! If God is this big almighty person that gave everyone life then sorry to burst your bubble but that would mean he gave me life too! Gandhi once said, 'I don't reject your Christ, I love your Christ, it's just that so many of your Christians are so unlike your Christ,' and I'm sorry to say this but if you are a real Christian then maybe you should stop judging others because does your Bible not say 'Thou shall not judge'… and hey, if I'm Satan's spawn, then let's fucking hope he looks like Dave Grohl; now that's a devil whose arse I would surely lick!"

"You, are …are..." The pastor spat straight into Dreanna's face, and made the sign of the cross with his fingers. "You are a Devil Child!"

Dreanna pulled down the sleeves of her cardigan and wiped the spit from her face. She stayed calm and not flustered.

"And you, my dear sir, are a complete cock. But I would like to say thank you, that's the first time ever I've been doused with holy water. Why don't you just go read your Bible and maybe pay attention to what Christ actually did and how he treated people… Now get off my fucking drive!"

The pastor walked backwards, his hands still forming the shape of the cross. He mumbled the Lord's Prayer and cursed Dreanna and Dreanna sarcastically blew him a kiss as she closed the front door.

Do You Understand all you See?

December 2004

The memory of Grace's visit still haunted Dreanna; she couldn't forget the horror this woman had faced and she thought it made her own life look like an easy journey. She struggled with the constant remarks on Facebook from other people, saying how these illegal immigrants should be returned home, abusing them publically, moaning that they had no right to live or work in the UK. In her own mind she couldn't understand how they were so quick to judge some of the people that had made the journey to England to re-build their lives. Of course she understood that some came over to her country under false pretences, to screw the system and take whatever they could, but she knew first-hand just what some were running away from. She always asked what these shallow individuals would do if they were put into Grace's shoes? But in reality she knew the answer, they would scream and shout, demand justice, demand help, and make their voices be heard – so unlike Grace, who quietly walked away and tried to re-build her own pitiful life.

She wished so many times that she had the courage to just walk away like Grace. To stop listening to the constant questions being asked by the needy people she saw every day. The household bills were piling up around her and Callum still didn't understand why she wouldn't charge for seeing these people. He told her over and over again that she was offering a service and so she had a right to be paid for her time and her ability, but Dreanna saw it differently. She remembered her Nan's words, "It's a gift to give with love," and no matter how broke they were, she would never charge a fee, even if it meant the electricity being cut off. She was detemined not to become one of those mediums who saw this as an easy way to make money, but yet again more confused thoughts troubled her mind.

Maybe all these gifted people were right. Maybe it was right to charge for the sittings – she had a need to feed and clothe her family just as they did. She only had one private sitting booked for this week and like most of them a call was taken that morning for the sitter to come to her home that afternoon. Over a very short period the sittings had changed from confabulating with deceased relatives to helping people overcome their problems. When people phoned asking for her help or advice she had to make sure they knew she wasn't a trained counsellor or life coach, but still they came un-phased by her honesty. Maybe they came because they were curious or maybe, like many, they just wanted something for nothing.

Her client arrived at 2.30 on the dot. Blossom was seven years old and the most beautiful little girl Dreanna had ever seen. Her hair was long and mousey brown, and she was tiny in height and build, with the biggest blue eyes. Her mother on the other hand was tall, obese and desperately looked like she needed a bath, a hair wash and her teeth scrubbed.

Blossom was the tenth child she had seen that month. Most of the previous kids suffered from anger issues, fears, phobias, or were genuinely being a pain in the arse and their parents could take no more. Each child she saw was different, and all of them were unique in their own way. As Dreanna had no experience or certificate in knowing how to counsel she just left it to the voice in her head to tell her how to help them. She had two rules: she would never see a child without a parent, and never see an anguished parent without the child being present.

Blossom sat upright on the chair next to her mother, who explained that her daughter had been diagnosed with an eating disorder, which in the future could turn into anorexia or bulimia.

"So what's the reason you've been given for her being diagnosed with an eating disorder?" Dreanna asked.

"They don't know, no one's told me. The doctors and people we've seen believe she just thinks she's fat and it's her own mind that's basically telling her to starve herself."

Dreanna turned her head away from both mother and child and gazed into space, in the place where the words, voices, and information seemed to appear. Daytime television appeared in her mind. The Breakfast Show that many watched was playing over and over inside the window of her brain. FOOD, FAT, blinked furiously in front of her eyes, DEATH came next, then a mathematical equals sign. And as always the message was completed with the same old finale, flashing continuously 'solve the puzzle Dreanna'.

Dreanna inhaled. 'Put the puzzle together,' she repeated over and over in her head. She turned to the girl, "Tell me Blossom, do you watch breakfast telly before you go to school?"

The child spoke quietly. "Yes." The puzzle was complete.

Dreanna turned to the little girl's mother. "Most of the things in life we learn from a very young age – our mind is an open book and a sponge, soaking up all we see and all we hear. Sometimes it can turn into irrational thoughts and fears. The trouble with learning in this way is that we pick out words and phrases, and we don't understand how they should be used in a productive manner. If things are not explained to us in a way that we can understand we are left to our own devices to make sense of them. Do you understand me?"

"Yes," Blossom's mother answered.

Dreanna looked at her. "It's my belief that Blossom has stopped eating because of what she's seen on television. If you want me to be precise, Breakfast Time TV. I'm not going to lie, I don't really watch much TV, but can you tell me if you've been watching anything of late regarding health and diets?"

"Er yes, I have the telly on most mornings before school and as I'm trying to lose weight I've been following the diet tips and stuff on their show, but to be honest I haven't actually started my diet as you can see," she laughed, wobbling her rather large stomach.

"Well there's the problem then," Dreanna smiled, "What Blossom has done is to take some of what she's heard and formed her own conclusion. From what I have just been given she has associated the words FOOD = FAT = DEATH."

Dreanna turned to Blossom, "Blossom do you think if you eat food it will make you die?"

"No," Blossom paused, "Mummy will die 'cos she's fat and I want to stay with Mummy, so Mummy doesn't have to die on her own... it's true 'cos that lady on the telly said so!"

Blossom's mother shook her head, "We've seen over ten psychiatrists and doctors in the last few months and not one of them has been able to find a reason for her behavior – and you've just done it in minutes!"

"Actually I didn't," Dreanna announced, "Blossom did. Sometimes we have to ask the right questions to find the answers we need, and where kids are involved you have to think like them and see the world through their eyes. Too much today is made difficult; life through a child's eyes is an adventure, they have their own built-in curiosity gene and a rampant imagination. Most of the world's problems would be solved if we listened to what the kids told us as they see the world as it is. They don't make excuses for things not being right, they just live to learn, and they live in a simple way; it's us adults that have the issues and problems, not the kids, because we've turned them into what we want them to be and not what they should be."

The next four hours Blossom and her mother sat undisturbed as they talked, laughed and played, and came to the conclusion and agreement that Blossom would begin to eat again if her mother would finally go on that bloody diet.

Many weeks passed and Dreanna received a phone call from Sue, Blossom's mother. In the past few weeks Blossom had been eating really well and had gained eight pounds. Sue had lost nearly ten pounds.

Dreanna's job was done.

February 14th 2008
Dreanna's days turned into months, the months turned into years, and the years seemed to pass faster than a speeding bullet. She had withdrawn herself

almost totally from the outside world. She saw no one unless it was for a sitting and spoke only to the people who rang up for a telephone reading.

As the years passed many of Patrick's siblings also died and Patrice's husband lost his battle to cancer. Nearly a whole generation of her family had gone and the rest distanced themselves from each other more and more. She could not understand why her family always claimed 'they were close' when they only ever met at funerals and only a select few were invited to family weddings. Most had some sort of angst with another family member and the rest only spoke when they had to. But was Dreanna happy? The answer was quite simply, yes. She felt in a very strange way that she had outgrown a lot of the people who had surrounded her all her life, and had outgrown the need to be part of a group or belong to a specific social sector of society. Spending so much time alone gave her the chance to really see the world through a completely new pair of eyes.

She used Facebook as a way of keeping a close eye on things and seeing just what made people tick in the 21st century. It has to be said that a lot of the comments placed on it she found crappy and humorous and her warped sense of humour made her aggravate many people with her outlandish or opinionated comments. She lost many so-called friends and some family, so why did she do it? In all honesty she saw a world full of pain every day, a world full of hatred which was becoming suffocated by each person's needs and wants. She actually began to hate human beings for their selfish manner and materialistic attitudes. Deep down inside all she wanted to do was climb into her computer and grab some of these people by the throat and show them just how much others suffered each day, but even if that was possible no one would have listened. It was her only reason for not giving up on the people who contacted her; at least she felt she was helping, and maybe in some obtuse way healing the world of all its pain. In many ways she didn't care; she saw the pain, she felt the pain, she had a life of other's pain and misfortune, so in the end why should she care if her words over a stupid social network actually offended people's intellect? As she saw it they were all fucked anyway.

It was many months since she'd had a personal visit from her guests in another dimension. Yes, she had joined one grieving relative with their dead counterpart, but no conversation between herself and 'them'. The last time they spoke to her was many months previously when in typical Dreanna fashion she had shouted, "Why the fuck aren't you talking to me?"

The response was short. "*It's only when you have nothing that you can see everything.*"

And she did indeed have nothing. Maybe hearing nothing from them made her study the human race without any intrusion, without any mind-conditioning taking place. Maybe she had to learn and work it out for herself to see just what the human race runs on, what makes it tick and what makes it often fail so miserably.

April 7th 2008

Dreanna was busy sorting out the washing, the endless piles of bras, knickers and clothes that came with having three teenage daughters. She held a g-string up and waved it in front of Callum's face. "What the hell is this all about? The girls may as well just go kamikaze for what dignity these would cover!"

Callum laughed out loud, "I think you mean commando?"

Dreanna flung the very small, very thin, pieces of material into a basket. "Oh ...do I?" she laughed, "whoopsies... well whatever it's called these things aren't worth wearing... Isn't it horrible how the girls are growing up so fast? It seems like only yesterday they were all running round making mud pies, and tents out of the table and sheets... and now," Dreanna sighed, "My babies are young women. God I feel old!"

"Well you know what they say, 'you're only as old as the man you feel', and as I'm three months younger than you, fancy a bit of a quickie? It might help you feel young again," Callum smirked, his eyebrows raised high.

"Behave! The kids will be home in a min, and I've got loads to do. For some reason I can't get Suzi out of my head; she's been playing on my mind for a few days now."

"What – your cousin Suzi? It's most probably 'cos she's pregnant, and you know what you're like with babies."

"Hmm probably." But Dreanna wasn't convinced.

Life is Cruel

April 8th 2008

The new mobile phone sat looking up at Dreanna and she sat staring down at it, too scared to touch it. The kids and Callum had bought it for her as they thought it was about time she 'got to grips with technology' and learnt how to use this modern device of communication, especially as her 'me time' was often spent alone in some woods or a reservoir somewhere.

Dreanna loved the stillness and calmness that Mother Nature made her feel, it was one of the only times her head was free from noise and confusion. She always made sure she timed it right so the 'me time' she had was when most people were busy doing their daily chores. The last thing she wanted was to have to make conversation with some stranger. All she wanted was a space to breathe and hear the sounds of rustling leaves, a bee, a bird, anything that made her heart sing, anything that made her respect just how beautiful this world is in its simplest form. She would often be gone for hours at a time, sitting, thinking, consolidating her thoughts. Her solitude meant that her knowledge of life was growing without her even realising it.

She picked up the phone and frowned at it, as she did so, it rang. 'Oh fuck, what do I press?' Her fingers pressed every button she could. It stopped ringing. Then rang again.

Dreanna held it to her ear, "Hello!" she shouted, "Can you hear me?"

A muffled voice was heard.

"Hello," Dreanna said again, holding the phone out in front of her.

"Mum! Put the phone to your ear and turn it the right way up!" It was Leticia.

Dreanna giggled a pathetic, 'I haven't got a clue what the hell I'm doing, how thick am I?' sort of snigger.

"Can you hear me now?"

"Yep, I can hear you ...over and out."

"Mother stop mucking about! I've just had a text from cousin James, Suzi's given birth to twins."

"But she's only 24 weeks pregnant!"

"It has something to do with the placenta coming away... Mum are they going to die?"

"Leticia please don't ask me things like that, you know I can't answer those sort of questions... keep me posted if you hear anything else won't you?"

"Yep will do. Send her a text or something."

"I can't, I don't know how to use this bloody piece of shit ...show me later, love you."

"Love you Mum, and please ask whoever it is to tell you about the twins."

'Please ask', the words rattled around and around over and over again in her head. But who was she supposed to ask? Her mum, her dad, her nan, any of the other relatives that had passed away over the last few years? Qulib, Seraphina, Jan, Susan..? Who was she supposed to ask? Apart from that one sentence none of them had spoken to her in months, and even if they did tell her, what was she supposed to do with what they told her? She couldn't exactly turn round to her cousin and say, "Yep, by the way Auntie Grace said the twins are going to be fine. Or …   heaven forbid ...not!"

Dreanna rubbed her face and left her hands resting on each cheek. She couldn't be the one to give information like that; surely she didn't have the right to ask? As she rested her head on the table the tears and fear for Suzi and her fragile babies exploded out of her. She wiped the moisture away with the cuff of her jumper, and looked out of her patio door.

A buzzing sound travelled through her ears. She shook her head to make it go away but it didn't, it moved further and further into her brain. She felt electricity shoot its way into the unknown spaces inside her head.

"Deanna, can you hear me?"

"What the flying fuckerty fuck was that, or even is this?" She felt as if her brain had imploded.

"Do you like our new way to communicate with you?"

"Er no! That fucking hurt... and this fucking hurts! My brain feels like I've got a million volts going through it."

"Now now Dreanna, a million? Really child, stop exaggerating."

"Well sorry for being human! But this is so uncomfortable... anyway who are you? I don't recognise your voice."

"I've waited so long to speak with you, how I've missed you."

"Missed me? I'm sorry I don't understand. I can't see you, where are you?" Dreanna trawled the depths of her mind, but there was nothing there.

"You see me everywhere. With every tree, plant, and blade of grass you look at, with the wind that blows, with the snow that falls, with the rain that pours, I am everywhere and you see me all the time."

Dreanna grinned. "Mother Nature."

"My name is Cia, but if you feel comfortable calling me Mother Nature then so be it. You are curious about the little angels that have just been born are you not?"

"Yes, yes I am, but in all honesty I would rather not know, it's not my job to be the bringer of bad news, to step in the way of what should be. It's not my job to step in the way of fate. No Cia, please... please don't tell me. I just need to know why. Why let them be born if... if they are only going to die?"

"Now you begin to ask the right questions. Each day we are asked so much; we see humans with their hands together praying, we hear their words calling us asking for answers. You have spent the last epoch of time answering the same questions posed to you by the people you see, you have felt upset by them, and you have in many ways felt the pressure that we face every day. The questions posed to us are no different from the ones people have asked you. The pity you hear in their voices, the words of despair that are spoken to you. The sorrow you have seen, the cries of help you have heard are no different from our world. People are so demanding and do not want to know the truth.

Sometimes people are all too ready to take it when it suits them but when it comes to changing or giving to others, the human race becomes selfish. You look confused, let me give you an example: 'when will I meet the love of my life, when will I meet my soulmate?' They want that reassurance that the person they can love forever is nearby, and those are the words they long to hear, what they don't want to hear is the truth. The possibility that before they meet their soul mate they have to change. People do not want to change.

You don't want to know the outcome of the children's birth but you are curious as to why they have been born. Remember what you were told Dreanna, the day of your birth and death is all that can be conceived as an accurate time, it was their time to be born. The experience that is to be had here is not the child's but the parents'."

"So are you saying that the babies were born because of something Suzi and Ben had to learn or experience?"

"Yes Dreanna. Neither of these young people have ever really felt love; they have felt desire, they have felt feelings of pleasure, but they have never known what it is truly like to love and love with no conditions. They do not know what love means, but this will teach them."

"Sorry Cia but that is cruel and just bloody horrible!"

"It is only through pain that you can change. When things are nice and trauma-free you humans take everything for granted, but as soon as pain and heartache is felt it changes your way of thinking. It changes you into a person with a heart rather than one whose heart doesn't beat in time with the universe. How much does it hurt your physical body to talk to us? How much does it hurt your physical body being surrounded by other people in pain? Think Dreanna, think. Why?"

"Because it teaches me to be more accepting of others, and not to judge. It teaches me to have hope in my heart and it shows me how to give unconditionally."

"The last few months have taught you well, I will see you soon sweet one, I will see you very soon, and remember I will never be too far away, for we are one."

April 29th 2008
She still didn't understand why Cia had said they were one. Was it because she shared the same love for nature that Cia so tenderly nurtured? Was it that eve-

rything in the universe was connected in some way? Maybe she just thought too much about it, maybe all she had to do was accept. But acceptance of her job or her role in society was one she knew she could never fully acknowledge, she could never fully believe any of it was real... Ever!

Today was also the day of the twins' funeral. Neither baby had survived, only living for a few days after their birth. Today was the day a young eighteen-year-old mother and father were burying their baby son and daughter. Tia and Tyler. Two babies born so others could learn. It didn't seem right; parents shouldn't bury their children, children should bury their parents, but who was she to argue, and what explanation could she give to the grieving parents for the death of their children? She knew questions would be asked as now all her family knew what she could do, but for years she had never said 'sorry' when someone died. Why would she? She wasn't sorry they died, she was jealous. She was jealous that they could now be so free of pain and heartache, free of physical life.

Dreanna had vowed at her mother's funeral she would never step foot into another crematorium or church ever again and she knew she never would, no matter who had died or needed her support. In all the places in the world nothing held so many turbulent emotions as the place we go to lay our loved ones to rest. Dreanna knew she had to protect herself; she was human, she was physical. She drove to the club where the wake was being held and sat silently in her car not wanting to move, and certainly not wanting to have to answer a barrage of questions from family members. But she had to go and show her respect and be part of this dysfunctional family that was so full of hate and jealousy.

She walked the twenty or so steps into the club, took a deep breath and entered. As always, she circulated the room, hugging each family member in turn, unsure why she did it as her affectionate advances never seemed to be returned, but she did it anyway. As much as she disliked the revulsion many of them had for other members, and as much as she felt agitated inside because of it, she still couldn't stop giving her affection to each one irrelevant of who they were.

Suzi's face was sunken and pale, her childlike features and purity jumbled and in disarray. Her emotions as expected were full of anger and confusion. Dreanna felt relief when the question she dreaded did not get asked; in fact no questions were asked of her until the time she was ready to leave.

Then Kerry, one of Dreanna's cousins, poked her on the shoulder. "We've never really had a lot to do with each other have we? If it wasn't for funerals I would most probably walk by you in the street and not know who the fuck you were." Kerry was a little wobbly due to the amount of Smirnoff Ices she had drunk.

"Same as," Dreanna answered.

Kerry's cheeks looked flushed, the sort of flush that appears when one too many passes your lips. "You know my nan, your auntie?"

"Yes Kerry of course, I know your nan, my auntie!"

Kerry was fidgeting. Dreanna would have told her to stand still if she had been one of her own daughters but she knew that this was a nervous fidget and waited for one of 'those' questions to be asked.

"Did you know she's not been that good lately?"

Dreanna shook her head. "No I didn't, sorry."

"Well I, I mean we," she pointed across to Suzi, "Can you tell us how much longer she's got, it's just we want to be sort of prepared ...if you get my drift?"

Dreanna looked at Kerry but through her at the same time.

"Within the next three weeks Dreanna, but please do not tell her this, tell her to show her how much she loves her, tell her to love her like never before."

Dreanna stared straight at her inquisitive cousin. "Tell and show your Nan that you love her so much, and let the next few weeks be the ones where nothing but your Nan's happiness matters."

"Okay," Kerry answered, "But that's not giving me a time is it?"

"Time isn't important, but the way you show her just how much you care is." Dreanna gave her cousin a brief but friendly smile and walked away.

May 9th 2008

Callum had taken a day off work as both he and Dreanna wanted to get the garden tidied and sorted before summer arrived. The weather was abnormally warm for the time of year but at least it meant they could do their chores in the warm sunshine instead of the typical wet British weather. Their only hindrance came from their new German Shepherd puppy who thought it was more fun to dig random holes in the newly turfed lawn than to tidy it up.

Dreanna felt sluggish and a quivering sensation kept weaving its way through her body. By lunchtime she just could not muster up enough energy or enthusiasm to continue with the gardening tasks, so she sat on the edge of the patio unable to move, think or even breathe.

"What's up with you?" Callum asked.

"Dunno, just feel sort of strange, like something's going to happen?" Dreanna was unsure of how to answer him.

"Well I can tell you what's going to happen, I'm gonna do all the bloody work while you sit watching me... I didn't take a day off work so you could just sit on your fat arse and watch me work you know!"

"Sorry, give me five minutes will you?"

The same sharp puncturing pain she had become accustomed to filled her head. She closed her eyes and breathed in deeply. 'Relax,' she told herself. 'Breathe in, hold, breathe out, breathe in, hold, breathe out.' The pain got worse.

"Today is the day Dreanna, we are expecting her today. Offer them your hand, give them your heart."

Dreanna called to Callum. "Cal, Auntie Kath is going to die."

Callum frowned. He hated what she could do and hated the fact that each day it got in the way of their lives. "What? For god's sake Dree, get it together!" He shook his head from side to side and puckered his lips. His voice was bitter, "Tell her to hurry up then as I need you to come hold this piece of fence," The words left his mouth cold and unfeeling.

Dreanna muttered under her breath, "Callous bastard."

The hands on the kitchen clock ticked by slowly and as they hit 5 o'clock Dreanna's phone rang, it was Kerry, crying and distressed.

"Nan's gone, she died in my arms, I don't know what to do... I don't know what to say to people. Can you, I mean would you... mind coming around? We are at Nan's house."

Kath's body lay on her bed, her dignity covered by an old duvet, her eyes closed tight, her children and grandchildren all taking turns to stare at her life-less form. Dreanna watched and listened as through their pain they began do-ing what every person does when a loved one dies. They remembered. They remembered the good times, the sad times, the arguments... but above all they remembered her, and her wicked sense of humour. Dreanna could do no more than hug her family, hold them close and join in their grief-stricken banter. Before long it was time for her to leave the room and her daughters-in-law to dress the body ready for the move to the mortuary, the chapel of rest and finally the crematorium.

As Dreanna sat in the living room watching the hustle and bustle of Kath's family; their mixed-up emotions and their numbness was the same numbness that she and her siblings had felt not so long ago. She stared around the room and her own memories slowly flooded back. Kath's home was very similar to Dreanna's family home as a child, full of nick-knacks and, second-hand fur-niture, cluttered in places but warm, clean and welcoming. Like most of her aunties' homes the doors were always open, people were never usually turned away... well in all honesty some were. Dreanna had the greatest respect for each one of her father's sisters.

"Proper old school birds," as Patrick always told her.

She liked them a lot. They didn't beat about the bush and they could talk the hind legs off donkey and often did so. They could be abrupt and forceful, but were all bought up with family morals, and family was the most impor-tant thing to them. They adored their children, they worshipped their grandchildren, and though they couldn't give them the material gifts so many other children enjoyed they smothered them in love and affection, along with the occasional slap on the back of the legs. They would defend them till their dying day.

Each aunt had special qualities of her own. Auntie Dot (or Dorothy) had emigrated to Australia with her husband Jack and their two sons many years ago. She was a large lady with a wart that sat precariously on the end of her nose. She had trained as a nurse in England and in the whole of Dreanna's life she had only had the pleasure of meeting her twice. The cost of coming back to England was too much for Dot and Jack to afford but their visits were special to Dreanna as a young girl. Both of them were so kind, with big hearts and smiling faces. Jack used to sit for hours with Dreanna teaching her how to draw and paint. He was such an amazing artist. Dot on the other hand, with Dreanna laying across her lap, told her stories of what is was like when she was young and all about this far away country she now lived in.

Patrick adored his elder sister and when the visits came to an end you could see in his eyes how heartbroken he was. But every week they wrote to each other, and once a month they sent each other a tape recording of different poems they had written and sometimes they recorded the fun times that went on in their individual homes. Dreanna loved her Auntie Dot.

Auntie Grace, well, she was a feisty old bird. She would tell you in no uncertain terms her point of view but she was one of the funniest women you would ever know. She could aggravate you until all you wanted to do was punch her in the face, but then once she had annoyed you to bursting point she would laugh and use her perverted sense of humour to get herself out of trouble. Grace was tiny, the complete opposite to Auntie Dot. She married her first love and they had two daughters. Grace lost her husband when Dreanna was very young, but she still remembered liking him very much; she always had trouble remembering their daughters and had to be reminded who they were at funerals. Grace was a character, a character full of mischief, but one of the most loving people you could ever know. Grace was fun.

Auntie Joy was the quiet one, almost shy in comparison to her sisters. Even though her real name was Ella she was known as Joy to most people. She had the same large frame as Dot and was one of the most amazing cooks – she certainly knew how to put on a feast for kings. She was married to Eric and they had produced two sons. It was with her family that Patrick, Iris and their children used to go on holiday with every year. Dreanna always laughed when remembering the time Auntie Joy couldn't be bothered to venture out of the caravan to go to the loo in the middle of the night and used a bucket instead. The only problem was the bucket had a hole in it and soaked the caravan floor. And the question has to be asked as to how did she manage to fit a rather large backside into a very small bucket? Auntie Joy was also an easy target for her sisters to ridicule, not in a hurtful or spiteful way but in a sort of 'take the piss' fashion. Joy was a sweet-natured woman... unless you annoyed her that is. Joy was homely.

Auntie Kath had it hard. Her first child was born a bastard – as they liked to call it in the olden days. But no matter what era, abortion was something this clan would never contemplate, not because of religious beliefs but because they believed a life was a life and no one had the right to destroy it or take it away. She married John and he was the biggest waste of time and effort that ever walked on two legs. The love of his life was alcohol and he spent every penny on it. Everyone knew what a pudenda he was, but for so many years Kath kept him in her home, and taking the last bit of money she had in her purse to go and get drunk instead of paying the rent.

Personality-wise she was as hard as nails, and who could blame her? She took no prisoners – she was a very strong woman. Kath and John had five children, six if you include Bruce, the son born out of wedlock, but Bruce was more of a father to his siblings than their own dad, and would often end up paying the rent on the council house in which they lived. Auntie Kath had sadness in her heart and Dreanna saw it in her eyes each time they met; she yearned for death everyday to take hold of her. She was never quite the same after her son Robin died and she missed him terribly. But now Auntie Kath had her wish, she was in the one place she longed to be, and she was finally reunited with the son she adored. Kath was strong.

Auntie Bet was the last surviving sister and the only one that had the dark skin and dark hair of their gypsy roots, and she too had her only child, a daughter, born outside the vows of marriage. It was actually Auntie Bet that told Dreanna when she was pregnant with Rebecca, "Ignore the comments of people calling you names for getting pregnant, it's actually a family tradition and anyway there's nothing wrong with being a slut in this family!"

Bet was fun to be around and finally found love with a man called Den. But yet again fate showed its hand and left her a widow. Bet was one of the only aunties that never removed herself from Dreanna's grasp when she gave affection. Dreanna loved being swamped by those rather large arms. Bet was secure.

Only Bet and Eric now survived, but for how long? Dreanna knew that a whole generation of her family that she had cherished, admired and loved, would soon be joining all the others, and now as she stared around the room with Kath's body upstairs she hoped that soon they would be all together again, moaning, grumbling about their children's squabbles... but above all else she hoped they would finally find eternal happiness.

Blood is Thicker than Water

February 7th 2009

After Kath's funeral the bond between Dreanna and two of her cousins grew stronger. Suzi was still consumed by grief and depression after losing her precious babies. Her nan and Dreanna tried everything in their power to support her and Dreanna felt proud that her three daughters all helped to try and lift their cousin Suzi out of the black spot she had sadly fallen into. It pleased Dreanna and lifted her heart so much to know that her children would never leave the side of a person who needed their support, and she felt humbled by their determination, generosity and affection.

Her other cousin, Kerry, was also suffering but it wasn't just through grief, it was the fact that her second born daughter, Regan, suffered from Rett Syndrome, a debilitating neurological disease that was slowly destroying this beautiful child.

Dreanna and Kerry never had anything to do with each other but their family bond was growing. They shared a warped sense of humour and now both had a need for each other's company. Dreanna couldn't understand why they were being pulled together. For what reason, after such a long time, could two people now need this friendship and support? Why was the love they now felt becoming an uncontrollable force of nature?

Regan was sitting on Dreanna's rug in the living room, her scrawny little legs protruding in front of her. The repetition of her hand to mouth action caught Dreanna's curiosity. "Kerry, why does she do that?" she asked, as Kerry lifted her third cup of tea to her mouth. The one thing Kerry did more than anyone else she knew was drink tea. Dreanna couldn't get her head around the vast amounts of the brown brew she could consume!

"It's part of the Retts. Kids with Retts often have repetitive hand movements, some of them wring their hands or clap. Regan has always put her hands to her mouth and chewed her fingers, it's just something she does."

Dreanna carried on watching this tiny child. "Kerry?"

"Yep."

Not one to keep her mouth shut, Dreanna asked the question most people shied away from. "What's her life expectancy?"

Kerry lifted her head and gazed into Dreanna's eyes. "We don't know. It's shorter than most people's but," she paused, "even though I don't like to think about it, I know that one day I'm most probably gonna have to bury my child.

I'm just going to enjoy what time I have with her... but fuck me, it's hard work, especially carrying her up the stairs!"

"Why haven't you got one of those stair lifts for her?" Dreanna asked.

"Because," Kerry sipped her tea, "the occupational therapist says our house is too small for a through-the-floor lift and they won't fund a stair lift. The help isn't there Dree – everybody assumes a disabled child gets what they need. We waited nearly two years for a bed with the sides on it to stop Regan falling out of bed at night. The OT told us to stick her on the floor while we were waiting. You would not believe how much we have to fight for. Everything we need just to give her some sort of quality of life is a constant battle. The whole system is complete bollocks. It sucks. big time."

Dreanna rubbed the bottom of her nose and bit on her top lip. "But what about the fund thing that was set up for her years ago by our cousin, is there no money in that to buy a stair lift?"

Kerry blew air from her nostrils sounding a little like a bull getting ready to charge the red flag, "No, not nearly enough. We need over eight thousand pounds to buy it, have it specially fitted to her shape and size and install it. It doesn't matter. I can cope, I have to don't I!"

The room fell silent as the cousins watched the little girl on the rug who would never know what it was like to walk, run, talk, play or grow into a mature adult. Her family had to make do and cope as best they could due to a system that was unable or even refused to acknowledge how much they needed help. It was a system that seemed to be strangled by rules and budgets and unsympathetic advisors who were unwilling to cut through the red tape and really help those who needed it most.

Dreanna jumped up from her chair slapping the tops of her legs. "Right! Here's what we're going to do. We're going to raise shitloads of money and buy the stair-lift thingy for her and anything else she needs too!"

"Dreanna, you're barking bloody mad! How the hell are we going to raise that sort of money?"

"Erm," Dreanna sucked in her bottom lip, "I haven't got a clue, but somehow we'll do it. The kids and Callum will help and I'm sure I can get some of the other family members to help too. If we can't help our own family, who can we help?"

Kerry answered with tears welling up in her eyes, "I... I don't know what to say."

"Shut up you old trollop-faced troll!" Dreanna gave a childish giggle as the nervous excitement shot through her body, "But what I will say is, if you're going to be spending more time around my house, you can bloody go and buy some tea bags 'cos I'm gonna need a second mortgage on my home because of your tea addiction!"

"Oi, Oi, who you calling a troll! You poisoned dwarf with short legs and dog-shit brown eyes!"

Instead of looking at Regan both cousins now fell about the floor laughing; through their laughter Dreanna knew that the hard work to raise the funds for Regan was going to cause her so much stress, but her heart was telling her 'this is what you should be doing'.

October 16th 2009

With the help of her own children, Callum, her niece Sadie, and Suzi, the amount of money in Regan's Fund now stood at £5,500. The work everyone was putting in to raise the money to buy this child a quality of life overtook all their lives. Dreanna even did the one thing she said she would never do and stood in front of an audience of people to give a demonstration of her abilities. Everybody assumed it was to raise money for Regan but Dreanna had a hidden agenda: she did it to prove to the people she loved that she could actually communicate with 'the other side', the apparent utopia that people hoped existed. One message after another came through and in one hour over twenty dead souls graced her with their presence. Would this finally have been enough for the acceptance she badly craved from the people she loved? Only the family members knew the answer to this, but Dreanna hoped and prayed that now the pointing fingers, the stares and the talking behind her back, would come to an end and she could hold her head high.

The final project for the year was a naked calendar. This had taken on the same format as the 'Calendar Girls' but the age range of the people involved ran from nineteen to well past middle-age. Friends who never knew Regan removed their clothes and their respectability, their wobbly bits and private bits only being covered by leaves, rugby balls, plant pots, and tinsel, in a bid to help obtain the equipment desperately needed to give Regan and her family some quality of life.

One picture and one month were left to be photographed, December. The women of the family decided that this was their month and Dreanna's living room was filled with naked family members, tinsel and a copious amount of tit tape. Callum, who had taken all the pictures to date, was again standing in the kitchen while each woman was positioned in place, their sexual organs being artfully hidden by tinsel or an elbow of the woman standing next to them.

Callum's embarrassment was obvious as he entered the room. It wasn't the nudity that bothered him as much as the fact that these women took no prisoners; if he screwed this up he would never live it down and be the butt of the jokes for years to come. The one thing you didn't mess with was the women in this erratic, often dysfunctional, but loving family.

David Bailey held nothing on Callum that evening. He was totally professional (once the embarrassment subsided) and clicked his tiny digital camera until over fifty pictures had been taken.

With Callum's job now complete and him safely in another room, the hustle and bustle of hoards of women getting dressed filled the living room. It was a room full of boobs, bums and the occasional "Ouch!" as the tit tape which held the tinsel in place was ripped from bare flesh. Dreanna struggled with her bra and hoisted it onto her shoulders then stopped and stared down at her breasts which seemed to now not fit into its cups. Two inches of space were between her skin and the black material. She spoke loudly and into the chaos of the room, "Er, I don't get it... my bra doesn't fit me anymore."

Kerry tapped her on the shoulder, "You stupid twonker, that's 'cos it's my fooking bra!" Kerry snatched back her underwear from her cousin, the bra thief, "You were wearing a white bra you reject, not black!"

"Oh!" Dreanna laughed so loud that she had to place her hands between her legs, and could do nothing but watch as tears of laughter filled the room. What a night, what a family, what a moment in time when all their differences were put aside and all that mattered was to help this one, cherished, treasured, beautiful creation known as Regan.

September 30th 2010
In the months that followed the Calendar, Regan's Fund had nearly hit its total of ten thousand pounds, the stair-lift was on order and sensory toys had been bought to help stimulate Regan's mind. What a journey the last year had been, but the point that stood out most to Dreanna was when Regan finally trusted Dreanna enough to talk to her through her eyes. Sounds stupid that someone could actually talk to you through their eyes doesn't it? But Regan did just that. She stared wide-eyed at Dreanna and blinked so slowly as if her eye control was being played in slow motion. She then held her eyes tightly closed before opening them wide once more and then slowly closing them – the sequence carried on for over ten minutes. Dreanna was so astounded that she couldn't blink back at her because tears were streaming down her cheeks. She had at long last built enough trust to communicate with the child she now loved so passionately. In her own way, was Regan saying "Thank you?"

October 1st 2010
With all her family out of the house Dreanna sat in front of the electric fire, the artificial flames lighting up the otherwise dark room. She drank her tea and began the arduous task of opening that morning's post. As always the brown-coloured envelopes were left to last. The last quarter's bills were due in and

in typical Dreanna fashion she never paid them until the last minute or when the bold red writing appeared on the letter reading 'Final Demand', but one envelope grabbed her attention. It was addressed to the founder of Regan's Fund and looked highly important. It was from the local voluntary association she had contacted three months before when she had enquired if she needed to obtain a charity number for their fund-raising group. It read:

'We are delighted to tell you that due to your efforts in raising money for Regan you are now eligible to apply for charity status.'

"Charity status," Dreanna said aloud. She didn't hang about but began that very moment putting pen to paper, making phone calls, and googling whatever she could to find any information as to how and what she had to do next to turn Regan's Fund into a charity to help others like her.

November 4th 2010
Dreanna was woken once again by Callum. She had for the third time that week fallen asleep at the dining room table trying to write her legal constitution, child protection policy, allocation of funds policy and all the other numerous amounts of paperwork she needed to complete before submitting it to the people in charge of making the decision as to whether or not she could become a UK-based charity. She lifted her head off the table, her eyes sunken, her exhausted body unable to move. She was even to tired to talk to her husband.

Callum rubbed his wife's shoulder. "Dree, its 5 o'clock in the morning! Can you please do me a favour today? Will you turn off the bloody phone and sleep? Even if you sleep the whole day, just close your eyes and forget about all this shit for a moment and get some rest, please!" He kissed her forehead and left for work.

She knew he was right, she did need some sleep. Her mind was muddled, disorganised and constantly going over all the things she needed to complete. It was at times like this she wished she had listened more in school so she could understand the long words and terminology that was being thrown at her. She couldn't help but ask herself time and again what she was doing it for, because in all honesty she didn't understand.

She lay on the settee covered by a fluffy pink blanket, her eyes feeling heavy and ready to close tight, but the other side of her life had other different ideas. The electric pulsating shock surged through her body and Dreanna held her head tight in her hands as the pain engulfed her.

Iris was standing in between worlds with another woman she did not recognise; in her arms lay a baby, so small so perfect so... so translucent? She handed him to Dreanna. "Dreanna, hold him, hug him, let him feel what it is to be loved."

When Dreanna held out her arms and nestled the baby close to her chest, the love she felt for him was instant, like the feeling she had when she held her own babies for the first time. She was head over heels in love with this flawless bundle of a see-through package. "I don't understand Mum. Who, what is he? I can see right through him. Why do I feel so much love for him? I don't understand."

"I haven't got long Dreanna, but I knew, we knew, due to the lack of communication in the family now, that it would be a while before anyone tells you. I'm sorry Dree I have to take him now, but 'hugs give love' – remember that."

For once all Dreanna wanted was for her mother to stay with her a little longer. To hold her and talk to her, to chat like they did before she became sick. But she had learned over the years that she did not have long. She never had long. It took a lot for a deceased energy to hold itself in the physical plane, so Dreanna just had to be grateful for the limited time they had together. And Iris was gone as quickly as she came, but the energetic waves of electricity still coursed through Dreanna's veins.

Seraphina was by her side. "Well, haven't we been a busy human?" The softness in her voice made Dreanna breathe a huge sigh of relief. "I have someone here who wants to say hello to you." She stepped aside to reveal the only surviving puppy of Dreanna's other two dogs' misdemeanors. The family had done so well at keeping the two German Shepherds apart, but nature's urges had taken control towards the end of their bitches season.

Two days before Layla, their bitch, gave birth she began scratching at the walls in the living room trying to dig holes in each corner, and the family knew the arrival of puppies wouldn't be long. Dreanna didn't bother going to bed as she wanted to be with her four-legged best friend when the fur babies arrived. At ten-thirty on the day of Dreanna's brother's birthday, Layla began panting and appeared uncomfortable and restless. A few hours later the obvious uterine contractions were seen to take place. Layla slept between each contraction but after a couple of hours everything stopped, Layla heaved herself into a standing position and a thick black substance left her vagina. Dreanna knew instantly something was wrong and made an early morning phone call to the vet. She hadn't been to bed for nearly thirty-six hours, but the fear she had for her best friend gave her enough adrenalin to keep going. Hendrix was born by emergency caesarian. The other puppies in the litter had died in their mother's womb. At five days old Hendrix began squealing like a seagull – the same horrible noise Fawn had made all those years earlier. Another emergency trip to the vet was needed. Hendrix was so small and weak and that he fitted neatly into the palm of their hands.

"I'm sorry," the vet said, "There's nothing more we can do for him."

Giving up without a fight wasn't something Dreanna, Callum and their daughters would contemplate; no one was going to abandon this tiny fragile life. They spent day after day and night after night feeding him with a syringe, stimulating his bladder and bowels and loving him like they would their own child. He was the family's four-legged *long-haired baby and there was no way they would accept that no more could be done. At ten months old Hendrix was still part of their family, still smaller than other German Shepherd dogs of his age, but he was theirs and still holding his own and enjoying his life to the max. But things took a turn for the worse as the spring weather began to change and the hot summer sun shone bright in the sky.*

The family was enjoying the last of that day's sunshine when Hendrix started to vomit. He didn't want to eat and struggled to drink, and didn't want to sit by Callum, which he did every night. Instead he never left Dreanna's side, following her wherever she went and curling his furry form around her legs. Dreanna knew in her heart something was wrong. She loved him like no other dog they had owned and was not prepared to acknowledge her own fear; she didn't want him to die, and would not accept what her consciousness mind was telling her, that Hendrix was going home.

The following morning Hendrix lay motionless on the kitchen floor and Callum rushed him to the vet once again. The diagnosis was a kidney infection and the necessary drugs were administered. He was kept in for observation and more tests and seemed to improve once the antibiotics got into his system, but Wednesday morning brought the news that none of the family wanted to hear: Hendrix's other organs had begun to fail and he was slowly and painfully dying. As always in her family the decision was a joint one, to allow the vet to terminate the life of this much-loved member. Each of them spent time in the vet's surgery saying goodbye and allowing their tears to fall with no embarrassment or shame. Callum and Dreanna were the last to see their beloved pet alive.

They sat on a blanket on the floor with Hendrix laying between them. He was unable to stand but still totally giving with his affection and constant wet sloppy licks. Dreanna watched as the vet filled the syringe with the liquid that would send Hendrix to an eternal sleep.

"When I administer the drug you may hear him cough and choke. Please don't worry about this – it is totally normal and nothing to concern yourselves with."

Callum and Dreanna both nodded. The vet leaned down and injected the 'sleeping forever' medicine into Hendrix. Dreanna was blind with tears and held his fur tightly between her fingers, not wanting to let him go. A choking sound filled the air but it wasn't from Hendrix it was from Callum. For the first time in over 28 years Callum cried, crying beyond meaning and measure. He cried like a child, like a grieving father.

For the next week Dreanna could neither speak nor sleep; she spent her time remembering the life that had just been ripped away from her. She couldn't understand why she was feeling such overwhelming grief when she, above anyone, knew that life was eternal. But grieve she did for she was physical; she felt pain and loss so completely it emptied her soul of everything else that was important.

Dreanna let her memories fade as she pulled the heavenly figure of Hendrix close to her, her face smothered in licks and kisses as the tears of happiness fell freely from her eyes. She didn't care if this was actually real or not, she was going to enjoy this brief moment in time with the dog she loved as much as her own children.

"You still struggle to believe, don't you?" Serephina asked.

"I will always struggle," Dreanna lifted her head.

"Let him go now Dreanna, we need to talk."

Dreanna released her grip on Hendrix and he ran off into a space of light.

"What is it you want? What is it you want to know?"

"I want to know everything, but at the same time I don't. I want to change the world but at the same time I just want it to suffer. That sounds so wrong doesn't it?"

"Explain child."

"The world is filled with so much pain and destruction; everything is so hard to understand. Regan didn't deserve the life she has, she's a child, it's so not fair. Take the charity status I'm trying to get. I don't understand it, I don't even understand the correct jargon that goes with it. All the sittings I've done, all the tears I've seen people shed, all the hate and the anger, the visits from dead soldiers, what is the point? I'm one person who wants the world to change, I've felt the pain, I've seen the pain, but how the hell is someone like me going to make all this work? Part of me just wants to sit back and say 'fuck it all', and anyway we all go to the same place when we die so why bother trying, the other side is better than here isn't it? And while I'm on one – who the hell designed the female body? We have to go through the pain of periods, the pain of child birth, the pain and hot flushes of the menopause, and to top it off you put our clitoris right next to the hole we pee out of so any rampant fumblings cause us to have bloody cystitis." Dreanna paused and smiled, "I think I've finished moaning now."

"Well, I'm so glad you got all that off your chest. I will try my best to answer all your questions. Let's begin with Regan and the womanly form that you already know the answer to, we are not in charge of the evolutionary tract of the human body as you well know. Please child, understand things go wrong and in Regan's case her genetics have a flaw, but know this, one day man will find the cure to her disease; it's closer than you think. As for being a woman, your body is designed to give new life and with all the changes comes the pain and trauma that is felt. It's just an inevitable fact of being in a physical life. Change equals a time of emotional and physical pain. A woman's body can take the different changes that life bestows on it."

"But what about women who can't have children, is that just another flaw?"

"Quite simply yes, but in some cases some woman have decided before they made the transition down to a physical existence that they do not want a child in this lifetime. They want to experience other aspects of life that they may have never experienced before. As for the charity, I need you to cast your mind back. You were told to study the shape of the pyramid were you not?"

Dreanna frowned and felt guilty that one of her teachers had given her a task to do, and in the physical throes of life she had totally forgotten ...bad student! "Oh shit yeah... sorry I forgot."

"The pyramid is a shape formed of solid sides to hold up and balance its structure. If we begin at the top of the highest point and work our way down you can see that the form increases in size, it doubles with each row that is built. This, child, is the pyramid effect. The ancient Egyptians knew that the pyramid held what is required to sustain life and the shape of the pyramid has been adopted by many cultures throughout the world, but sadly people have forgotten why this shape is so needed for life to flourish. You see my sweet Dreanna, you are the pyramid, you help one life at a time, this then makes that person go back to their family happy and fulfilled, then their family go about their daily chores with more confidencey and reassurance and that changes the attitudes and disturbances of others around them. Thus you are changing not only one person but many. All human life at this stage in its existence needs each other to survive, but for you to continue you have to find your balance; a pyramid's structure is only as strong as its foundation. You must save the children Dreanna for they are the future. This is your job, and this is your destiny, child."

"But how? How can I save the children? Look at our history, look at all the people that have in some way changed this world for the better. Gandhi, who changed the world and showed everyone that change can happen by demonstrating in a peaceful non-violent way; Florence Nightingale who helped the poorer classes and healed their wounds and sickness free of charge; Martin Luther King who ended the segregation and again did it in a non-violent manner; Princess Diana who touched people with AIDS and changed the views of the world for an infected person; Nelson Mandela who led the way to free Africa from the apartheid movement; John Lennon and Michael Jackson who tried hard to change the world through their music, and now you give me the job of trying to save the children!

How many times do I have to tell you? I'm a nobody, I don't have a talent or a gift. I'm not special or in a position of status, I'm just me, so insignificant and in all honesty I'm as thick as shit and wouldn't know where to begin. You can't give someone like me this job, you can't put this on my shoulders. I don't have the knowledge or even the willpower to undertake a task as great at this! I don't even have the willpower to give up smoking, so please give this job to someone else who can make that difference, someone who has the experience and the know-how. Please Seraphina, I'm sorry I just can't do it, I can't!"

"You will. You will show the world that its future does not lay in how rich a country is but how it nurtures its children. Children on Earth are being suffocated and their voices are being taken away; help them find their voices, help them build a better world for all to enjoy. We believe in you, now please believe in us."

Dreanna slowly drifted into sleep but the final words belonged to her, "I can't believe, I'm sorry, I just can't..."

A Hug is a Handshake from the Heart

March 25th 2011
It had been months since Dreanna submitted her paperwork and she had all but given up getting a response from the 'powers that be' regarding her charity status. She sighed deeply as she finished the washing up. Undecided whether or not to phone them yet again to find where she was in the queue of other hopefuls, she chose not to waste any more of her time and carried on with her own life and painting the downstairs bathroom.

There was a knock on the front door. Dreanna carefully climbed down the rungs of the ladder. Her and ladders didn't mix, and her clumsiness had often left her battered and bruised from the times she had fallen off, so her policy was always one step at a time when it came to any kind of DIY.

It was the postman. He gave her a handful of letters, one by recorded delivery that needed her signature.

"Oo! I wonder what this is?"

The postman looked at her as if she was stupid. "Well if you open it you'll find out, won't you?"

Dreanna fumbled with the edge of the letter, opened it and scanned the words. Her face broke into a huge smile. "Oh my God! We've done it. Woo hoo!"

"Good news then?" the postman asked, shuffling the rest of the letters.

"Oh yes, really good news." Dreanna grabbed hold of the postman and planted a kiss on his cheek; he turned a bright crimson. Inside the house she picked up the phone and dialed Callum's number. "Callum we did it, we did it! We are now a UK-based children's charity. Oh my God, I'm so excited, I've got to tell everyone… I can't stop crying, I can't believe we actually done it… Ooooo, I can't breathe…"

Callum interrupted his hysterical wife, "Dreanna – you did it, not we… I'm so proud of you. Well done… I can't talk now as I'm down a hole wrestling with a gas pipe, but love you and speak later okay?"

Dreanna went through every number in her phone and called everyone she knew. The tears of joy constantly fell, her heart was saying 'You can do this' while her rational, conscious brain was asking 'Can you really?'

June 6th 2011
Within the first week of gaining charity status Dreanna phoned numerous other charities asking their advice on how to build up her newly-formed organi-

sation. She was shocked at how some of the larger more recognised charities refused to speak or advise her. One in particular, another registered children's charity, actually said, "Why would we help you? You are our competition," while others just hung up immediately. But a few were friendly and offered her guidance and instruction. She wrote it all down in her little black book and started the task of going through all the advice they gave her. One useful piece of assistance they told her was to get a patron for her charity, a well known figure that people recognised and admired. They said this would help with public awareness – it figures that the higher the celebrity the more interest you get.

So over four thousand letters and emails were written to management companies of the rich and famous, over two thousand to large corporations and famous high street stores and over one thousand to the smaller organisations and businesses, all within the first week of receiving that magical seven-digit charity number.

The weeks passed and slowly emails were being replied to, and letters were arriving from the managers of the celebrities she had approached; they pretty much all said the same thing:

> "As you may be aware we receive numerous letters like yours asking if we can offer support to your venture but unfortunately we cannot help everyone. At this present time our client (name of the celebrity) helps with many other charities, (list of the well known charities everybody has heard of) but we wish you luck."

Over three thousand emails and letters were answered, each one near enough saying the same thing, each one declining help.

Dreanna sat on her living room floor unable to suppress her sadness. In front of her was yet another letter from a family with a daughter who was critically ill and needing help; next to it was a pile of rejection letters. She cried. The outside world was silent to her and she sat wallowing in her own self-pity. She hadn't heard the front door open and now Rebecca was standing in front of her. No words were exchanged but her first-born child took her mother in her arms and hugged her tightly. She wiped away her mother's tears, took her face in her hands and spoke softly to her.

"Mum, what you've done and what you've achieved makes us all so proud of you. You don't need these famous people to get there, you just need to have faith in yourself. We believe in you, now believe in yourself."

There were those two bloody words again: Faith and Belief.

The two generations sat holding each other tightly, both now crying, and in Dreanna's heart it wasn't the words Rebecca had spoken that helped give her back a small percentage of faith, it was her actions. It was her arms that held her tight and the hug she gave her mother. It was the love the hug could give that brought her back from her own negative state of mind. And that was why Dreanna's small charity would always be different from the thousands of others that were out there. Her charity was not going to become just another business, just another public organisation that relied on the rich and famous to succeed. Her charity would give a pair of open arms to anyone who needed help, free of charge and with love. They were building their own pyramid, not out of bricks and stones but out of hope.

Dreanna worked so hard trying to build up this tiny charity. The phone rang constantly with calls from families asking for help or advice, and she gave each one her time, even if it was 3am in the morning. She was exhausted but this time she felt tired in a good way. Her tiredness soon turned into anger and frustration but this time it was aimed partly at the eternal beings who had given her such an enormous task. How was she, with a tiny charity, supposed to overcome the red tape and corruption that was part of a system which was supposed to help to feed the starving, shelter the homeless and stick up for the underdog? She had discovered that some of the celebrities who were praised for their charity work actually took a big fee for attending a function. Money was sidelined for expenses rather than the people it was collected for, and religious organisations that were supposed to help people were now rife with child abuse allegations. She was angry that there seemed to be so much hypocrisy in the world and that she had no idea how to deal with it. She couldn't understand. Or was this just the nature of the beast and what man has become through evolution, greed, power and control? To what degree are we prepared to rape a young person's mind and destroy what little hope for a future they might have? How much longer would they be deprived of the essentials they require for life to be sustained?

Thousands of questions flooded her brain. But she wasn't going to give up. She knew that people only found the passion and desire to help others when they had to live through an experience themselves, but when would they open their eyes and see the truth behind human existence, and the art of giving for nothing more than a 'thank you'?

Many events were arranged to raise their funds or help other non-profit organisations reach their target amounts. Dreanna worked up to seventeen hours a day, seven days a week, and still found time to do her sittings, look after her home and family and the animals that they shared it with.

Dreanna sat alone, confused as to what to do next. She was drained but kept smiling, trying to work out what was becoming of her life. Of course she was happy that she had finally achieved something that could seriously help others, but still could not understand 'why her?' Part of her wanted to go back to the person she was years ago, when her secret was hidden from family and friends. She wanted to go back to the endless piles of other people's ironing and even the cleaning and scrubbing of toilets in the evening. But her life had changed; her body was changing and mid-life was now upon her. The evil throes of the menopause kept her awake most nights as she sweated profusely and the hot flushes took away her sleep. The knowledge that she would never be able to give life to another child, or hold one to her breast, hurt her and made her feel worthless. She was in a tunnel that had no end, in a life that made no sense, perplexed as to what her future held. But she felt humbled when she heard other's stories of struggle and woe – yet at the same time she still felt angry.

Her anger was aimed at the politicians who could change this world and feed the starving and shelter the homeless; she felt angry at the way the vast wealth of religious organisations was hidden away in vaults instead of being used to help those in need; she felt angry at the people who couldn't think for themselves and believed every newspaper article and thought that everything they saw on television was true; she felt angry at the hypocrisy of the world but most of all she felt angry with the eternal life force that had spoken to her since a child. She couldn't understand. She wanted to believe, she needed to have faith, but she just couldn't. She lay down on the settee and stared at the clock on the wall. It read 12.20pm. She closed her eyes, hoping that when she awoke she would feel different and the rage that burned inside had been extinguished.

Her body was freezing, but the electrical energy and high voltage vibrated throughout her whole being, and her heart pumped like never before. Her translucent shape was once again standing apart, staring back at her own physical body. She was free. With one final glance back at herself she lifted upwards, not concerned with the boundaries or her own limitations. She looked up towards the sun and with the anger still burning inside she hoisted herself towards her target. The sun got closer and she went through it. But where was she?

She was floating in water. A man on a small rowing boat beckoned her to get into the boat and her body lifted itself out of the water. Her body wasn't wet – it was dry, and she was different. Her skin was as pure as snow, no tattoos, no old skin spots, no blemishes. It was untainted by life and all the physical abuse it had endured. Instead of a scruffy old pair of ripped jeans and a Nirvana tee-shirt she was covered in what could only be described as a toga, a material so beautifully soft to the touch. It draped her feminine form, and it was covering her, yes, but it felt part of her own skin. She was once again baffled. The man stopped rowing as they approached land and ushered her to get out of the boat. She stepped out onto ground that looked like Brighton beach before the tide went out, full of pebbles of different shapes and sizes. It was rough to her feet but didn't cause her pain. She bent down to touch the ground that looked so harsh but felt so soft. Hundreds, thousands of people were rushing around; a group of people this size would normally have made her turn on her heels and run in the opposite direction, but she walked forward.

A line of people stood in front of her and she tapped one on the shoulder. "Where am I? Who are you?"

A boy no older than seventeen looked at her. "You really don't know do you Dreanna?" he laughed. "It's not my place to say where you are," he paused. "But who are we? We are reporters. We are the ones that report what is going on, on Earth; we're also the ones who can give information and ideas to you and your kind. You shouldn't really be here, this isn't your place. Walk towards the light Dreanna, walk towards the light."

Dreanna turned her head and started walking towards a brightly coloured light that shone at her side. She walked through it and towards a bench that stood in front of her. She held out her hand to touch it and it too was soft and smooth. A dog ran into her vision. A woman appeared sitting on the bench.

"Ah, look at him play. You know he couldn't walk for years before coming here. His old bones were so crippled, but now look at him, finally he is free to do whatever it is he wants to do."

Dreanna bent down and held the woman's hand. "Where am I? What am I supposed to do?"

"You, child, should ask your dogs what to do. They have all the answers."

"Er, what? Do you mean I've gotta start rolling about in fox shit and pissing up a lamp post? 'Cos in all honesty that is not deemed acceptable behaviour where I come from."

"No Dreanna, I do not mean that! I mean you should live for the moment and not worry about tomorrow, next week or even next year, just enjoy the here and now, the moment you're living in." She was gone and so was the dog.

A man took hold of Dreanna's hand, a look of concern on his face. "My daughter, have you seen my daughter? She was supposed to be here ages ago, I can't find her, I've looked everywhere. I can't stop and talk to you, I must find her, I just must." He was gone.

Dreanna stood alone, unsure of where to go or what to do next. Wherever this place was it was so beautiful. The vibrant colours stood out in a three dimensional sort of way. She was transfixed by a leaf. She had never before seen the way the green hues shone, as if they were being lit from within by an internal force.

"There you are Dreanna. We've been looking for you. Come, come follow us." Two women who had spoken in unison took hold of Dreanna's hands and walked her through another beam of light. They were both oriental in appearance and both wore a kimono that fitted their shape and size perfectly. Their hair was black, pulled tightly back to form a neat bun, their eyes were as dark as onyx and shimmered when the filtering light hit them. They were perfection and beauty and they wouldn't stop talking at the same time!

"Don't be afraid, walk this way," they said in harmony with each other.

Once through the light she found herself standing on a beam of grey slate. At the end of the beam stood four pillars, each holding up a roof so high Dreanna could hardly see it. There were no walls, and the whole structure was surrounded by the clearest cerulean water. They sat Dreanna down and washed her feet; the water was warm, their touch velvety. She didn't know what to say or do, she had so many questions but she could not speak; all she could do was watch as her feet were dried delicately and without haste. "We will always look after you Dreanna, we are always here for you." They giggled childishly. "Now you must go that way." They pointed to their left where another luminous glow appeared. Dreanna walked over it and at the end of the beam stood Seraphina and Qulib. Every family member including Dreanna's parents, grand-parents, aunties, uncles, plus a host of people she did not recognise lined the way, their feet washed over by the free flowing water. She wanted desperately to run into the arms of her Dad, but he made no sound or movement, he just stared at his daughter, nodded his head and smiled. He looked so young, so healthy, so happy.

Seraphina held out her hand and Dreanna took it and walked with her into a mist of nothingness. She was mesmerised by the sights she was seeing; pillars stood all around her, each one engraved with markings she had never seen before. The pillars stood so tall, with no roof or sides. Dreanna could do no more than stare.

"Welcome home child."

Dreanna turned and looked at Seraphina. "What? Am I ... am I dead? Please don't tell me I'm dead, I didn't get a chance to say my see-you-laters."

"No sweet child, you are not dead, you are what we call in a transferred state. You will be going back. But the time has come for you to receive just some of our knowledge. We have much to teach you, and you have much to learn."

"I'm not ready, I'm not the right person you should be telling this to." Dreanna felt fear rise inside her.

"You are ready and you are the right person. You see, you do not follow others' words, you do not believe that a truth is spoken and must be adhered too. You know inside we all have to find our own truth through the experience of life, not because one other physical creation has said it is so, but because of the feeling that you hold in your heart. You, my child, are the right person; but tell me why after all this time do you still not trust us and believe in us? Your mother Iris came to you and showed you the baby, did she not? The same baby your nephew lost through miscarriage, on precisely the same day and time it happened, yet you still do not believe. You have reported back to many grieving families their loved one's final words, and in our reckoning this has happened over three thousand times, yet you still do not believe. You have been visited by many in your lifetime, you have glimpsed what life after death is, yet you still do not believe. What would it take for you to trust us, have faith in us and believe in us?"

Dreanna lowered her head and spoke in a calm soft voice. "I don't know... I really don't know. I struggle every day to fit in and be accepted. I've spent years being a 'yes man' agreeing with people and what they say just so I don't have to let them see the real me, just so I don't have to be ridiculed by anyone. I've been laughed at and spat on. I've been given so many labels by people that don't even know me. But I struggle, as I don't even know who I am anymore. I try and change things, I try and give people hope to continue with their lives, and as I try I hit yet another brick wall, another obstacle that stops me moving forward."

"Do you want recognition for what you have achieved?"

"No of course I don't! I don't want to be placed on that pedestal, I don't want to be admired and worshipped. Why should I want that? Isn't life about giving to others without wanting anything back? Isn't life about making your journey worthwhile and reassuring others that they are not alone? Isn't life about just being honest and being true to yourself...?"

"But you are not being true to who you are and what your capabilities are, are you? You hide each day behind a shield... a shield that you think protects you from others' irrational words and thoughts. Some may say you are embarrassed by what you can do. Are you ashamed and embarrassed Dreanna?"

"No, no, I'm not ashamed and not embarrassed, but I just don't understand one thing. Why? Why can so many others who claim to do what I do manage to stand with their heads held high, have no worries or feel the physical pain that I do when we talk? Why can they be allowed to do this work and still enjoy a physical existence and experience such things as being in a crowded room without feeling their brains are being fucked senseless? Why can they have that life yet I have to struggle?"

"Because they are not you, because they do not see what you see, because they do not feel the pain and remorse, because their job on this journey is to report the messages between worlds. You have reported, you have given every part of your being with no charge, with dignity, and with the one thing we here feel every day. You have given every inch of yourself with the emotion that is love, and that my sweet child is why you are different to them.

You talk about struggle and not being able to be near others. Ask yourself one question; do you need others? Do you need the company of others to feel complete?"

"I get lonely sometimes, but that feeling doesn't last long, so the answer is no, I don't need the company of others to feel complete. My completeness comes when I'm alone watching the birds and the insects and the wind blow through the trees. Solitude isn't an issue as I can be whole without company. I need Callum though. Without him I couldn't survive ,could I? His wages pay the mortgage, feed us and keep us warm in winter, but that sounds so harsh and so selfish. I couldn't live without him even though most of the time he is a pain in the arse!"

Seraphina smiled. "Then maybe you should understand that he was given to you to take care of your physical needs so you can be the person you need to be. Haven't you ever asked yourself why your relationship has worked for so long, when the pair of you are so different? The answer my child is you need him to be able to fulfill your destiny. He provides and protects you in a physical sense, but as much as you need him, he needs you to give him the clarity and security, the trust and the abundant love that you both share.

Now we must move forward; we have a lot to tell you. Let us go back to the pyramid. When you leave here write down all the numbers that hold meaning to your life. You have always stated three is the magic number. It may help you understand why you are the pyramid we spoke of before. Work it out and understand child, life is an equation but the conclusion has to be solid. Only you can build the solid structure, build it well and build it with love."

Seraphina stood with her blonde hair flowing in abundance down her back. Her beauty still made Dreanna gasp as she thought just how perfect Seraphina was – not Mary Poppins perfect (no one can be as perfect as Miss P.) – but perfect all the same. Dreanna's mind began picturing Seraphina hovering through the air then lowering herself to the ground with a talking umbrella. A vision of a woman so beautiful that any living creature, male or female, would die to see, and let's face it most did have to die to witness what stood before her. Seraphina was practically perfect in every way... except that in Dreanna's thoughts Seraphina was talking to an inanimate object.

Dreanna smirked to think such stupid thoughts when she was supposed to be serious. She looked at Qulib, and noticed the stern expression on his face that only a teacher would have when his pupils were not paying attention.

"You knew what I was thinking then, didn't you?"

"Yes, yes I did. Now once you've finished analysing can we begin?"

"Sorry boss, Mr, Sir, I mean Qulib. Sorry but before we begin I have to say that that is one of the most stupidest names I think I've ever heard. It sounds like you have something stuck in your throat when you say it. Quullibbbb," Dreanna spoke deep into her throat and growled his name.

"Dreanna, you still after all this time have not worked out why I have told you my name is Qulib? I, my child, am Balance, I am Equilibrium!"

"Ah now I get it, you are balance and you used the letters in your name to form a shorter version of who you are. That's so cool. Aren't you a clever dead person?"

"I'm not a 'dead person', I am a Keeper... now please can we begin, and child may I ask you to please try and be serious?" Qulib nodded his head in a displeased manner.

Dreanna began her nervous verbal diarrhoea mumblings. "Sorry, I just had one of those moments, you know when all you want to do is sort of be stupid and childish. I blame Seraphina personally 'cos if she wasn't here then I wouldn't have had the picture of her being Mary Poppins in my head." All eyes were on Dreanna. "Whoops," she said and pursed her lips together and pretended to sew them up. She looked at Qulib, her eyes wide, her mouth sealed, her mind open to all he would tell her.

Qulib sat crossed-legged, his fingers toying with his long white beard that went into a point just above his navel. His white hair hung past his shoulders. He was clothed in the same garment that covered Dreanna's ghostly figure. He was so very old. He spoke in the same soft manner as Seraphina but his voice had some sort of accent to it that she could not decipher. Qulib rubbed his hands together, looked at his pupil and began.

"The universe is a vast and open space. A void in time and a doorway to much more than the human mind could ever believe to be true. It holds many secrets that man will actually never know the truth of until the time when the inevitable happens and death prevails.

For thousands and thousands of years people have ventured and travelled persistently around the globe, searching for the real truth. Tombs have been unearthed, fossils have been found and scrolls have been deciphered. The continuation for a reason as to why and how the human life was formed is still the focus of many arguments where people claim they have the 'real truth' behind your existence. But, as we have seen, the arguments do not just stop at words but turn into hatred and needless lives being destroyed.

Over time much of the 'real truth' has been lost. The truth behind all humanoid existence still lies dead and buried beneath the rock formations, the wide expanse of the ocean and closer to the Earth's crust. So how can it be that one religion, faith or scientific evaluation knows everything about the reason 'why' a physical life is felt? The true answer is they don't. They would all like to believe they can solve the mysteries of all civilisation, and will continue to try and prove that their way is the only way there is.

To follow one particular faith or belief may give a person hope, and a feeling of a central knowledge structure to their lives. For many this is not enough, they feel they have to have an explanation for every possible thing that has ever manifested on Earth. The hows, whys and wherefores are really not important, as somehow, someway, Man will survive and religious beliefs or scientific evaluations will not seem quite as important in the greater scale of things. There are a few things that are required by man to live a satisfactory life:

Light and Warmth, Water, Food and Shelter. These things enable you to survive, and continue your existence. On an emotional scale you need and crave more, but to flourish in an exultant life you only need another three possessions:

Hope: That life does not end when the last breath has been expelled from the lungs.

Faith: That one day all wars will cease and every human will have enough food, water and shelter.

Enjoyment: Life should be enjoyed. Emotions you have to feel are at times inevitably painful, but enjoyment is the experience of life.

Each and every human has to go through a transitional stage of being. This stage begins when the first beat of the heart is drummed inside the womb. From there on each day that the heart beats is another day closer to a physical existence. You know through science that the growing life goes through a metamorphosis of changes. Each organ grows stronger daily, each cell, muscle and nerve, will begin to change shape and evolve into the form of a human. But it is the human brain where a great deal of work must be done. Its structure is remarkable, it holds the power to control and mould the person. It can manipulate the body, give it false hope and give it pain. It is the vessel that makes you the person you are.

Many seek solace in the knowing that all life was created at the finger-tips of one great being. They believe that, with one touch from him, he gave life to all we see on the sphere where you reside. What if the world wasn't created by the one source? Would this destroy many people's faith? Would their lives seem empty and would a great void appear in their hearts? The answer to this is most probably yes. For these devout believers cannot and will never see any different reason for why life exists. They have become mesmerised into a chain of others' views and have formulated even in the 21st century what has become a powerful tool to control the masses. All it takes is for one person with considerable knowledge, a person who has convinced many with their words and you end up with an equation of: "Follow me, I have the answers to life, the reason behind our existence, the reason behind our pain, and if you don't, then you will suffer more pain for eternity."

To understand why humans behave the way they do, we have to revert back to the naturalistic side of life. For every animal that you cohabit with has to prove its own strength, and this strength enables it to survive. Nature is all about the survival of the fittest. Many battles take place in nature every day. These battles decide who the leader is and who the followers are. The pack of wolves, the pride of lions, the herd of elephants, all have to be led by the strongest and most intelligent of their kind. They are chosen through the strength of their physical bodies and by their astute and dexterous minds. Whoever wins the battle gives the victor the power to take control and lead their species to the next stage of their existence, thus the same hypothesis can be used in the evolution of man. For it is the strongest of men that lead nations and religious institutions. Their strength comes from a play on words rather than the strength of their physical bodies, just like a colony of ants busy working to provide for the masses and building extensions of different routes and roads that lead back to the main nest, so too, the homo-sapiens builds towns and roads on the orders of one man's or one women's words. So you see we all have to be governed by 'one' who has proved they are worthy to take control. You all have to be a leader or follower. In many ways it is the most common rule of each species; it is the Rule of Nature.

Time and time again man has made some extreme mistakes in governing nations. These mistakes have led to many innocent lives being lost. Their mistakes have left countries without the basic requirements which are needed for life to flourish. Why is this so? The answer is simple, they desire power. They have more greed running through their veins than is actually required. Their desire is to become the most pow-

erful of all humans. It is like a disease, a catastrophic disease that mutilates the most evolved incarnation there is on your planet, and yet, if we trail through the history books and records, we see nothing does actually stop these rebels from changing their thought patterns. Countries and many vast civilisations have been wiped out of existence, just because of one man's determination to ergonomically grow the perfect race. So this actually begs the question as to why you govern your nations in such a way, that one day leads to war and destruction. History actually shows you that through every war that has ever been fought, lives are wasted unnecessarily and there is no real winner, just another proclamation that 'war' has to take precedence over 'peace'.

Political and religious dogma has created an evolved species to become susceptible in the formulation and transit of the human way. For it is said that quite blatantly the human way should be nothing more than a simplified existence and balance between nature and its surroundings. To survive you need nature, but for nature to survive it needs nothing more than the sun, rain and the plant-life that grows abundantly wild in every corner of the globe. In conclusion, man needs nature, nature does not need man. If man did not exist, nature could flourish and species of many different forms would not have become extinct. Their chances of survival would have been greatly increased and your planet would hold a more balanced way of life.

Your generic ancestors of many thousands of years ago knew this fact and they built harmony and a belief system on this hypothesis. They realised that with nature they had a better chance of survival. This was known around the world, from whatever ethnic minority you had been born into. From the time your planet came to exist, the two planets that aided your existence were the sun and the moon. The sun gives you the necessary warmth and light, whilst the moon controls the tidal influences and the cycle of the womanly form. Without either of these two planets your world as you know it would be a cold, dense and dark environment.

The sun and the moon are no different from any other living matter; the composition of the sun's genetic make-up has changed over a great period of time. In human terms you are born, mature, grow old and die. So too the same hypothesis could be said about your surrounding planets, including Mother Earth. For some believe that we all at some stage of eternal life choose to reincarnate, and it must be assumed that this same occurrence of reincarnation would happen to other forms of living matter. If planets dissolve over a cycle of time into a multitude of gasses and chemicals, it would be predictable that a new chain reaction would begin to form again another variation of what existed before."

Dreanna fidgeted.

"Are you tired Dreanna, shall I stop?"

"No, please don't, please... please continue."

"Very well. Now where was I? Ah yes. So for the natural world to thrive and prosper the sun has never been just another planet, but a requirement for the purpose of life.

It is no wonder that ancient civilisations worshipped the sun, as they saw that without its warmth and light their existence would become an involuntary death, and these past humans began to see the sun as the 'Giver of Light' or 'Giver of Life'. So many deities were grown and formed using this basic knowledge structure, and it comes as no surprise when we look back and see a common belief system evolved.

Sun = Life Nature = Life

Life did not just happen, religion and different belief structures did not just happen, they have all evolved and changed to suit the needs of your ancestors and the needs of the human being of today. If we glance at science and knowledge of the past we can see that most species, whether physical or spiritual, do not just exist alone. This is where the wisdom of your historical benefactors and past civilisations knew and understood. They knew more about the truth than you do in the 21st century. The reason why they were more aware is simple; they were not conditioned into believing something of which they had no prior knowledge as their beliefs were simplified into an understanding and awareness. They did not care and were not bothered who was right and who was wrong, their thought patterns were not evolved to destroy, but just to survive."

"But Qulib, there are so many theories about who or what created life – which one is right? All these people who claim to know the 'truth' all fight and argue over and over again and proclaim their way is the correct path, they say their way is the only way. Like you said, lives are being destroyed, wars are being fought, because of a presence, a great being, a God. Surely this isn't what you wanted? Or what is needed?"

"Child, nothing is hard to understand, life is a simple adventure, but your race, your species all make it harder than it could or should be. Whose theory is correct you ask? Quite simply child, they all are. Close your eyes Dreanna. I ask you to use the one piece of your mind that you all have, and that is your imagination.

Close your eyes tightly and what do you see? With your eyes closed tightly you can see no more than a deep darkness, a void into an infinite passageway. This is the universe, a dark hole of never-ending space. After a short period of time your vision begins to show you tiny atoms of moisture, particles of dust which slowly join together and form magical colours of different shapes and sizes. The colours are brilliant, dazzling and vivid; reds, blues, greens, and yellows. Your dark universe has now become a multitude of effervescent, lurid, animation. You now have a kaleidoscope, a vast amount of colours, shifting and creating a symmetry of patterns. With each rotation, more colours, more shapes are being formed. Your kaleidoscope has now formed into a collective magnitude of vibrant auras. Here is the Big-Bang, this is the beginning of a chemical chain reaction process, molecules and tiny atoms are now forming together. At the same time as Earth was forming and evolving, other components and elements still continued to merge and blend together. These translucent orbs began evolving too, after a transitional transformation of gasses they evolved into higher conscious beings then into the consciousness energies of light that many call God.

Let your mind now take you forward to many thousands or even billions of years later. Evolution has made its entrance, your diverse, translucent orbs have developed and evolved, your planet has developed and evolved. The consciousness or energy of light over time acknowledged that all living matter is no more than a balance of chemicals, an equation that can be changed and altered. But Dreanna, nothing in the universe exists alone, where one light being was formed so too were many. You have met Cia, the very first Keeper. We have tried over the eons to let information seep through to all on Earth, placing ideas, words, thoughts, theories into the minds of man. We find it humorous how you interpret and use such information. Take Cia for instance, we gave an idea, we gave a clue as to what the perceived God or higher being could be, you used her name for man's own benefit rather than to understand what we are.

You look confused Dreanna; think for a moment, think about her name."

Dreanna sat saying Cia's name over and over again in her mind. 'Cia, cia, cia,...' She spelt the letters c.i.a., c.i.a., C.I.A. She laughed as the penny dropped. "You, the Keepers, are nothing more than a Central Intelligent Agency! Oh my god, that is so brilliant. Qulib, C.I.A." She laughed some more.

Qulib smiled too. He actually smiled! "Yes indeed it is humorous to you Dreanna, but for us it can be a little frustrating. We try and give you reasons and the truth, but you and your kind always use what we tell them for their own self gain. The human in many ways has still not understood. Every piece of information has been given as to the whys and the hows, but still you do not do the one thing you should in order to prolong your species. You do not communicate your findings and collaborate. If all the belief structures conversed instead of tried to prove they had all the knowledge, your world would be one of harmony and peace and the same can be said for the politics that govern your nations. Shall we continue?"

Dreanna moved her feet around, stretched out her legs, and laid down on her stomach, her head resting on her elbows for support. If she was going to be here for some time she may as well get comfy. "Yes," she replied, forcing all the new information into her tiny human brain.

"Many religious scriptures tell the tale that God wanted to see himself in physical form. They were right. We the Keepers watched as the Earth was evolving and changing. We saw from the very beginning the first pustule on Earth and its vast structural changes. We observed the way life was being formed and it was our wish to experience what a physical life was like. The first pustules evolved and mixed with other enzymes and slowly transformed the world. Single-celled organisms were swimming around in great quantities and where the water and land cross, other parasites grew copiously. Time passed, how much time is really immaterial as we realised just how long it took for us to evolve and we were more than happy to wait patiently to view the results and see the world change. We also realised that we too could aid the existence and mould life. We used the same matter that was flying abundantly free in the universe and used it to

make new life, new species, and a new world. Over time we understood that our energy could be transferred into a physical existence. We could aid life by becoming life, but the one thing we could not do was to reproduce without having a conscious existence.

Once a vessel was formed that was strong enough to hold our consciousness energy we manipulated the Earth in such a way that made each vessel reproduce of its own accord, and this gave birth to something extraordinary, this taught us that with the manipulation of evolution and assistance from our life force all living matter after death could transform into energies of light. Every living thing you see on Earth including the plantlife may well die, but like I said before it reincarnates itself into the next stage, you have seen with your own eyes the life force that seeps through the plants and vegetation in our world. In many ways life is no different in the physical state or consciousness state because in both places it exists, the only real difference is we live in a state of harmony, balance and love.

In the early stages of evolution and our growth we learnt that new life forces could be made with each birth of a physical vessel, but these consciousness energies were erratic and caused mass destruction on Earth. We had to step in and reincarnate ourselves to stop the devastation from occurring. Until we managed to create a balance, this balance was one that is still used today. So you understand it Dreanna the equation is:

Herbivores eat vegetation, carnivores eat the herbivores. Not one is allowed to overtake the other, as if it did life would cease to exist. Your world would die and in many ways we cannot let that happen or we too would not be able to feel the life force that is a conscious existence.

The theories mankind has, regarding magical and mythological creations, are also correct. Every theory man has is correct. Vampires, werewolves, cyclops, mermaids, each one of these creations has at some stage lived on Earth, and if only the eyes of the world would open you would understand this, and understand why they were not the perfect vessels to continue being allowed to have life.

A vampire had the strength, the dexterity and the longevity that we have been searching for, but they were the biggest predator there was, they destroyed life in an instant. They had done everything in their power to attract their prey. In many ways man still uses what power they had. You see, man or woman preens themselves, they make their bodies smell appealing to attract a mate. A vampire used this power for sustenance instead of reproduction.

A werewolf, cyclops and mermaids too had the attributes for a life force that could hold our energy, but these creations were unstable, often clumsy and their longevity and physical bodies were more prone to the natural diseases that were manifesting and growing on Earth.

You look as if this is actually difficult for you to believe Dreanna, but the genetics of long ago still make their appearance today in your world, children are still born with abnormal amounts of bodily hair, or webbed fingers, legs or toes, or skin that resembles scales. The truth is around you."

"Okay, but you have to understand this is a lot for me to take in, I still struggle in believing in you, let alone vampires and stuff! But I'm curious. Tell me this: if your energy and mine are reincarnated so we can reproduce, why do you as 'The Keepers' destroy life through wars when you said yourself you believe in harmony and peace?"

"Do you really think that we want to destroy what has taken us billions of years to create? We don't want to destroy it Dreanna, we want to keep it alive. Many of the wars in your world are man-made and are not made by us, but sometimes we intervene so life can change. What is the war you remember?"

History wasn't Dreanna's strong point. Actually nothing taught at school was, but she answered him with what little knowledge she had. *"Well it has to be the Second World War. I wasn't born but it's the one Dad used to talk about, so it must be Hitler and his need to build the perfect race."*

"And there child is your proof, how does your saying go? Ah yes, you have hit the nail on the head."

Dreanna sniggered. *"Nail on the head! Qulib I think you might have to get an Urban dictionary 'cos times are changing fast and that saying is a bit old hat."* She laughed some more, *"We have new words nowadays like 'boof' and 'fob'."* Dreanna again realised she wasn't being the attentive pupil Qulib wanted. She coughed and put her straight poker face back on, *"Sorry Qulib, I will be serious I promise, but in all honesty you've lost me mate, I don't know what the hell you are on about."*

"Hitler wanted to build the perfect race; we the Keepers of Life want to build a vessel that can carry our consciousness energy with no flaws. When life is conceived man has no recognition of what happens after death. Sometimes, it has to be said, some memories, some thoughts, come back. When Hitler was growing we gave him the thought of building the perfect race, we allowed him to have a glimpse of what we were trying to do."

"Hang on one bloody minute, are you telling me you made that arse-hole murder, maim, torture and kill millions of innocent people in a horrific manner, because you wanted him to do it!" Dreanna was dumbfounded at what she just heard.

"We had to Dreanna. You see the world and its people were becoming separated from each other. You had spilt and segregated your world, on one side you had the rich, the other the poor, one side you had black skin the other you had white, all the diverse religions also segregating themselves, you were becoming a world of non-acceptance and it was growing beyond measure. We had to make a change happen and through all changes come pain – you know this. But look at how man finally saw that the colour of a person's skin does not matter, their material wealth becomes irrelevant. This war, this tyrant, proved that you can as a species stand side by side, and all your differences are unimportant. That one experience of war gave your world a new chance to accept.

But like everything, man forgets what has been taught before and now we see the same obtuse views once again appearing on your planet. We the Keepers are now faced with how to teach man to accept again."

"So you're saying another war is on its way, another complete wanker like Hitler is going to be born?"

"We do not want to make war happen again, and that is why so many energies have chosen to reincarnate themselves, to help change the way the eyes of the world see each other, and you Dreanna are one of them."

"Sorry Quilib, er... nope, I don't believe in all this ascension bollocks, rainbow children shit, and 2012 prophecies crap. Sorry but in my opinion all children are special and deserve a quality of life without all the labels that go with it, and ascension with all its theories about our DNA changing, and the prophecies, well sorry but they're no more than guidelines. The Mayans were a gentle tribe using the power of the planets and nature to help them survive, and if people actually looked at the evidence they would see that the Mayans never counted leap years so in reality the 'end of the world' should happen in summer 2011 not the winter solstice of 2012! And also the world has evolved since many of these prophecies were written, and you said it yourself, you are not in charge of evolution in its different devices, so prophecies are no different from religious manuscripts – they're all subject to change in a changing evolving world."

"We have taught you well Dreanna, we have taught you to think for yourself and not be blinded by others beliefs, and that my sweet child is why you have been chosen. Because in life you all have to find your own truth, you all have to use the one remarkable piece of equipment you're are born with… the power of your mind. This tool alone will take the human race into the next stage of its evolution, and this device alone can and will make another war on a gigantic scale unnecessary if people woke up and saw that your race needs each other for survival.

Your job Dreanna, your role in this life, is to save the children…"

Dreanna's body convulsed as her energy transferred itself back into her physical form. She gulped for air, her body as cold as the inside of a freezer, then she shivered and opened her eyes. Her vision was distorted and her painful head throbbed like never before. She lifted her hands to her face, rubbed her eyes and blinked over and over again in a bid to make her sight return. She tried to stand but fell backwards; she inhaled as her heart thundered inside her chest. She inhaled again, and stood slowly; her body was still in disarray and didn't feel like it was hers. She looked at her hands and watched as her physical form returned; she was becoming a solid mass of molecules and atoms once again.

The ticking of the clock on the wall took her attention away from her own self. "I don't believe it," she said out loud. "How can this be?" The clock on the wall read 12.20pm. "I feel like I've been away for hours, but time hasn't moved. I couldn't even dream so much in such a short space of time… could I?"

What We Teach can be Bequeathed

August 2011

The last year had been remarkable; it brought tears, it brought laughter, it brought so many cheques being written to a wide range of people. She and her team were helping change the lives of children all around the UK. It also brought Dreanna back to a place of confusion, a place where she felt trapped, a place with no windows and no doors. So many would have just felt proud and have accepted that the long hours and sleepless nights, the hard work, was a moment to sit back and admire all that had been achieved. But Dreanna felt nothing. She felt numb, she didn't feel proud, and not once did she look at her own reflection smiling and telling herself "I did that."

With all the endless days she had spent trying to fill the emptiness inside her she still had to deal with the everyday occurrences that happened in every family. She watched as her daughters struggled to cope with relationship break-ups; she watched helplessly as tears fell from their eyes. She watched and listened to their words of pain until it hurt her just as much as it hurt them. This pain they suffered, this heartache that strangled them, ate its way through her heart like nothing else she had ever experienced. She held them and spoke words of comfort; she wanted to right the wrongs and make them happy and take their pain away, but she knew she couldn't because this was their life, this was their journey, and all she could do was be there for them, no matter what.

The family of five sat at the table enjoying what was left of their Sunday roast. The conversation soon turned into one about all things womanly. Periods and hot flushes really didn't impress Callum so he got up and lay on the living-room floor watching a game of golf on television and leaving the mixed-up emotional females to carry on their discussion.

Dreanna was unusually quiet and it wasn't long before Leticia asked why. "Mum what's the matter?"

"Nothing," Dreanna smiled "I'm fine."

"Yeah right," Fawn said, "you always say you're fine when something's wrong, so c'mon what is it?"

"Nothing – just tired that's all."

Leticia looked directly at her mother, her long dark hair falling neatly onto her shoulders and those massive brown eyes staring right at her. "That's bollocks! And you know it!"

Dreanna didn't know how to explain the dark empty feelings she had, "I'm just, I mean I ... Oh I haven't a clue what I'm trying to say or even how to say it."

Leticia glared at her, screwed up her nose and with head tilted to one side replied, "Mum we're used to you talking shit and we're used to your mummer-isms, so – just say it."

Dreanna lifted her gaze from the table and looked straight out of the patio doors into their garden."I just don't know if I can do this anymore... I mean the charity, the readings or sittings, whatever you wanna call them. I... I'm losing the will, I mean ... I don't seem to have any compassion left inside me. Nothing seems to upset me anymore or shock me or even make me feel sorry for these people. I think my heart's grown cold."

Rebecca spoke. "Mum you've seen and been through more than most people. You've heard from complete strangers some of the worst atrocities that life can spit out. It's no wonder you don't feel compassion anymore, because nothing alarms you anymore. Don't you see, there's nothing on this planet now that would make you wince at how cruel life can be?"

"I know what you are trying to say, Becks, and I understand, but if my heart has grown cold then surely it means I have nothing left to give?"

Fawn hadn't spoken up yet, but she was a thinker, an old head on young shoulders. She was wise beyond her years. "What is it you've always told us?" Fawn made full eye contact with her mum. "When you feel there's nothing left then you've got to search for that tiny bit that's hiding 'cos there's always something left inside, it's just you are looking in the wrong place. Maybe you just need to go look for it?"

"I know... I know you're right, but right now I just don't know if I can be bothered, I just don't know if I have the energy left." Dreanna answered.

Rebecca leaned forward resting her elbows on the table. "You just don't see what you have achieved and done do you?"

Dreanna stared out of the window, hoping that the sights and sounds of nature would give her a clue. "No... no I don't."

Rebecca continued, "At our Charity Ball, you got a standing ovation; you Mum, no one else. People listened to you, people cried as you read your speech, and people stood at the end of it and applauded you! And do you know why they did? It was because you said it like it was, it was because you read aloud what that pervert did to you as a child, you shared your story and look what happened – strangers came up to you and told you their stories....these people who had been raped as children, for the first time in their lives actually didn't feel ashamed any more. You've done so much more that you realise."

Dreanna lit up a cigarette. "But people also walked out of the room."

"Because they couldn't handle the truth Mum," Leticia answered. "They couldn't handle it and didn't want to see or know that these things happen. They would rather ignore the fact that shit like this happens and they will always carry on shutting their front door to the world because they are basically shallow pricks!"

"Say it like it is Leticia," Dreanna smiled.

"Mum," Rebecca asked, "what is it you want? What is it you want to do?"

Dreanna sighed, "I want to change the world."

"Oh Mother!" Leticia screamed. "Most people want to go on holiday, wanna buy a new car or pair of shoes, but you! You want to change the fucking world! Can you not see how different you are to most people? For someone whose heart has nothing left in it you still want to do something to make things better for everyone. Your heart ain't grown cold, it's beating exactly the same as it always has."

Droplets of moisture began to form in Dreanna's eyes, "Maybe I can do it on my hedgehog and ride off into the sunset carrying my sword carved out of a pumpkin."

"What?" Fawn asked.

Leticia explained, "I phoned Mum the other day saying I was gonna pop in for a cuppa, and in typical Mother style she said to call before coming round as she had to go save the one-legged wonky-eyed unicorn from the snizzleflips, but as her hedgehog had a flat tyre she wasn't sure how long she would be. I told her hedgehogs didn't have tyres and she said that her prickly friend had his legs bitten off by the cheese-eating belly-button fluff monster so she had to make special wheels for him... you really don't want to know the rest."

"Actually Leticia," Dreanna announced "If you're gonna tell the story you should tell it correctly. It was the snozzleflops, the snizzleflips are a totally different tale." She stood up and piled the dinner plates on top of each other.

As Fawn handed her mother her plate, she grabbed hold of her wrist. "You know Mum... you know how you say that the dead or Keepers, or even the turnips in the sky as you call them, often speak to you in cryptic; well it may be you are looking at this all wrong."

Dreanna sat back down and Fawn continued. "Maybe your job isn't to save the children as such, may be it's one of us that need to do this, or even one of our children, or even our grandchildren, because you've planted the seed inside us. You've taught us how to care and give hope back to people and maybe that's all you were supposed to do. As you keep saying, this world is so young and still learning, still evolving, but that seed you've planted in us will grow and you never know, when the time is right, it could bloom into something that none of us could've ever imagined."

Dreanna stared round the table at each one of her daughters. "How did you lot get so knowledgeable?"

And in unison they all replied, "We had a good teacher Mum!"

Dreanna's bottom lip quivered and silence fell as each woman finally allowed their tears to flow unchecked.

Leticia sniffed in deeply and pounded her fists on the table. "Right, enough of this bollocks! You know what we need don't you… We need," she paused, "Bon Jovi, and I know just the perfect song."

She walked to the iPod and flicked a switch then played air guitar in the middle of the room. Rebecca and Fawn joined her, each holding a remote control and singing into it like a microphone.

> *This one goes out to the man who mines for miracles*
> *This one goes out to the ones in need…*

Dreanna jumped off her chair, picked up a spoon and joined her daughters, singing like she had never sung before. When the song finished the four women collapsed in a joyful heap on the floor.

Callum tore his eyes away from the television for a moment and looked at each one in turn. "Fucking women!" he shook his head and turned back to the men hitting a little ball with a stick.

The End … Or is it?

She is Life and Love

August 2011

Dreanna was in a state of disarray, still thinking about Qulib's words, still wondering what she was supposed to do next, and still laughing and feeling satisfied that her daughters had listened to all she have ever told them.

She sat quietly in her home empty of its other cohabitants and listened to the children next door squabbling over some toy or another. Their squeaky raised voices got louder and louder and her body went cold. She felt the rising flow of currents gush through her again, and held tight to her head as it cramped with spasms shooting through every vein, capillary and muscle in her body.

"Dreanna are you ready to begin again?"

No, no," she begged, "Please, please leave me alone, I can't take any more pain. Why are you telling me all this? I don't want to know any more, I want to live my life, please I beg you no more, please just leave me alone."

"I'm sorry Dreanna we cannot leave you alone. Please relax and the pain will ease. We have never met before, my name is Lucina and I am the Keeper of reason and logic."

"Wait!" Dreanna shouted, "You have to know I've decided to give everything up, I've decided to throw in the towel and admit defeat. Lucina I just can't do this anymore, I can't take the pain and I can't keep fighting. I surrender. The white flag is raised."

"You may not want this to happen anymore, but we can make you listen. You, my sweet, sweet Dreanna, are carrying the world on your shoulders and your body is being weighed down with all the misery you see and feel. You feel angry don't you?"

"Of course I feel fucking angry. I'm angry that no one listens, I'm angry that we live in a society that has so much but gives so little. I'm angry that so many people sit and moan and grumble then do fuck all to change anything. I'm angry that everybody wants to take and take some more, irrelevant of the harm it does to others… I'm angry that …that I can't find it inside me to continue fighting a fucked up system in a fucked up world!"

"Did you not listen to what Fawn said? It may not be your job. Do you want it to be your job?"

"I don't know! If it isn't my job then why do I feel that it is? Why feed me all this stuff? Why make me continue to want to ride off in the sunset on my hedgehog and shove a marrow up all of those people in power's arses that could, I mean really could, change this planet…? If I've done my bit why don't I feel complete?"

"Maybe you are just wanting too much too soon? Is it not possible that the time for all the changes you speak of is not now but in the distant future? You are fearful of something too."

"Yes, yes I am. As you well know as you are reading my thoughts... don't!"

"Your mind is an open book to us, so shall we deal with this fear before moving on to what needs to be spoken of?"

"'Spose," Dreanna sighed.

"Every event in your life indeed does revolve around the number three. You know this as you have worked this out for yourself. You are scared that because this year your physical age hits forty-five something awful is going to happen... am I correct?"

"Yep! I know that everything happens for a reason and in some very weird way everything in my life seems to happen every three years. I even ended up having my three very own Witches of East Grinstead as my daughters. What if this year when I turn forty-five something bad happens? And before you say it I am aware that it's not always bad. Some of the things that have happened are good I know this, but in all honesty I really don't think I can handle any more bad shit right now."

"What would you do if it was another bad occurrence? But I know you better than you know yourself and I know what you would do Dreanna. You would cry until you couldn't cry any more, then you would brush yourself down and find a way to cope and move forward and carry on. It's what you always have done is it not?"

"Jeez, thanks for that! I was hoping you were going to tell me not to worry and this time I was due something nice. But instead you still leave me thinking that the worst could happen... Cheers!"

"Fate Dreanna, accept your fate like everyone else has to, patience is a virtue and time is on your side. Now shall we begin?

Each human being is a mirror image of another, each human holds a duplicated existence. We have since time began used the same mould that you see in your reflection each day. This mould is and has been used time and time again, this is why so many times you see people who look the same but are not related. These similarities begin to change and evolve due to the genetics of your race. Do you understand?"

Dreanna heaved a sigh, "Here we go again. So what you're basically saying is the reason so many people look the same as others, you know the ones that can make a living out of looking like a celebrity, is because you have used the same 'mould' as you put it and that's why some of us look the same and the rest simply change the mould due to our own evolution and genetic make-up. So what you are saying is many thousands of years ago we actually all looked the same as each other? If a duplicate existence is a plausible factor in life on our planet, where people that have never met look very similar or almost identical to each other, could it also be that there is another Earth with other more evolved forms of humans that reside on it?

If you analyse life you see that everything has an opposite; up-down, back-front, man-woman... like I was told before, we have the sun to bring light and life and the moon to bring darkness and rest. If we continue down this same path and understand that we have life and a physical existence, then can't we assume that with death must come a transition into another possible dimension? And this dimension again floats around in the endless space that is between more than one Earth, more than one Universe, more than one duplicated mixture of the same compounds and components? Surely then there must be another Earth somewhere and maybe more Keepers of life... Am I correct or am I barking up the wrong tree, or quite simply just going barking bloody mad?"

"For someone who doesn't want our knowledge you are curious. More than one Earth yes, more than one Universe yes, and that sadly is all I am allowed to tell you. But we the Keepers are the very first of our type; we have been around since time itself began. We are more than just life – we are knowledge. We helped to mould Earth and humankind into what it is and will continue to help until the day arrives and we have built a vessel strong enough to hold our consciousness energies for eternity, with no hate, no disease, no pain. But this day is many millennia into your planet's future."

"But why would you want to? You reside in a place where the only emotion felt is love, where peace exists, why the hell would you want to be physical for eternity? When... where you come from is so perfect?"

"What you see before you is no more than an apparition. We are energy."

"So what the hell do I see when I sit here with your face in my mind. I'm staring at you now, your short brown hair, black eyes, perfect skin, what am I seeing then?"

"You are seeing whatever image I choose to be. I am using your own mind to create what you see before you, I am using your own imagination."

"Hang on a minute! So in all honesty I am imagining all this. What's happened all my life is just my imagination, nothing more?"

"Yes and no Dreanna. You know how this works, you have been told before it is in the state of your altered imagination where we converse with you. When you see us or even members of your physical family, they and we are placing those images of what you recognise into your mind. When the human form dies it no longer has a physical form, it becomes energy. This energy is one you have witnessed before; the white crystal-like shapes that form before you, the expanse of translucent light is what we are. This is what you can see until we are able to make a connection with the abyss of your mind and instill a shape that becomes coherent to your logic."

"So you in your correct form are like the er... beings in the film 'Cocoon'...yes?"

"Is that the image I can see in your mind as we speak?"

"Yes, that's what I perceive you look like in your natural state."

"Then my child, I have to acknowledge that it is very similar to what you become after death, with one or two differences, but that you will find out when it is your time to depart Earth. To evolve the human mind has to be undertaken slowly, and at this stage in the process of evolution the human mind only uses a very small percentage of itself; imagine what its capabilities could be if every cell were to be used."

"Too much too soon, and we're all brain fucked like I feel now I suppose."

"As always, your eloquent use of language is exact and to the point, but yes the answer is yes. Humans evolve at different stages and for some their minds just could not handle progression like others. In your mind now you have the images of winged beings, angels as you call them. You want to know if they are real, don't you? Well they are real if you believe they are. They are real to many who believe in them. Just like everything else in life you create your own tangible reality and after life has finished your heaven becomes what your thoughts believe and this is why everyone who believes they see angels in a certain form will after death once again see what their own nirvana will be like, but the one thing you must know is whatever you choose your reality to be you can never take away what we are... and what we are is nothing more than the purest form of life. We hold no hierarchy, we do not sit on thrones of gold, and there are certainly no pearly gates or any one living thing that is abandoned to hell, for hell comes to many in life. Hell can come too in death when some lose their physical body and remorse sets in. They suffer, yes, because they finally feel the love we have here and the wrongdoings they have done in life fill their persona with repentance. You are now thinking of the 'fallen angels' again – they are real but not in the way you think. A fallen angel is a being in a reincarnated conscious existence who was given a job a role to do to change the formulation of life on planet Earth and for reasons sacred to them they decided not to undertake the role they were given."

"But what about the Bible and other religious manuscripts?"

"Ah yes, I had wondered when your curiosity would bring into question the meaning behind such literature. These narrative novels were written in a manner so people of that time could relate and understand. Yet again in all that has been written the similarities to the creation of life and its purpose are all equal, they just use different terminology, symbols, words, winged beings, horned beings, but they are all one of the same. Let us look at the Bible. You are led to believe that the female gender was created from the rib of Adam, this is an interpretation of how reproduction happens. You see, the rib of Adam is a phallic symbol for the male genitalia; this then is inserted into the female giving a new life. The story of Noah is again proving that nothing on Earth can ever survive alone, every species has to have a mate, a habitat. Do you understand?"

"Er no, not really. We have creatures that can reproduce alone that are both sexes – they don't need a fuck buddy to do this because they're born with both male and female genitalia, so no I don't get it, I don't understand."

"You are correct, but did you not listen to what I said? As well as 'mate' I also said 'habitat'. The ark is the container that holds the copious amounts of different life forms; the Earth is the ark. Do you understand now?"

"Yeah I think so. But what about Jesus? What about all the other mythological sons of gods or goddesses?"

"Jesus was a man, nothing more nothing less, but he was a man that gave unconditionally. He was in retrospect no different to you; he gave to aid so others could live, and he too heard our words, he too listened to our voices. Ancient mythology tells you

the truth about existence, but like every message reporters receive, it is a conundrum of the truth that has to be understood and observed in a simple way. It is not difficult to understand but it is difficult for humans to change their thought pattern to believe every word written could be nothing more than a fabrication of the truth.

Children at this present time in your world are being used as pawns in a game of spiritual power, a physical and spiritual crusade, but they are also having their minds conditioned and confused in a manner of destruction. The segregation of years gone by is once again forming. Religions are not mixing with other beliefs. The different colours of skin are once again giving rise to the non-integration of a race that is slowly re-living the days of the past. When will you all see that the future of the planet is down to what knowledge the younger generations hold? Look at your world Dreanna. If the children are not taught, given a chance and shown the way, what sort of world do you think it will become?

We are trying to re-incarnate as many energies that have experienced life in its simple form without the modern day conformation of money and power, but these energies are struggling. You see they came from an era where the greatest limitation they had to experience was survival; now they are living in a world full of technology and a world that is full of activity which spends its time engaged in taking what they want instead of what they need. These children are being categorised and identified as mentally challenged.

You have seen for yourself that many of these children experience problems with learning; they experience problems with understanding the transit of the human way, but these children have gifts that if only you on Earth gave them a chance you would be able to see just what they can teach you. Many are still in their own minds living with their memories of days gone by, many are fixated on the living world as it was in the beginning, creatures that are extinct. Architecture and mathematics are just some of these children's talents. They understand so much but are not being allowed to integrate. They can aid and change life as it is now and they can teach the adults the simple way forward to help mankind continue with an existence that can help it advance and not go backwards. We have tried making a human that gives unconditional love but sadly with the brain as it is at the moment it could not cope with how we engage in our emotional thought pattern and mental consequences have been seen."

"Tell me one thing. Why on this planet do we still see children in parts of the world starving, being murdered and going without? How can you let this happen? Why do you let this happen? Why haven't you intervened and stopped this before? Because out of all the good that is done some tit wank comes along and destroys it all! All because they are greedy, all because they want to be that most powerful human that has ever lived. It doesn't make sense, none of what goes on in life makes sense. Life at the moment is nothing more than political and religious dogma; it's all crap and bollocks!" A burning rage slowly grew in Dreanna's belly.

"You ask why, Dreanna. Think about what you have just said and the answer is in your final sentence. Life in your time is built on a theory of 'control', and the majority of people have allowed it to happen because of fear. People are too frightened to make their voices heard in case they lose the material possessions they own, but fear like everything else in a physical existence is only real if you believe it to be. You see you have to believe, have faith and acceptance, to have the life your heart desires."

"You're talking about cosmic ordering, asking the universe, the secret, spell casting... aren't you?"

"It has been given many names, but if you believe with the whole of your heart and have faith that when the time is right your wish or desire will come true, and accept that beyond a shadow of a doubt that all life is only there for you to enjoy, then and only then will you live a life of freedom where control of the masses is not needed to aid its survival. The energy that is around you becomes you; if you are negative in your mind-pattern your life will too be negative, if you are positive then this will lead your life to a more favourable and exultant existence. In order to reach that balance, in order to reach that level of tranquility, you must first undertake the changes your life needs, and as you are aware change is never easy. Anything is possible... anything.

Your energy can also change the energies of another to help them to share in the blissful appreciation that life can give. It is called transferable energy. When two negative atoms meet we have a cosmic collision. Why do you think your world, your Earth, has planets surrounding it?"

"But it's hard to remain positive all the time. I know I've got the tee-shirt, the DVD and the book! Science Lucina, per-lease! I got thrown out of my science lessons, so the only reason I can think of is that these planets must help us in some way to protect us from all the shit stuff that is floating around in the universe; without them, maybe our planet would not be able to survive. A cosmic collision of emotions and maybe a cosmic collision of planets too?"

"You see, yet again all we have done in creating your world is to try and protect it; a cosmic collision on a planetary scale would end all life, it would have a negative outcome the same as with physical emotions when emotions of a negative value collide and join forces they too have a damaging and destructive effect on life. Many will spend their time trying hard to find the answers to this simple equation, but life is not an equation that was meant to be problematic or challenging – it was meant to be effortless and un-complicated.

For every problem, for every sickness that has manifested, there is an answer, there is a cure around you. If a disease has been created in the physical world, the physical world will hold the cure, there will be a cure laying somewhere in the undergrowth, laying somewhere in nature's pathway. There is never a problem that cannot be changed, there is never an illness that cannot be cured, because Earth has been designed to have balance, an opposite to every creation, every disease, and every outcome."

"I know it sounds daft but it's a bit like if you get stung by a stinging nettle a dock leaf grows nearby that will take away and counteract the sting. So okay, if everything in life is simple and balanced and nature holds these remedies why has man with all his knowledge not found a cure for cancer, and why do innocent children die from it, and why like I've been told do people reincarnate to push the boundaries?"

"These children, like your own mother, made the decision before their birth to be the ones to push the limitations further, to push man's knowledge of how to heal, to push man's capability of one day building a vessel that no natural disease or man-made sickness could destroy, enabling us all to eventually live a physical existence without pain and sickness. Man has to be the one to find the answers, we aid but cannot give. Do you remember what you said to your father when you were a child about cancer?

"I think I asked why they don't kill cancer with another virus."

"Others were given this information also and since then many tests and experiments have been done, but also have been stopped. If only man continued with these, cancer could be obliterated because a bacterium like everything else has its purpose. Man does not see that all sickness has a cure, he sees sickness as another way to make money, he sees sickness as another way to be in control and be powerful; he has not learnt that life is simple, for man makes problems where problems do not need to be. The key to man's problems lay in the voices of the children. Let them speak, let them lead the way and right the wrongs of the generations that have lived before. They are the future."

"Forgive me Lucina, all this information is hard to accept. It's hard for someone like me to have the acceptance you are speaking about. But even if what you say is true, even if all of what I've heard in the last couple of days is 'how it is', please tell me what the hell I am supposed to do with all this information. Nobody will listen to me, people will think I'm off my rocker! Take all the rejection we have received for the charity. Yes I know we are able to help some kids, some families, but we are never going to be able to compete with the large organisations – we can't even get help from the people that, let's face it, at the end of the day could offer their support and assistance, because we… I live in a world where fame is everything. People follow fame, they want fame, they yearn for fame, they kiss the arses of the rich and famous, and all they want is to be that mirror image of their hero. The celebrities won't help us to help others because there's nothing in it for them. We can't give them the publicity, we can't pay their fee, and we'll always be just another organisation that tries but never quite succeeds. And now you tell me all this for what reason for what purpose? I can't get support, I can't make people listen and to be honest no one is going to listen. In my world no one is even going to listen to the kids. How many times do I have to say it? I'm just an insignificant person!…And the kids, well they're just the ones who yet again will pick up the pieces and probably suffer more than they are now. It's a circle of destruction, a circle of dis-ease."

"Oh my sweet Dreanna, I can't tell you what is to become of all you have achieved,

but I can tell you to pick up a pen and write. Write all we have told you, write all your thoughts and feelings, everything you know to be real and true. The people who are meant to read it will, the people who will take you on yet another of life's adventures are waiting patiently. Do not be the person others want you to be; be honest, be open, be true to the child we call Dreanna.

I will leave you with this, Dreanna. It will be a woman who will make the eyes of the world open, for she is on the Earth now but does not realise her destiny: the love in her heart will be felt; the freedom of her soul will extinguish the hate many carry. She is unlike those that have been before; she will heal the hearts of many, she will shine like the brightest star in the night sky. She is life and love, she is the nurturer, she is the carer, and she is the voice of reason and hope.

We love you completely, because you are us and we are you, just have faith and believe Dreanna, and hold hope close to your heart."

"Right...okay then... well, whoever she is, tell her to get her finger out of her arse and get on with it then, because if she doesn't hurry up the world is going to be fucked right in the anal pit!"

"DREANNA! Are you taking any of this seriously?"

"Erm, possibly not. The only thing I know for a fact is that each time I talk to you I end up with the most epic bad head and body twinges. You have to understand this all sounds too bizarre to be true, it's like the best sci-fi film ever."

Lucina tittered. "No matter what you say, no matter how many times you try and ignore all you have been given, the woman I speak of is closer than you think. It has been written so shall it be done. I love you."

With one shuddering volt and convulsive quake Dreanna was back in her own body. She stared longingly into open space trying so hard to understand, to make sense of everything and have the faith and belief she had spent her life searching for. She cried so hard her tears splashed to the floor like rain drops before thunder. She felt so alone with so many words echoing around inside her mind. How could she, a common working class woman whose favourite word was 'fuck', ever write a book?

She only wished that whoever this female was who was going to change the world would appear soon and show her the way, because she was lost. She felt nothing more than a shadow in a dark world of mixed up emotions. All day she sat without moving, her mind turning over and her head full of words, plus the last remnants of pain from her consciousness guest.

Callum was home from work and came to where she was sitting. She looked up at him with puffy red eyes. "Callum, hold me, please hold me."

"You're freezing. Why are you so cold? It's over thirty degrees outside and like an oven in here?"

"You wouldn't believe me if I told you." Dreanna leant forward, her face inches away from her husband's. "Please don't ever leave me – no matter what is to come, please say you'll always be by my side?"

"Hmm. Well I don't know about that - you see it all depends on how often you are going to continue to dance naked under a full moon. If you carry on doing that once a month I think I'll possibly stay," he grinned at his wife.

When Dreanna pursed her lips and kissed him, he didn't reject her advances. His hands stroked her flesh, she smelt his skin.

"We cannot touch or smell in the manner you do," the words escaped her mouth.

Callum pulled away. "What?"

Dreanna's body began to tingle as the returning heat coursed its way through her veins. Should she tell Callum of her journey that afternoon? Would he understand? Would he believe her? Would he even care? All she knew was she had to disengage from her spiritual quest. She moved closer to Callum, her finger tips brushing the side of his face. "It doesn't matter. In all honesty none of it really matters. Because we are here to live in the moment. I think we should make some more memories don't you?"

"I'm always up for making memories," Callum replied his face now full of a schoolboy grin.

Dreanna's skin prickled with expectation. She needed to let go of all her senses. Within seconds Callum's sensual lips were on hers. Their lips lingered on each other's before their mouths opened and their tongues danced in the darkness.

Breathlessly Dreanna disengaged. With a deep longing in her heart, she looked deep into Callum's eyes. "I will love you for eternity"............

Epilogue

Dreanna's Notebook

The Bird on a Wire

I am the bird on a wire, staring down upon your face
I am a swan so mystic that moves with care and grace
I am the badger, I am the hare, I am the fox, I am the hound
I am the Earth, I am the sod, I am the black tarmac ground
I am the day, I am the night
I am the stars that shine so bright
I am the ocean, I am the shore
I am peace and I am war
I am the beating of a heart, I am the ticking of a clock
I am the chains, I am the mask, I am the bolts, I am the lock
I am heaven, I am hell
I am silence, I am the tolling of a bell
I am a word, I am a chapter, I am the cover of a book
I am a glimpse, I am a stare, I am an unadulterated look
I am fear, I am passion, I am love and I am hope
I am ribbon, I am string, I am cable and I am rope
I am each breath that you inhale
I am a ship without a sail
I am entrapment, I am prison
I am blindness and I am vision
I am ignorance, I am wisdom
I am a kaleidoscope, I am a prism
I am an aura, I am light
I am an eagle in full flight
I am the UNIVERSE and I am trying
To stop your pain and to stop your crying
I am the Earth, Air, Water and Fire
I am the bird upon the wire.

"If your desire is to make a name for yourself, if your desire is to be remembered, the only way you can achieve your goal is to share your dreams. Life is not a popularity contest; to turn heads you must turn words into reality..."

ঔঔ

"Without Hope we have nothing...
but without nothing we can appreciate things a lot more."

ঔঔ

"When you think you've come from the 'school of hard knocks', and blame others for the way you are, it's time to stare at your own reflection and realise that no one else is in control of you and your actions but yourself; only you can make changes happen, so what's stopping you?
Don't blame others, stand in your own power..."

ঔঔ

"It is through the illusion of life and truth that people struggle to find out what and who they really are.
They will search in many places and walk down many roads until instead of drawing on their first breath they exhale their last,
and it is only at this point that they realise they are then truly free..."

Tomorrow, Together…

Won't somebody take away my pain?
Won't somebody help me see clearly again?
Won't somebody take away my sorrow
So I can have a brighter tomorrow?
Won't somebody take hold of my hand
And lead me to a peaceful land?
Won't somebody fill the void in my heart
So I don't feel like I'm falling apart?
Won't somebody stop the clocks and time,
Won't somebody make life mine,
So I can smile and be set free
From all I feel, from all I see?
Is this life, is this really it
The pain, the trauma, the endless shit?
I try and smile, and let it go,
But it always comes back, it continues to flow.
Should I try harder, and change who I am?
Should I become like every other child, woman and man
And not care, hurt many and take what I desire?
Should I kill, stab, abuse, should I become a liar?
But I can't change who I am, I can't become a new breed,
So I will continue to see everyone as equal, whatever their creed.
For I have more to give, I have a heart full of love,
I am your angel on earth, and have been sent from above,
So take my hand, and follow me,
I will suffer your pain as well I will set you free.
I will give you my heart, my love and my soul,
And we will continue this journey, and make life our goal,
We will experience many trials along the way,
But for now we will step into tomorrow, as it is a new day…

Please Help Me Wake Up
Do I laugh, or do I cry?
Do I live, or do I die?
Do I smile, or do I scream?
Am I awake or is this a dream?
Am I in heaven or am I in hell?
One thing's for sure only time will tell.
One day I will awake and open my eyes,
Then I will realise just how time flies,
So which path now should I chose?
I may win or I may lose,
Won't somebody help and decide for me,
So then I can be eternally free?
Free from pain, and stress, and strife,
So I can enjoy this sacred life,
Am I flamboyant or am I meek?
Am I strong or am I weak?
Am I destined to be so alone?
My only friend a quiet phone.
I have two choices, and that's for sure,
So through life my soul can soar,
Do I laugh or do I cry?
Do I live or do I die?
I must decide my own fate,
Before time has gone and it's too late,
We can ask many, just what to do,
But the fact remains it's up to you,
Make the right choice...

ℬℛ

"Perfection isn't something that is made or can be taught, it is something
that you have to accept and see with physical eyes..."

Are You Sure You Want To?

Put down your gun, lay down your weapon,
Look into the eyes of the man you're going to kill,
Does it make you feel brave, does it make you feel strong?
Does it make your heart pound, does it give you a thrill?
Put down your gun, lay down your weapon,
Look into the eyes of the man you're going to kill,
As you cock that trigger, and let the bullet go,
As it hits its target, you watch the blood flow,
Put down your gun, lay down your weapon,
Look into the eyes of the man you're going to kill,
You watch your target fall, you see them on the ground,
Their screams you hear, but you make no sound,
Put down your gun, lay down your weapon,
Look into the eyes of the man you're going to kill,
As they take their last breath, as their life slips away,
Can you really forget the events of this day?
Put down your gun, lay down your weapon,
Look into the eyes of the man you're going to kill,
Remember the sorrow, the tears and the pain,
Can you live with the anguish, can you live with the shame?
Put down your gun, lay down your weapon,
Look into the eyes of the man you're going to kill,
Remember pulling that trigger and holding that gun,
Remember one day the victim might just be your son...

ßℜ

"The world cries yet more tears today and more innocent children have
died, but we still continue to kill innocent lives every day throughout the
whole world. When are we going to realise that war is not the way forward?
How many more children have to die because of the need
and greed of adults?"

Who Are You?

Can you feel desperate, but not needy?
Can you take without being greedy?
Can you weep, but never cry?
Do you give hope, but never lie?
Can you feel in pieces, but not be broken?
Do you think words that are never spoken?
Can you feel lost but not be missing?
Do you stop wanting and stop wishing?
Can you feel lonely, but not be alone?
Are you a bird that's never flown?
Can you feel happy, but never smile?
Do you see life as an ongoing trial?
Can you feel, but never touch?
Do you see, but not that much?
Can you listen, but never hear?
Do you care, or shed a tear?
Can you be alive, but still feel dead?
Are you optimistic, but still feel dread?
Are you hope without a cause?
Are you love without a clause?
Are you being who you're meant to be
Or are you trapped, when you should be free?
Are you the ocean, without a shore?
Do you pretend the world doesn't exist, and slam the door?
Are you a friend, or are you a foe?
Do you believe war is the way to go?
So who are you deep down inside?
Do you conform, then go and hide?
Do you take but are not prepared to give
And tell others how they should live?
The words you speak, are they words you took
From somebody else's experience, from someone else's book?
So who are you really, with the words that you speak?
Are you making a difference, when you prey on the meek?
Are you really that special and just craving fame
Or are we all unique and just pawns in a game…?

Remember

Remember the soldiers that gave up their lives,
Remember their families, their children, their wives,
Remember them in uniform, their desert attire,
Remember them when they came under fire,
They fought their last battle upon foreign lands,
The blood soaked crimson sea, that was once golden sands,
Remember their fear, as in battle they did go,
Not knowing who was their friend or who was their foe,
We must remember the pain that was in their eyes,
We must remember the torture of the families that have to say their goodbyes,
Do you take a big sigh, and say it's a shame?
Do you see their lost lives as part of the game?
It's now time the politicians made all the wars cease,
But to these brave young men in uniform, let them finally
Rest In Peace.

The Beauty Of Nature

I sit and stare up at the sky,
And watch the clouds gently float by,
My eyes then fall to the old oak tree,
Its strength, its power, its branches spread wide,
A blue tit, a robin nesting deep inside,
Flowers galore are beneath my feet,
A daffodil, a rose, a tiny weed,
Which all grew from a tiny seed,
An ant, a beetle, a bird of prey,
Make me rejoice in each new day,
A dormouse, a badger, a graceful swan,
It would break my heart if these things were gone,
A fox, a toad, a blackbird's tune,
The pure white light of a full Moon,
Be it dusk or dawn take a step outside and see,
The beauty of Nature is yours for free.

Memories
As I stare out across the moor,
There is inner peace, throughout my soul,
I lay down upon the dampened grass,
And watch the day slowly pass,
The clouds are floating way up high,
My eyes begin to fill, I start to cry,
I remember the days when I was young,
With Mum and Dad, and the family,
I remember the times when we all sung,
At Christmas time around the tree,
I remember the smell of fresh baked bread,
The washing on the clothes-horse or the back of a chair,
The crisp cotton sheets that lay on my bed,
My little brown teddy bear,
My family showed me just how much they care,
Life is so simple, when you are small,
You are given the world, and you take it all,
If only I'd given a little bit more,
My innermost self, right to my core,
The sky's gone dark, and begins to rain,
My memories will have to wait again,
But in my mind they will always stay,
For recognition another day.

ᗰᗽ

"Stop for one second and look into the eyes of a child. Do you see a fun-loving free spirit who is struggling to understand what life is all about? Do not tie a child down as this is the only time that they really have the freedom to be whom and what their imagination tells them to be...

Through My Eyes

What do you see, when you open your eyes?
Do you really see the world in all its beauty,
Or do you just see what you want to see?
What do you see when you open your eyes?
Do you see the birds flying free in the open skies,
Or do you just see wars, and pain and ask yourself why?
What do you see when you open your eyes?
Do you see the beauty of nature, the swan that glides with such grace,
Or do you just see hatred on every person's face?
What do you see when you open your eyes?
Do you see flowers and trees, that grew from tiny seeds,
Or do you see the children, that nobody wants or needs?
What do you see when you open your eyes?
Do you see the sun with its warmth or billowy clouds,
Or do you just see people in a rush, pushing through crowds?
What do you see when you open your eyes?
Do you see the changes in the weather, the pouring rain,
Or do you just see loved ones dying in pain?
What do you see when you open your eyes?
Do you see fields upon fields with barley, wheat and clover,
Or do you just see destruction and starvation, the whole world over?
What do you see when you open your eyes?
Do you see the serenity of a rose or a tiny weed,
Or do you just see humans filled with so much greed?
What do you see when you open your eyes?
Do you see hope and love that seeps from your heart,
Or do you just see a world falling apart?
So honestly, what do you see when you open your eyes?

If I Could I Would...

If I could change your life what would I do?
I'd try my God-damned hardest to make your dreams come true.
If I could change your life, what would I do?
I'd take away your grief and sorrow,
So you could rejoice, in a brand new tomorrow.
If I could change your life, what would I do?
I'd make your spirit fly so free, so you can soar through the open skies,
I'd wipe away all your tears that fall from your sad eyes.
If I could change your life what would I do?
I'd take away your physical pain,
So you could feel like you've been born again.
If I could change your life, what would I do?
I'd take away your anger and rage,
So you could start a new chapter, with a new page.
If I could change your life what would I do?
I'd give you back the hope you need,
So your family you could feed.
If I could change your life, what would I do?
I'd put love back into your broken heart,
So you didn't feel like your world was falling apart.
If I could change your life, what would I do?
I'd give you a brand new pair of eyes, so you could open them and see,
The beauty that surrounds us, that is given to us for free.
Life doesn't have to be full of worries and strife,
This is your new beginning, enjoy it as this is your life...

The Love of A Child

The sky is grey high up above,
The air is still, but filled with love,
The children are nestled in their beds,
With magical thoughts,
Dancing through their heads,
The life we lead can be a strain,
With tears and heartache,
And agonising pain,
With one child's smile,
And another's kiss,
Let's live in harmony,
And in bliss.

Wipe Your Tears

My life maybe over now,
But do not cry nor shed a tear,
As now I am without a fear,
Remember my hair and the colour of my eyes,
But do not sit there and start to cry,
Remember my mouth, my lips, my face,
Remember the times I moved with such grace,
Remember my hands, my feet, my heart,
And know that we will never be apart,
I may not stand there by your side,
But I will always be there to guide,
Remember the good times, and not the bad,
This is not a time for you to feel sad,
This is a time to be happy and full of glee,
As now my soul is eternally free,
Life is given and taken away,
So please be grateful for each new day,
Remember my clothes or my favourite song,
And remember life really isn't that long,
When the sun rises up from the East,
Know that this is your time, on life you must feast,
When the sun sets, and goes down in the West,
Rejoice in life, and always do your best,
So wipe your tears, and hold your head up high,
This is just see you later and not goodbye…

ʚ̵ɞ

"When you feel like you're being pulled under
I will reach in and pull you up.
When your tears are falling I will wipe them away.
When mess and chaos surrounds you
I will sweep and clear you a path.
When no one seems to understand
I will always be there to listen.
Love will conquer pain and my love for you is your shield
because I am your mother and I will always be by your side
in life and in death for eternity..."

ʚ̵ɞ

Titles from The Wessex Astrologer
www.wessexastrologer.com

Martin Davis	Astrolocality Astrology From Here to There	Joseph Crane	Astrological Roots: The Hellenistic Legacy Between Fortune and Providence
Wanda Sellar	The Consultation Chart An Introduction to Medical Astrology Decumbiture	Komilla Sutton	The Essentials of Vedic Astrology The Lunar Nodes Personal Panchanga The Nakshatras
Geoffrey Cornelius	The Moment of Astrology		
Darrelyn Gunzburg	Life After Grief AstroGraphology: The Hidden Link between your Horoscope and your Handwriting	Anthony Louis	The Art of Forecasting using Solar Returns
		Lorna Green	Your Horoscope in Your Hands
Paul F. Newman	You're not a Person - Just a Birthchart Declination: The Steps of the Sun Luna: The Book of the Moon	Martin Gansten	Primary Directions
		Reina James	All the Sun Goes Round
		Oscar Hofman	Classical Medical Astrology
Jamie Macphail	Astrology and the Causes of War	Bernadette Brady	Astrology, A Place in Chaos Star and Planet Combinations
Deborah Houlding	The Houses: Temples of the Sky		
Dorian Geiseler Greenbaum	Temperament: Astrology's Forgotten Key	Richard Idemon	The Magic Thread Through the Looking Glass
Howard Sasportas	The Gods of Change		
Patricia L. Walsh	Understanding Karmic Complexes	Nick Campion	The Book of World Horoscopes
M. Kelly Hunter	Living Lilith	Judy Hall	Patterns of the Past Karmic Connections Good Vibrations The Soulmate Myth The Book of Why Book of Psychic Development
Barbara Dunn	Horary Astrology Re-Examined		
Deva Green	Evolutionary Astrology		
Jeff Green	Pluto 1 Pluto 2 Essays on Evolutionary Astrology (edited by Deva Green)	John Gadbury	The Nativity of the Late King Charles
		Neil D. Paris	Surfing your Solar Cycles
Dolores Ashcroft-Nowicki and Stephanie V. Norris	The Door Unlocked: An Astrological Insight into Initiation	Michele Finey	The Sacred Dance of Venus and Mars
		David Hamblin	The Spirit of Numbers
Martha Betz	The Betz Placidus Table of Houses	Dennis Elwell	Cosmic Loom
Greg Bogart	Astrology and Meditation	Gillian Helfgott	The Insightful Turtle
Kim Farnell	Flirting with the Zodiac	Christina Rose	The Tapestry of Planetary Phases

Lightning Source UK Ltd.
Milton Keynes UK
UKOW04f1616051114

241163UK00001B/15/P